Office 365 User Guide

A comprehensive guide to increase collaboration and productivity with Microsoft Office 365

Nikkia Carter

BIRMINGHAM - MUMBAI

Office 365 User Guide

Commissioning Editor: Vijin Boricha
Acquisition Editor: Akshay Jethani
Content Development Editor: Jordina Dcunha
Technical Editor: Varsha Shivhare
Copy Editor: Safis Editing
Language Support Editor: Rahul Dsouza
Project Coordinator: Nusaiba Ansari
Proofreader: Safis Editing
Indexer: Rekha Nair
Graphics: Jisha Chirayil
Production Coordinator: Tom Scaria

First published: April 2019

Production reference: 1300419

Published by Packt Publishing Ltd.
Livery Place
35 Livery Street
Birmingham
B3 2PB, UK.

ISBN 978-1-78980-931-2

www.packtpub.com

`mapt.io`

Mapt is an online digital library that gives you full access to over 5,000 books and videos, as well as industry leading tools to help you plan your personal development and advance your career. For more information, please visit our website.

Why subscribe?

- Spend less time learning and more time coding with practical eBooks and Videos from over 4,000 industry professionals

- Improve your learning with Skill Plans built especially for you

- Get a free eBook or video every month

- Mapt is fully searchable

- Copy and paste, print, and bookmark content

Packt.com

Did you know that Packt offers eBook versions of every book published, with PDF and ePub files available? You can upgrade to the eBook version at `www.packt.com` and as a print book customer, you are entitled to a discount on the eBook copy. Get in touch with us at `customercare@packtpub.com` for more details.

At `www.packt.com`, you can also read a collection of free technical articles, sign up for a range of free newsletters, and receive exclusive discounts and offers on Packt books and eBooks.

Contributors

About the author

Nikkia Carter is the Worldwide Modern Workplace Tech Lead at Microsoft, covering Office 365, Microsoft Teams, Windows, SharePoint, Office, and Security and Compliance. She also serves on Microsoft's VFI taskforce. In 2001, she started as an applications developer, before adding in intranet development. In 2009, Nikkia changed to SharePoint, later adding Office 365 and related tech. She ran a Microsoft partnership for seven years, before selling it in 2018. She has worked with clients in the government, commercial, and non-profit spaces. Nikkia is an accomplished speaker, event organizer, former community leader, former Microsoft MVP, and a Microsoft and Microsoft Partner board member.

I want to thank my editors and reviewers for helping me to finish this book, and to my readers for their patience.

About the reviewers

Yvette F. Watson is a solutions architect for Microsoft collaboration solutions based in the Philippines. Her experience with a Microsoft Partner exposed her to Office 365 deployments and Exchange Online migrations for various large and multinational companies. Among her certifications are **Microsoft Certified Solutions Expert** (**MCSE**): Productivity, **Microsoft Certified Solutions Associate** (**MCSA**): Office 365, and **Microsoft Specialist** (**MS**) in Administering Office 365 for Small Businesses. Yvette is also a regular resource speaker on Microsoft technologies, invited by numerous colleges and universities in Manila. She graduated summa cum laude from Treston International College with a bachelor's degree in computer engineering.

Born in Zugdidi, Georgia, **Dima Sitchinava** showed a keen interest in technology from childhood. He was 15 when he finished schooling and enrolled himself at Georgian Technical University, where he graduated from the information technology faculty. This was followed by a master's degree obtained from Shota Meskhia State Teaching University. After obtaining his master's, he started working as a manager of computer laboratories at his alma mater. Having worked with a myriad of organizations, he currently works as a lecturer of vocational programs.

Packt is searching for authors like you

If you're interested in becoming an author for Packt, please visit `authors.packtpub.com` and apply today. We have worked with thousands of developers and tech professionals, just like you, to help them share their insight with the global tech community. You can make a general application, apply for a specific hot topic that we are recruiting an author for, or submit your own idea.

Table of Contents

Preface 1

Section 1: Understanding Office 365

Chapter 1: Exploring Office 365 7
  Technical requirements 7
  Microsoft Office and its versions 8
    Overview of the services of Office 365 9
      Exchange 10
      Skype for Business 10
      Microsoft Teams 10
      SharePoint 11
      OneDrive for Business 11
      Office Professional or Professional Plus applications for desktop 12
      Office web and mobile apps 12
      Security, transparency, compliance, and privacy 12
    Logging in 13
    A word about browsers 14
  Summary 16

Chapter 2: Understanding More about Office 365 17
  The home page 18
    The suite bar 18
    The app launcher/switcher 19
    The Office 365 link 20
    Notifications 20
    Settings 22
    Help 22
    Your profile picture 28
      Changing your profile picture 29
      My profile 30
      My account 34
        Personal info 35
        Install status 38
        Subscriptions 40
        Security & privacy 42
        Password 43
        Contact preferences 45
        Organization privacy statement 46
        Additional security verification 47
        Updating your account security phone numbers 47
        Managing app passwords 48
        App permissions 50
        Settings 52

Profile picture for Microsoft Teams   54
Configuring your personal settings   55
The search box   57
Themes   58
Start page   60
Software   61
Language and time zone   63
Your app settings   64
Licensing   64
Office 365 consumer   64
Office 365 commercial   65
Business plans   65
Summary   67
Further reading   68

Section 2: Managing Microsoft Exchange

Chapter 3: Understanding Exchange   71
Background and History of Exchange   71
History of Exchange   72
Getting into Exchange Online   80
Outlook via the Office 365 Home   80
Outlook via the app launcher   81
Parts of Exchange Online   83
Email   84
Calendar   84
Contacts   85
Tasks   86
Summary   86
Chapter 4: Sending and Receiving Email   87
Parts of Mail in OWA   88
#1 The list of your emails   89
#2 Displaying an email message   90
#3 Focused and other filters   91
#4 Filter   92
#5 Action bar   92
The New menu   93
The Junk menu   94
The Move to menu   95
The Categories menu   95
The open menu   97
#6 Mark all as read   98
#7 Search   99
#8 Folders   100
#9 Groups   100
#10 Outlook apps   101

Email options   101
Parts of Mail in Outlook   102
  #1 List of emails   104
  #2 Display of email   105
  #3 Focused and other filters   105
  #4 Filters   106
  #5 Search   107
  #6 The tabs   107
    The Outlook backstage   107
      Info   108
      Open & Export   109
      Save As   110
      Save Attachments   111
      Print   112
      Office Account   112
      Feedback   115
      Options   116
      Exit   116
  #7 The ribbons   117
    Home   117
    Send/receive   119
    Folder   119
    View   120
    Help   120
  Tell me what you want to do   121
  Favorites   122
  List of email accounts   124
  Outlook apps   124
  Email options   126
Summary   126
Chapter 5: Using the Exchange Calendar   127
Parts of the calendar in OWA   128
  #1 Action bar   130
    New   130
    Add calendar   132
    Interesting calendars   132
    Share   136
    Print   139
  #2 Month/year navigation   141
  #3 Calendar   141
  #4 Calendar views   141
  #5 Selected day's events   142
  #6 Search   142
  #7 Month calendar navigation   142
  #8 Calendars and groups   143
  #9 Outlook apps   144
Parts of the calendar in Outlook   144

#1 The tabs 147
The Outlook backstage 148
Home 148
Send/receive 149
Folder 149
View 150
Help 151
#2 Tell me what you want to do 151
#3 Calendar navigation 152
#4 Weather 152
#5 Search 153
#6 Calendar 153
#7 Another calendar navigation 153
#8 List of calendars 154
#9 Outlook apps 154
Summary 155
Chapter 6: Using Contacts in Exchange 157
Parts of people (contacts) in OWA 158
#1 The action bar 160
#2 The main window 162
#3 Search 162
#4 Left navigation 163
#5 Outlook apps 164
Parts of contacts in Outlook 164
#1 The tabs 166
The Outlook backstage 167
Home 167
Send/receive 168
Folder 169
View 169
Help 170
#2 Tell me what you want to do 170
#3 Left navigation 170
#4 Search and filtering 171
#5 List of contacts 171
#6 Contact details pane 173
#7 Outlook apps 174
Summary 174
Chapter 7: Getting Familiar with Other Exchange Settings 175
Creating an email signature 175
Creating an email signature via Outlook on the web 176
Creating an email signature via Outlook 176
Option 1 – creating an email signature in Outlook via a new, forward, or reply email 177
Option 2 – creating an email signature in Outlook via the file backstage 178

Setting the out of office reply   178
   Setting an out of office reply via Outlook on the web   179
   Setting the out of office reply via Outlook   180
Creating email rules   180
   Creating email rules via Outlook for the web   181
   Creating email rules via Outlook   182
Setting a forwarding email   182
   Setting a forward email via Outlook on the web   183
   Setting a forward email via Outlook   184
Summary   187

Section 3: Skype for Business and Microsoft Teams

Chapter 8: Understanding Skype for Business and Microsoft Teams   191
  History and Background of Skype for Business   191
  History and Background of Microsoft Teams   192
  The parts of Skype for Business   192
   #1 Personal note   194
   #2 Presence, location, and photo   194
    Presence   194
     Green/available   194
     Red/busy   195
     Red with dash/do not disturb   195
     Yellow/be right back   195
     Yellow/off work   195
     Yellow/appear away   195
     Reset status   196
     Sign out   196
     Exit   196
     White with question mark/unknown   196
     White/offline   196
    Location   196
    Photo   197
   #3 The contacts, conversations, and meetings tabs   197
    Contacts   198
    Conversations   199
    Meetings   200
   #4 Settings   200
   #5 Finding someone   202
   #6 The add people button   203
   #7 Sub-tabs   204
    Contacts   204
    Conversations   205
   #8 The main section   206
   #9 Selecting primary device   206
  The Parts of Teams   208
   #1 Search box   209
   #2 Your profile picture   210

#3 The minimize, maximize, and close buttons   210
#4 New chat button   210
#5 Back and forward buttons   211
#6 Left navigation   211
#7 Location and menu   212
#8 The tabs   212
#9 Adding a tab   212
#10 Public/private indicator   213
#11 The main app screen   214
How to get into Skype for Business   214
Getting into Skype for Business via Office 365   214
Getting into Skype for Business via the app   215
How to get into Teams   215
Getting into Teams via Office 365   216
Getting into Teams via the app   216
The Way Forward with Teams   219
Summary   219
Chapter 9: Using Skype for Business   221
Knowing the presence settings   222
Available   222
Busy   223
Do not disturb   223
The aways   223
Be right back   223
Off work   224
Appear away   224
Offline   224
Unknown   224
Working with contacts   224
Options by hovering   224
Options by dropdown   225
Instant messaging, calls, emails, and meeting invites   226
Removing a contact   226
Copying and moving contacts   227
Tag for status change alerts   227
Change privacy relationship   228
Working with groups   228
Instant messaging   229
#1 Text box   231
#2 Message area   231
#3 Message options   231
#4 IM button   231
#5 Call buttons   231
#6 Presentation button   232
#7 More options button   237

#8 Participants list 238
#9 Add more participants button 239
Initiating calls 239
Working in meetings 240
Sending a meeting invite 241
Sending via Outlook online 241
Send via Outlook on your desktop 242
Summary 243

Chapter 10: Using Microsoft Teams 245
Exploring presence settings 246
Available 246
Busy 247
Do not disturb 247
The aways 247
Be right back 247
Appear away 248
Offline 248
Unknown 248
Working with contacts 248
Adding chat contacts to groups 250
Adding call contacts 252
Instant messaging 255
Initiating calls 256
Working in your Teams 256
The Teams and channels panel 257
Privacy indicator 257
Using more options for Teams and channels 258
More options for the selected Team's channel 260
The tabs 260
The main window 262
Join or create a Team 262
The manage Teams settings 264
Working in meetings 265
Sending a meeting invite 270
Sending a meeting invite via Teams 270
Sending a meeting invite via Outlook on your desktop 274
Summary 275

Section 4: OneDrive for Business

Chapter 11: Understanding OneDrive For Business 279
History and background of OneDrive for Business 279
Getting into OneDrive for Business 280
Parts of OneDrive for Business 282

#1 Search box   282
#2 Your OneDrive navigation   285
   Recent   285
   Shared   286
   Recycle bin   286
#3 Sites navigation   287
#4 Extra options   288
#5 Action bar   289
#6 View options and detail pane   290
#7 Main window   296
How is OneDrive for Business different from OneDrive   296
Summary   298

Chapter 12: Working with Files in Your OneDrive for Business 299
  Adding new files   299
   Creating new files   300
   Uploading files   303
  Editing files   304
  Deleting files   305
  Parts of the Office Online file   306
   Open in the full desktop version   306
    AutoSave   306
    Easy way to rename file   307
    The simplified ribbon   307
    The tabs and ribbons   308
    Getting back to your OneDrive for Business 309
    The backstage   310
     Save As   311
     Print   312
  Sharing files   313
   Giving access   313
   Editing or removing access   316
   Things you should consider   320
  Move to   320
  Copy to   322
  Summary   322

Section 5: Collaboration Using SharePoint

Chapter 13: Understanding SharePoint   325
  Background and history   325
  Editions of SharePoint   327
  Getting into SharePoint Online   327
  The SharePoint home   328
   #1 Search   329
   #2 Left navigation   333
    Following   334

Recent 335
Featured links 335
#3 Creation options 336
#4 Message 337
#5 News from sites 338
#6 Frequent sites 338
#7 Site card 338
#8 Get the mobile app 339
Navigating SharePoint 340
The anatomy of the SharePoint page 342
The classic page anatomy 343
#1 Office 365 suite bar 343
#2 Settings 344
#3 Help 345
#4 Promoted actions bar 346
#5 Search 346
#6 Tabs 348
#7 Logo 348
#8 Global navigation 349
#9 Left navigation 349
#10 Breadcrumb 349
#11 Web parts and app parts 349
The modern page anatomy 350
#1 Office 365 Suite Bar 350
#2 Settings 351
#3 Help 352
#4 Promoted actions bar 353
#5 Page actions bar 353
#6 Global navigation 353
#7 Logo 353
#8 Breadcrumb 354
#9 Search 354
#10 Left navigation 355
#11 Page header 355
#12 Web parts and app parts 355
#13 Feedback 356
Summary 357

Chapter 14: Working with SharePoint Lists 359
What are Lists? 359
The different List types 360
Communications 360
Tracking 361
Custom lists 361
What is a List View? 362
Adding items to any list using a list view 362
Editing items using a list view 366
Deleting items in a list view 370

Adding/editing/deleting items in the calendar view 372
Summary 373
Chapter 15: Performing Different File Operations on SharePoint 375
  What are libraries? 375
  The different library types 376
    Document 376
    Form 376
    Wiki page 376
    Picture 376
  What is a library view? 377
  Using the document library 377
    Adding files 378
    Creating new files in the Modern Experience 380
    Uploading files in the Modern Experience 382
    Editing files 383
    Deleting files 384
    Naming conventions 386
    Version history 387
    Checking files in or out 388
      Checking out 389
      Checking in 390
    Coauthoring 394
  Sharing files 394
    Giving access 394
    Editing or removing access 398
  Move to 398
  Copy to 400
  Summary 401
Chapter 16: More on Using SharePoint 403
  Quick edit mode 403
  Exporting to Excel 406
  Creating a link 407
    Alerts 410
      Creating alerts 410
      Managing alerts 412
  More on views 413
    Creating a personal view 413
    Switching between views (to view, edit, or delete) 422
  The different ways you can find data 423
    How to use list/library filtering 424
    How to use searching in a list/library 425
    How to search sites in SharePoint 425
    Searching via the SharePoint home 425
  Site contents 426

The recycle bin   426
The danger of the Share button   428
SharePoint permissions and what they allow you to do   429
How to request access   430
Summary   431

Other Books You May Enjoy   433

Index   437

Preface

The purpose of this guide is to give the reader an understanding of the use of Office 365 from a beginner's perspective. This guide will focus on the main areas: email via Exchange, Team communication via Skype for Business and Microsoft Teams, Team collaboration via SharePoint, and Business document storage via OneDrive for Business. It will give you an understanding of how to perform the most common tasks, which will help you begin your journey into one of Microsoft's most popular cloud technologies.

Who this book is for

If you are an IT professional who wants to upgrade your experience to include Microsoft Office 365 and you are new to it, then this book is for you. New users looking to learn about the Office 365 environment in their organization will also find this book useful. Some understanding of the Microsoft Office suite and cloud computing basics will be beneficial.

What this book covers

Chapter 1, *Exploring Office 365*, looks at the background of Office 365 and goes through an overview of its major parts: Exchange, Skype for Business, Microsoft Teams, SharePoint, OneDrive for Business, Office desktop, web and mobile apps, and security. We'll also look at how to log in, and include an important word about browsers.

Chapter 2, *Understanding More about Office 365*, looks at the various parts of Office 365 Home and your personal settings. We'll also look at the difference between Office 365 Commercial and Consumer and their licenses.

Chapter 3, *Understanding Exchange*, explores the background and history of Exchange, arguably the world's most popular mail server. We'll also see how to get to Exchange Online and look at its parts.

Chapter 4, *Sending and Receiving Email*, introduces the different parts of the Outlook web app and Outlook on your desktop, and their functions.

Chapter 5, *Using the Exchange Calendar*, looks at the different parts of the Outlook calendar via the web app and via Outlook on your desktop, and their functions.

Chapter 6, *Using Contacts in Exchange*, explores the various parts of Outlook Contacts via the web app and via Outlook on your desktop, and their functions.

Chapter 7, *Getting Familiar with Other Exchange Settings,* covers the other settings of the Outlook web app and Outlook on your desktop, such as creating an email signature and creating email rules.

Chapter 8, *Understanding Skype for Business and Microsoft Teams,* looks at the background and history of Skype for Business and Microsoft Teams. We'll also look at how to get into Skype for Business and Microsoft Teams, the various parts of each, and their functions. Lastly, we'll point out the path that Microsoft is taking with Teams.

Chapter 9, *Using Skype for Business,* explores the functions of Skype for Business, such as presence settings, instant messaging, and working in meetings.

Chapter 10, *Using Microsoft Teams,* covers the functions of Microsoft Teams, such as presence settings, instant messaging, and working in meetings.

Chapter 11, *Understanding OneDrive For Business,* explores the background and history of OneDrive for Business. We'll also look at how to get to OneDrive for Business and examine its parts. Lastly, we will look at how OneDrive for Business is different from OneDrive.

Chapter 12, *Working with Files in Your OneDrive for Business,* looks at adding, editing, and deleting files using OneDrive for Business, and the parts of the Office Online file. We'll also look at sharing, moving, and copying files.

Chapter 13, *Understanding SharePoint,* goes into the background, history, and editions of SharePoint. We'll also look at how to get to SharePoint and the various parts of SharePoint Home. Lastly, we'll look at navigating SharePoint and the anatomy of a SharePoint page.

Chapter 14, *Working with SharePoint Lists,* explores what a list is and the different list types. We'll also explore list views, as well as how to work with them.

Chapter 15, *Performing Different File Operations on SharePoint,* explores what a library is and the different library types. We'll explore library views, as well as how to work with them. We'll also look at naming conventions, version history, coauthoring, and checking in/out, as well as sharing, copying, and moving files.

Chapter 16, *More on Using SharePoint,* covers other SharePoint functions, such as using the quick edit, creating and managing alerts, different ways to search, and the dangers of the share button.

To get the most out of this book

In order to walk through the examples in this book, you will need an Office 365 Business subscription, preferably Business Premium, E3, or E5.

Download the color images

We also provide a PDF file that has color images of the screenshots/diagrams used in this book. You can download it here: `https://www.packtpub.com/sites/default/files/downloads/9781789809312_ColorImages.pdf`.

Conventions used

There are a number of text conventions used throughout this book.

`CodeInText`: Indicates code words in text, database table names, folder names, filenames, file extensions, pathnames, dummy URLs, user input, and Twitter handles. Here is an example: "Via this tab, you can open a calendar file (`.ics` or `.vcs`), a `.pst` file, or a `user` folder shared with you."

Bold: Indicates a new term, an important word, or words that you see onscreen. For example, words in menus or dialog boxes appear in the text like this. Here is an example: "Click on the bell to open the **Notifications** panel and see what notifications you have."

Warnings or important notes appear like this.

Tips and tricks appear like this.

Get in touch

Feedback from our readers is always welcome.

General feedback: If you have questions about any aspect of this book, mention the book title in the subject of your message and email us at `customercare@packtpub.com`.

Errata: Although we have taken every care to ensure the accuracy of our content, mistakes do happen. If you have found a mistake in this book, we would be grateful if you would report this to us. Please visit `www.packt.com/submit-errata`, selecting your book, clicking on the Errata Submission Form link, and entering the details.

Piracy: If you come across any illegal copies of our works in any form on the Internet, we would be grateful if you would provide us with the location address or website name. Please contact us at copyright@packt.com with a link to the material.

If you are interested in becoming an author: If there is a topic that you have expertise in and you are interested in either writing or contributing to a book, please visit authors.packtpub.com.

Reviews

Please leave a review. Once you have read and used this book, why not leave a review on the site that you purchased it from? Potential readers can then see and use your unbiased opinion to make purchase decisions, we at Packt can understand what you think about our products, and our authors can see your feedback on their book. Thank you!

For more information about Packt, please visit packt.com.

Section 1: Understanding Office 365 **1**

In this section, readers will learn about Office 365 in general and will be given some information on how to make it more useful.

The following chapters will be covered:

- Chapter 1, *Exploring Office 365*
- Chapter 2, *Understanding More about Office 365*

Exploring Office 365 1

Office 365 is one of the many Microsoft cloud solutions, and it seems to be the most popular. Since its general release in June 2011 as the successor to **Business Productivity Online Suite** (**BPOS**), Office 365 has grown to have over 120,000,000 active monthly commercial users and 28,000,000 active consumer users.

Since the start of Office 365, there has been a lot of confusion about what the difference is between Microsoft Office 365 and Microsoft Office. To add to the confusion, there are the Office 365 Commercial and Office 365 Consumer versions, and the Commercial version has many versions. Many business owners purchase the Consumer version and believe they have services available in the Commercial version. Because of this confusion, I believe it is imperative that you understand the different versions and what comes with each.

For starters, Office 365 has only been around since being beta-tested in 2010 and released in 2011, while Office had been announced in 1988 and was released in 1990.

In this chapter, you will learn about Microsoft Office, along with its different versions and the services provided by it. You will get a brief overview of all these services. You will also learn how to log into your Microsoft account.

In this chapter, the following topics will be covered:

- Microsoft Office and its versions
- Overview of the services of Office 365
- A word about supported browsers

Technical requirements

To follow along with the lessons in this book, you will need an Office 365 Business Premium, E3, or E5 subscription..

Microsoft Office and its versions

Microsoft provides different versions of its Office suite, which differ in the applications they include and are designed so that customers can buy only the applications that they need. Office has a few versions of its suite:

- Office Home & Student
- Office Home & Business
- Office Standard
- Office Professional
- Office Professional Plus
- Office Professional Academic

Each version of Office includes the following programs, products, and features:

Programs, products, and features	Office Home & Student	Office Home & Business	Office Standard	Office Professional	Office Professional Plus	Office Professional Academic
Excel	Yes	Yes	Yes	Yes	Yes	Yes
OneNote	Yes	Yes	Yes	Yes	Yes	Yes
PowerPoint	Yes	Yes	Yes	Yes	Yes	Yes
Word	Yes	Yes	Yes	Yes	Yes	Yes
Outlook	No	Yes	Yes	Yes	Yes	Yes
Publisher	No	No	Yes	Yes	Yes	Yes
Access	No	No	No	Yes	Yes	Yes
Lync/Skype for Business	No	No	No	No	Yes	No
InfoPath *	No	No	No	No	Yes	No
SharePoint Workspace	No	No	No	No	Yes	No

The previous table is referencing Office 2010 since it is the last version of the Office suite, before the cloud versions complicated things. Office, the non-cloud version, is purchased via a one-time fee of between $60 to ~$400 retail. When I say one-time, I mean one-time until you need to upgrade.

Conversely, Office 365 comes in a lot more versions than Office and, rather than paying a one-time price at retail or volume cost, you lease the software by paying a small sum monthly or annually. Office 365 can be Office only, Office with other products, or no Office included whatsoever.

The main versions of Office 365 are as follows:

- Consumer versions:
    - Home
    - Personal
    - Home & Student
- Commercial/business versions:
    - Business
    - Business Essentials
    - Business Premium
    - Pro Plus
    - Enterprise E1
    - Enterprise E3
    - Enterprise E5

Those are the core ones, but there are more versions for government, non-profit, and academic use, but they are very similar to the Business through E3 versions, aside from the cost and a few other particulars.

In `Chapter 2`, *Understanding More about Office 365*, we will discuss licensing in more detail. Just note that in this book, we will cover the Business version of Office 365.

Overview of the services of Office 365

Office 365 subscriptions vary, but the following are the services in Office 365 for most plans. There are more services than what I have listed here, and each of these services can be assigned to users individually with some exceptions. For more details, see the Business plans at `https://products.office.com/en-us/compare-all-microsoft-office-products?tab=2` and the Enterprise plans at `https://products.office.com/en-us/business/compare-more-office-365-for-business-plans`.

Exchange

This is the engine behind Outlook. It supplies you with email, calendar, contacts, tasks, journaling, and notes capabilities. This portion of Office 365 gives an enterprise-grade, professional email with 50 GB of space using your company's custom domain. You also get the ability to share calendars with others in your organization. Exchange is included with the Business Essentials, Business Premium, E1, E3, and E5 plans. If you have an E3 or E5 plan, you will get a 100 GB mailbox with unlimited archiving.

Skype for Business

This application started as Lync in the first release of Office 365 and is different than Skype, which is the consumer service. With this service, each user has their own account where they can see the presence of people in their personal list and have the ability to instant message and schedule or initiate impromptu online meetings with audio or HD video conferencing for up to 250 participants. No more sharing meeting accounts! It also allows the host(s) to share surveys, polls, and whiteboards with the attendees, and attendees as well as the host(s) can share a meeting notebook or take notes on an individual basis via OneNote integration. Invited attendees do not have to have the Skype for Business application to participate in the meeting.

Skype for Business is included with the Business Essentials, Business Premium, E1, E3, and E5 plans, and were initiated after around 24 August 2018. Any plan initiated after this date will only have Microsoft Teams available, as Teams is replacing Skype for Business in purely cloud Office 365 tenants. Your organization will still have the ability to have a Skype for Business server on premises if desired and if the appropriate additional server (not Office 365) licenses are purchased and deployed. If you have an E5 plan, you may also get a phone number assigned to you from this service and have the ability to dial out and receive calls via this application.

Microsoft Teams

Microsoft Teams is one of Microsoft's newest services and a direct competitive service to Slack. It is a real-time and persistent collaborative work space that's easy to quickly set up and integrates instant messaging, meeting, notes capabilities, and file management, as well as the ability to easily integrate in other Microsoft and third-party apps. This service gives teams of people, internal and external, the ability to have their own work space and collaborate on a single source of truth.

In organizations with purely cloud implementations of Office 365, users with Skype for Business and Microsoft Teams will eventually be migrated to Microsoft Teams only. Microsoft Teams is included with the Business Essentials, Business Premium, E1, E3, and E5 plans. If you have an E5 plan, you may also get a phone number assigned to you from this service and have the ability to dial out and receive calls via this application.

SharePoint

SharePoint is Microsoft's original collaborative work space and has been around even before its initial release as SharePoint in 28 March 2001. SharePoint was added as a service to Office 365 and renamed SharePoint Online. Since then, it has evolved into its own evergreen version during the life of SharePoint 2013 and on a life of its own, widely diverging its capabilities from the SharePoint on-premises versions of 2013, 2016, and 2019. Still, SharePoint Online has capabilities above and beyond those offered by Microsoft Teams and is the backbone for Microsoft Teams. This service gives you the ability to share documents and manage projects, like Microsoft Teams, but also to create online forms, dashboards, automated workflow, and much more.

In SharePoint, your organization starts off with 1 TB of storage space, which can be upgraded to as large as 25 TB. SharePoint Online is included with the Business Essentials, Business Premium, E1, E3, and E5 plans.

OneDrive for Business

This application started in Office 365 as SkyDrive for Business and is not the same as OneDrive, which is the consumer service. OneDrive for Business gives you your very own 1 TB of business file storage that can be synced with PC, Mac, and/or mobile devices. You have the ability to easily create and share files with internal and external people (depending on configuration) and control who can see and/or edit the shared documents. OneDrive for Business is included with the Business, Business Essentials, Business Premium, Pro Plus, E1, E3, and E5 plans.

Office Professional or Professional Plus applications for desktop

Plans offering gives you either licenses for Office Professional or Office Professional Plus. Each user with this license will have the ability to download Office on up to five mobile devices and five PCs/Macs. Office Professional Plus includes Outlook, Word, PowerPoint, Excel, Publisher, Access, Excel, and OneNote, and Professional offers all of these except Publisher. The version of Office in Office 365 is evergreen, much like SharePoint Online. InfoPath, which has been a part of Office Pro Plus since Office 2003, has been removed from the Office suite, but is still available for download separately via the Office 365 downloads. Office Pro is included in Business and Business Premium plans, and Office Pro Plus is included in Pro Plus and in all Enterprise plans.

Office web and mobile apps

The web app and mobile app versions of Office give you the ability to create, access, edit, and share Word, Excel, PowerPoint, and OneNote files through OneDrive for Business, SharePoint, and Microsoft Teams. You also get the ability to co-author documents with those who have edit access. Co-authoring is the ability to open and work on a document simultaneously with others. Office web and mobile apps are included in the Pro Plus plan, as well as all Business and Enterprise plans except E1. For E1, only the web apps are available.

Security, transparency, compliance, and privacy

In addition, Office 365 is security-hardened and compliant with a plethora of government and industry standards in the US and abroad. Your data is your data and it says private to you and your organization, and your organization has the ability to see where the data is and who has access to it. There are more measures and capabilities than what I have outlined here. You can read all of the details on Microsoft's privacy, compliance, security, and transparency measures via the Microsoft Trust Center: http://trustoffice365.com.

Logging in

You need to log into Office 365 to use all of its features. Once you have an Office 365 account, you can login using the following steps:

1. Go to `https://www.office.com/` and click the **Sign In** button:

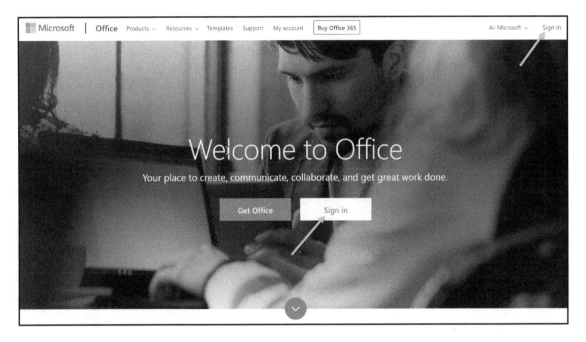

2. You will be taken to a page similar to the following, where you can enter your email address for your account and then your password:

3. If you have logged in with different accounts before, you will see something similar to the following screen. Choose an account:

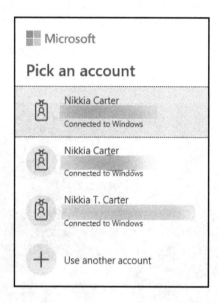

You can go directly to the sign-in page by going to `https://portal.office.com` instead of `https://www.office.com/`.

Now, let's look at the different browsers that you can use for Microsoft Office.

A word about browsers

Microsoft says that Office 365 works on all popular, up-to-date browsers, which is true, but not all work well. Here is the ranking from best to worse:

- **Internet Explorer 11 (IE11)**: This Microsoft browser is still the best for all features and functionalities of Office 365 and SharePoint. I realize that this browser is decrepit and mostly useless for anything else but this.

I have noted **IE11** since no other version of IE will work well, and any other version is no longer supported.

The first three browsers offer most of the features and functionality of Office 365 and SharePoint:

- **Edge**: Microsoft's newest browser, which was meant to eventually replace IE. The word on the street is that Edge should replace IE soon but, at the time of writing this book, there is no anticipated date.
- **Firefox**: This browser can actually work better than Internet Explorer in one regard: it can be easier to move things around in SharePoint when designing at times because it was designed for web development.
- **Safari**: This is the browser for Mac. On Mac, the user can get Firefox but not IE.
- **Chrome**: This browser, by Google, is a hugely popular one, but in the case of Office 365 and SharePoint, you should make this browser your last choice. Google does not readily share browser code changes with Microsoft, and those changes can happen at the drop of a hat and usually without warning. You could literally leave your desk for a few minutes or even go from one page to another and suddenly the screens may look different, have things missing, and/or look broken. The sudden code changes cause problems with SharePoint and Office 365.

  Things could be different and, if you are not intimately aware of the environment, you may not even realize that you are missing possible valuable pieces of information. Due to this possible sudden issue, I highly advise you to use Chrome for everything else for Office 365 and SharePoint. If you do use Chrome for SharePoint and Office 365, note that you will be doing so at your own possible peril.

  I would even go as far as to highly recommend that you set your default browser to any of the other browsers because some of my clients have had trouble launching Skype for Business meetings when clicking on the **Join Skype Meeting** link (and this may also be the case for Teams meetings). When the link is clicked, the user is first taken to the browser while the full Skype for Business or Teams application is searched for. If the application is not found, the user is offered the ability to use the web app version. The browser that's used when the meeting link is clicked is the default browser.

Summary

In this chapter, we discussed Microsoft Office and its versions, the services of Office 365, as well as important information about how to log in and an important note about browsers.

You learned about the history and different parts/services of Office 365, such as exchange, security, transparency, and the business services, such as Skype, teams, and One Drive. You also learned how to implement the login process in Microsoft Office and about how different browsers handle the features and functionality of Office 365 and SharePoint.

In Chapter 2, *Understanding More about Office 365*, we will go deeper into Office 365 by exploring the Office 365 Home page and setting your personal settings.

2
Understanding More about Office 365

Like any other cloud service, understanding Office 365's home page and how to use it is essential to making effective use of the service. The home page gives you access to all of the services that are available under your subscription plan, access to recent documents, and so on. It's a page you'll visit very often, especially when you first start using the service. A basic activity you need to learn about in Office 365 is setting up your personal settings. These settings help you accurately set your preferences and make your use of the service optimal. Finally, it's important to understand the various licenses for Office 365 and pick one that is appropriate for your needs.

In this chapter, you will explore your Office 365 Home page, learn how to set your personal settings, and examine the available licenses and what they offer. You will click through different sections of your home page to look at the features and actions that are available to you. You will change a few details such as your profile picture and update your security phone number. You will also learn about Office 365's background and the parts of Office 365 that make up this platform as a service.

In this chapter, the following topics will be covered:

- The home page
- Configuring your personal settings
- Licensing

The home page

Like any web-based service, Office 365 has a home page through which all subscribers can access all the essential services and features of their subscription. When you first log in to Office 365, you are greeted with the Office 365 Home page:

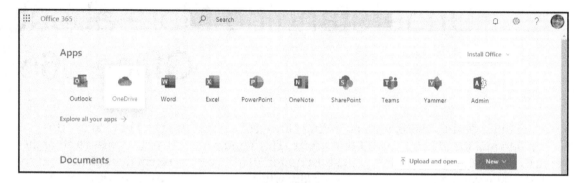

This home page may greet you every time, depending on what type of user you are. It may be replaced automatically if you are an admin, or manually if you change the settings yourself. We will look at how you can change your settings in a bit but, for now, let's explore the Office 365 Home page and the Office 365 suite bar. We'll start at the top, moving left to right, and work our way down the page.

The suite bar

The suite bar is the bar at the very top of the Office 365 screen in your browser. This bar is always there for you and can be accessed no matter where you go in Office 365, with the exception of Microsoft Teams. Microsoft Teams has its own suite bar of sorts, which will be discussed in `Chapter 8`, *Understanding Skype for Business and Microsoft Teams*:

In some Office 365 applications, some of the options may change, such as those under **Help**, while others such as the app launcher/switcher will always be present with the same options.

You can still get to the Office 365 Home page by clicking on **Office 365** in the suite bar, as shown in the following screenshot:

You can also get to **Office 365** by going to `https://www.office.com/?auth=2home=1` in a new tab or in the same tab in the browser that you are currently logged in to **Office 365** within.

The app launcher/switcher

This is also known as the Waffle menu, and contains the applications that are available to you through the **Office 365** platform as per your **Office 365** license. Your license may be different than that of your peers, so you may have more or fewer applications than them. The Waffle, which travels from application to application, allows you to get around **Office 365** with ease. The following is a representation of what you may see in your Waffle, depending on the applications you have access to and your role in your organization:

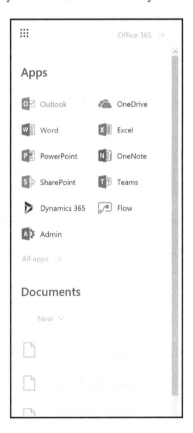

As you can see, you get a truncated list of apps with an option to see your full list. After this list is a list of recently used documents.

The Office 365 link

The Office 365 link immediately follows the Waffle. This link allows you to get back to the Office 365 Home page if you ever want to go back to it for whatever reason. Most users decide to configure their settings to start the day in the portal at a different point than the Office 365 Home page, but they may need to get back to Home for several reasons. One reason could be to access software downloads easily as this is one of the elements that is easy to access from Home rather than from within an application.

Following the **Office 365** link may be an indicator of where you are in **Office 365**:

For instance, in the previous screenshot, you are in **SharePoint**. After the words **Office 365**, you can see the words **SharePoint**. In SharePoint's case, this is clickable and will lead you to the **SharePoint** home page.

Notifications

The bell on the suite bar is where your notifications will show up. The notifications you can expect are for emails, as well as meeting and appointment reminders. To check these notifications, perform the following steps:

1. Click on the bell to open the **Notifications** panel and see what notifications you may have. You may not see any notifications for a while if you just turned **Notifications** on under **Settings** or if the notifications were turned off:

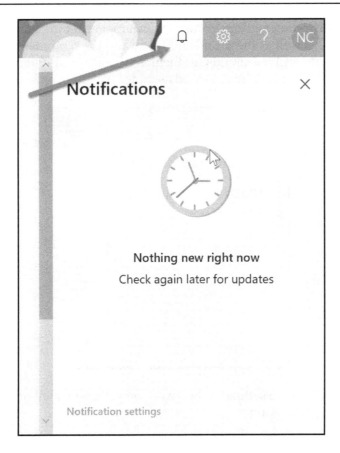

2. To change the settings for your notifications, click the **Notifications settings** link at the bottom of the panel or click on **Customize settings**:

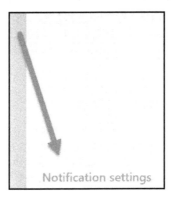

3. In the **Notification settings** panel, you can toggle getting **New mail** notifications on and off, as well as the sounds for them, and the reminders for meetings and appointments and the sounds for them, too. You can also toggle notifications themselves on and off here, as well as under **Notification settings**:

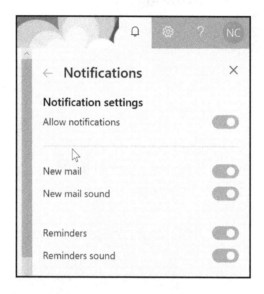

Once you are done with these settings, whenever you get a new mail or reminder, you will receive a notification with a sound.

Settings

There are a lot of settings that you can control as an end user. There are so many to explore that I gave them their own section in this chapter. I will go into more detail about these settings in the *Configuring your personal settings* section of this chapter.

Help

The content of the **Help** menu you get in Office 365 can vary, depending on where you are in Office 365 and/or if your web page has fully opened or not. Clicking on the question mark icon will open the **Help** menu. If you open it from the Office 365 Home page and your page has fully opened, you have the ability to search through help topics and view the **Featured Help** topics. Also, at the bottom of the panel, you can click on links to the **Legal |** **Privacy & cookies** information:

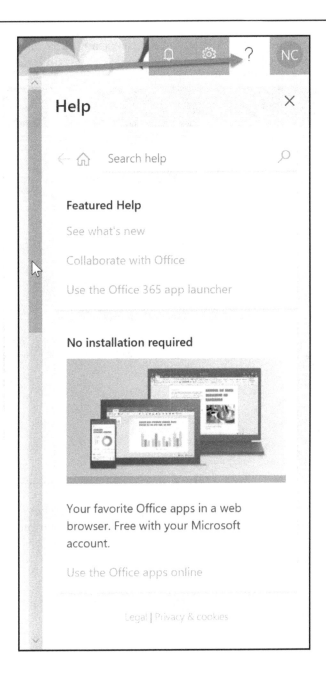

If your page doesn't completely open or if you are in certain parts of Office 365, you may see the following **Help** menu. Notice that the search box is missing:

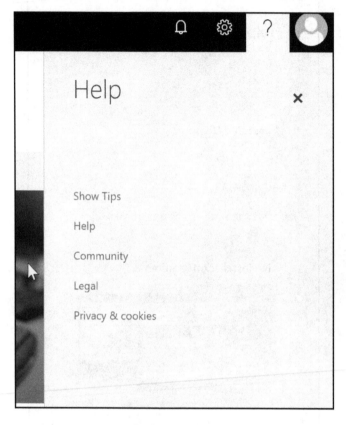

When in Outlook, you may get the following **Help** menu. Notice how the topics here are a bit different than those on the Office 365 Home page. Most of the topics here focus on email capabilities:

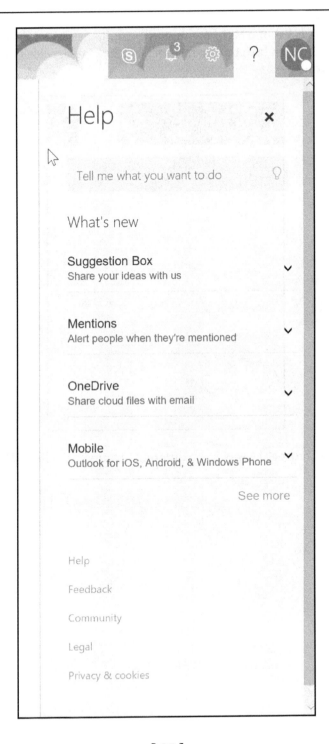

In other places in Office 365, the **Help** menu may be quite generic, such as in the following screenshot. There is a search box, but there aren't any links to articles pertaining specifically to the place where you are:

The **Help** menu in **Microsoft Teams** has a different location than most **Help** menus in Office 365:

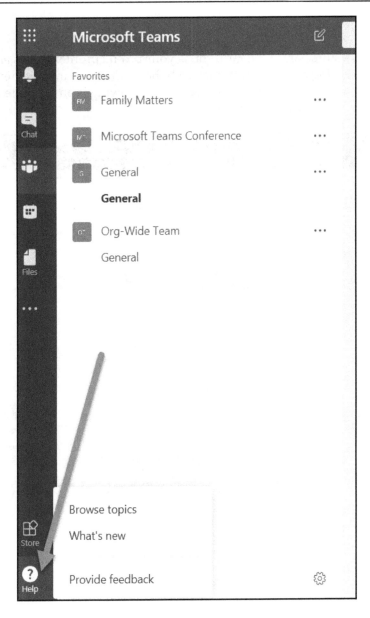

It is actually at the bottom of the left navigation panel instead of on Office 365's suite bar.

Your profile picture

Also on Office 365's suite bar, to the far right, is your profile profile. This is an image of you, or an image representing a person or perhaps a bubble with your initials (depending on how your admin has set up your organization). The following is an example of what you may see if you have chosen an image of yourself:

Here are the examples of what you may see if you have not chosen an image of yourself:

- A generic silhouette:

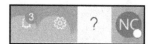

- Your initials:

When you click on your persona anywhere in Office 365, except for Microsoft Teams, a side panel opens:

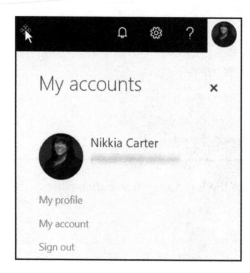

In this panel, you can click on the links to view your profile, view your account, **Sign out**, or change your profile picture.

Changing your profile picture

One of the first things you may want to do is change your profile picture. In an organization, using a profile picture can help others identify you easily, especially in Microsoft Teams.

To change your picture, perform the following steps:

1. Hover over the profile picture bubble in the open panel and then click on the camera icon:

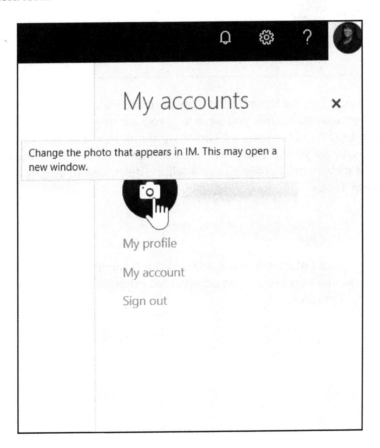

2. Another page will open, where you will be able to browse images and choose the one you want to display. This will give you a preview of the image:

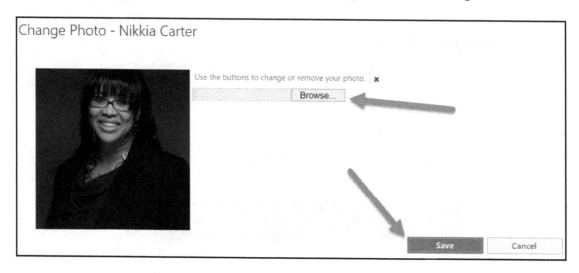

3. Once done, click the **Save** button. Your picture should show up in the suite bar almost immediately after you save it. If you are using Skype for Business, it may take up to 15 minutes before it shows up there. For Microsoft Teams, you will have to change your picture in Microsoft Teams separately. Changing your persona picture in Microsoft Teams will be discussed in Chapter 10, *Using Microsoft Teams*.

My profile

My profile is a section of Office 365 that contains your basic information. Depending on the kind of organization that you are in, you can also see other members of your team and click through to their own profiles.

Clicking on the **My profile** link will take you to Delve.

You will be required to sign back in for security reasons.

From Delve, you will be able to see the details of your profile that you have already filled in and can choose to add more details or edit those details by clicking on the **Update profile** button:

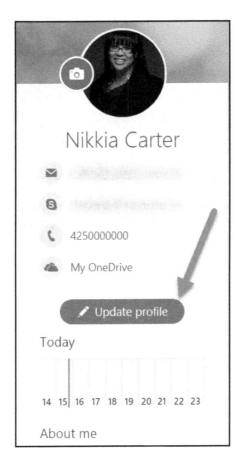

You can also choose to click on the **Add about me**, **Add projects you are working on**, **Add skills and expertise**, or **Add schools and education** links to add details about those areas directly:

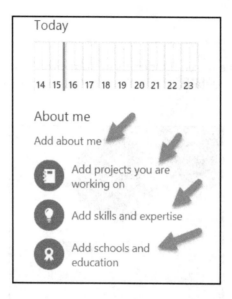

When you click on the **Update profile** button, you will be taken to a page where you can enter details for your contact info, projects, skills, education, interests, and/or give a summary about yourself:

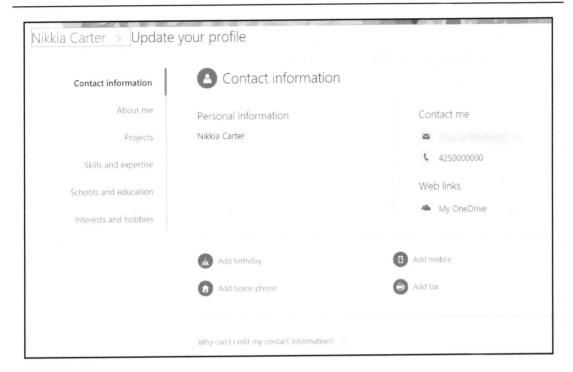

 Some of your details may be un-editable, depending on if and how your organization is managing those details for you.

Keeping this page updated will help people in your organization contact you efficiently as this is the information available to them through all Office 365 apps.

My account

Clicking on the **My account** link takes you to the **My account** page:

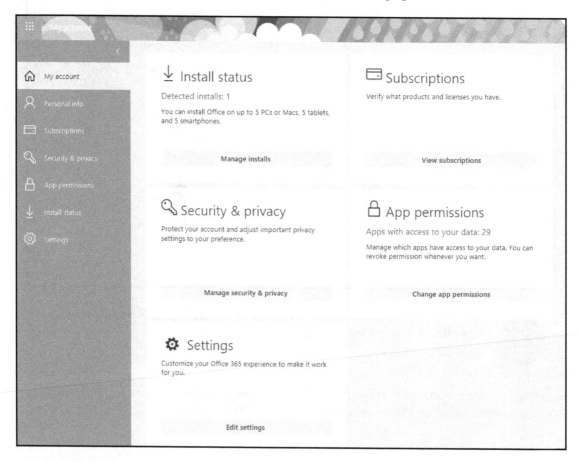

On this page, you can do the following:

- See the number of devices that you have Office installed on
- Manage a mini version of your profile
- See the products in Office 365 that you have access to
- Manage other settings for app permissions, security and privacy, and customization

Personal info

Personal info is another option that you can use to view your contact information. To view or edit your personal information, follow the steps:

1. Click on the **Personal info** link in the left navigation bar:

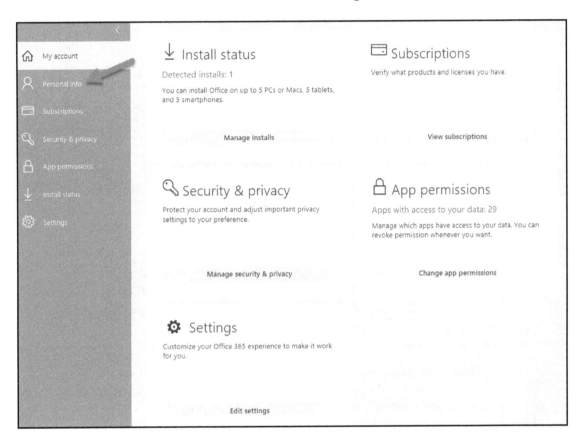

Once you click on it, you will be taken to a page where you can enter or edit some of your personal information and change your picture:

The details that you can enter or edit here aren't as abundant as what you can add via the **My profile** link under your persona button in the suite bar. If you need to add or edit details, such as projects you have worked on, you will need to go to the **My profile** page instead. Some of your details may be un-editable, depending on if and how your organization is managing those details for you.

2. To edit any of the details in any of these sections, simply click on the **Edit** pencil in the upper right-hand corner of that section:

3. Click the **Save** button once you're finished:

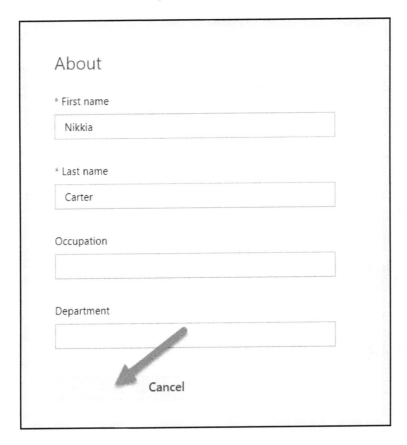

Once you click on this button, your personal information will be updated.

The **Save** button will not activate until you actually make at least one change. If you don't change anything, the button will remain grayed out.

Install status

The install status shows you how many installs of the desktop version of Office you have completed and how many you have left. You can see the number of installs you have completed in the **Install status** block of the **My account** page. You can click on the **Install status** link in the left navigation bar or click on the **Manage installs** button in the **Install status** block to get to the **Install status** page:

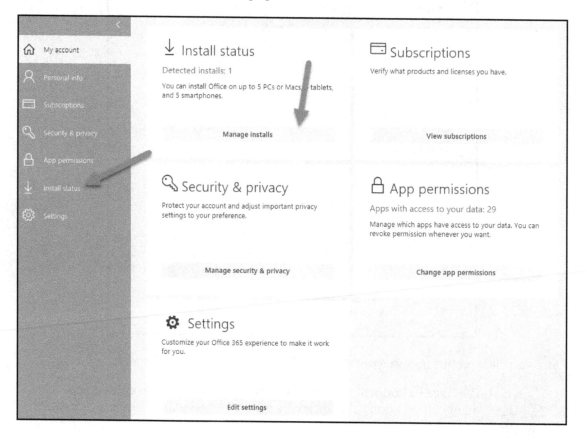

 You must have a subscription that gives you a license to download the desktop version of Office.

Once you're on the **Install status** page, you will see a block for each installation of Office that you have completed. There will also be a link that you can use to install Office. You can see the device name and type from here. You also are able to **Deactivate** any installations that you are no longer using or no longer have access to:

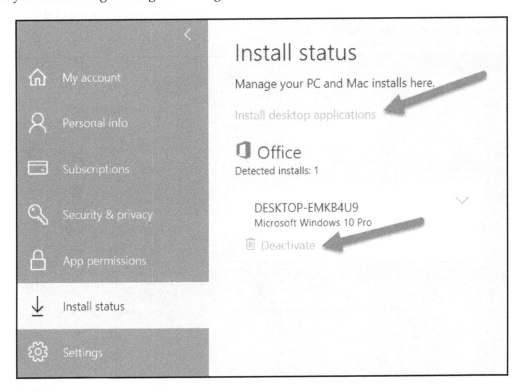

You may find that you need to uninstall Office on a computer that was lost, stolen, or damaged. That way, when you get a new computer, you will have a license to install Office there.

Subscriptions

Subscriptions shows you what software you are licensed to access as per your subscription, and any add-ons that have been added to your user account. Click on the **Subscriptions** link in the left navigation bar or click on the **View subscriptions** button in the **Subscriptions** block to get to the page:

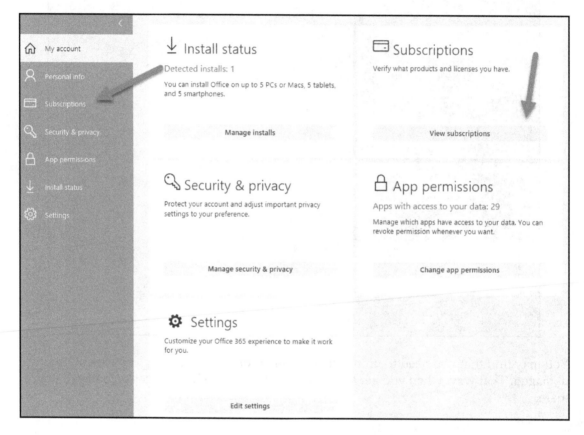

When you click on this option, you'll see the following page:

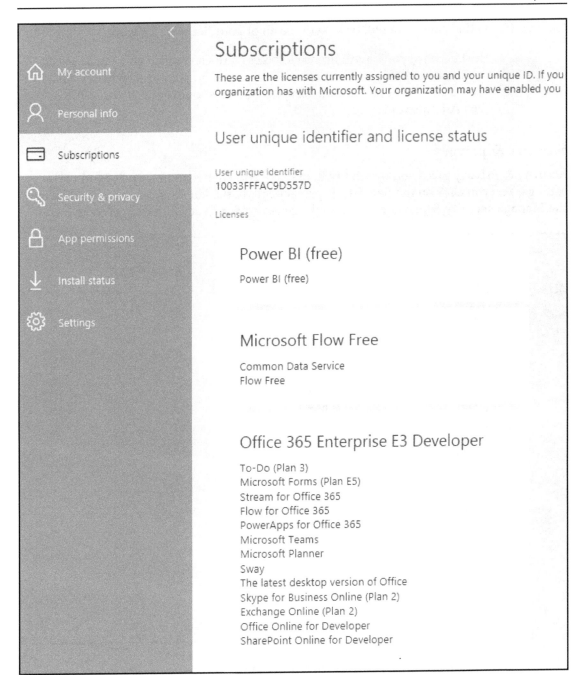

Subscriptions

These are the licenses currently assigned to you and your unique ID. If you organization has with Microsoft. Your organization may have enabled you

User unique identifier and license status

User unique identifier
10033FFFAC9D557D

Licenses

Power BI (free)

Power BI (free)

Microsoft Flow Free

Common Data Service
Flow Free

Office 365 Enterprise E3 Developer

To-Do (Plan 3)
Microsoft Forms (Plan E5)
Stream for Office 365
Flow for Office 365
PowerApps for Office 365
Microsoft Teams
Microsoft Planner
Sway
The latest desktop version of Office
Skype for Business Online (Plan 2)
Exchange Online (Plan 2)
Office Online for Developer
SharePoint Online for Developer

Sidebar menu:
My account
Personal info
Subscriptions
Security & privacy
App permissions
Install status
Settings

Once you're on this page, you will be able to see all of your licensed software.

 Just because you have a license to access it doesn't mean you can access it easily or at all. If you don't see an application on your app switcher but you can see that you have a license to it, you should contact your Office 365 Administrator.

Security & privacy

Security & privacy gives you the ability to manage and change your security and privacy settings. You can click on the **Security & privacy** link in the left navigation bar or click on the **Manage security & privacy** button in the **Security & privacy** block to get to its page:

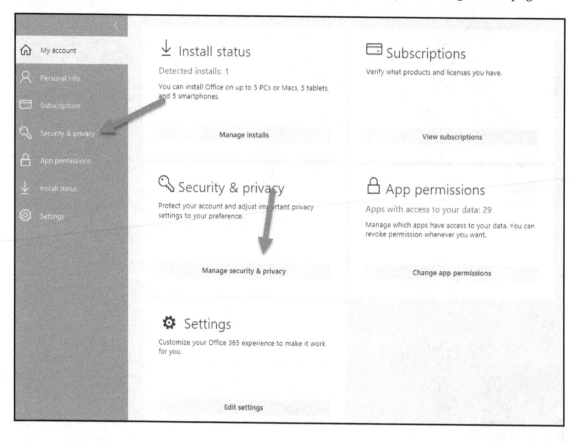

Once you click this button, you will be taken to the **Security & privacy** page:

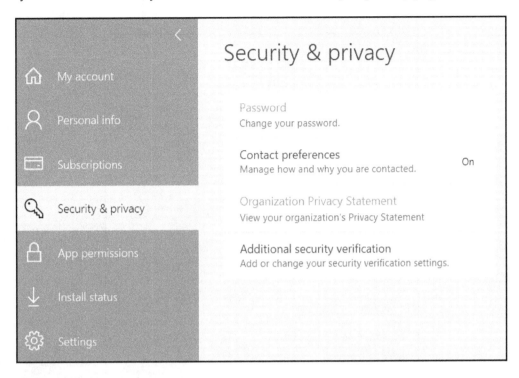

Once on the **Security & privacy** page, you will have options for changing your password, changing your contact preferences, and viewing your organization's privacy statement, and have access to security validation settings.

Password

It's always important to change passwords at regular intervals. Your organization may have a mandatory interval that you need to comply with in terms of keeping your password updated. It's also important to know how to change your password if you suspect that your information has been compromised or if Microsoft puts out a security warning about password security.

Let's look at how we can change our password in Office 365.

When you click on the **Change your password** link, it will open a new page where you can change your password:

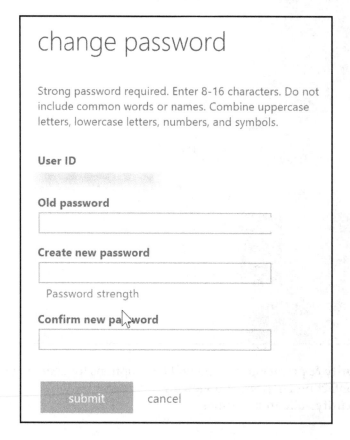

Remember to click the **Submit** button once you have finished.

 Once you have changed your password, you will be logged out and will need to log back in with your new password. Changing your password may not be an option for you if your organization is managing your password for you.

Contact preferences

When changing your **Contact preferences**, you can choose whether you want to get helpful emails from Microsoft. If you are an admin for your organization, you will also be able to set your email and **Phone preferences** for communication with Microsoft partners, and other offers and tips about Office 365 from Microsoft:

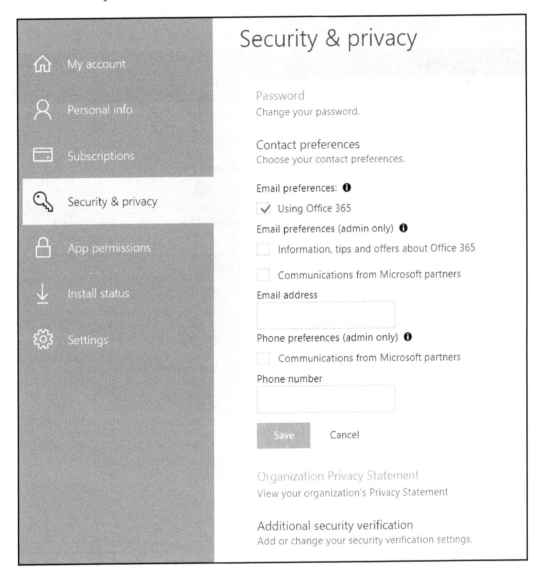

Remember to click the **Save** button once you have finished editing your options.

Organization privacy statement

Privacy concerns is one of the most talked about topics in the always connected age that we live in. It's important to understand the privacy status of your information, even in your work accounts. Such information safeguards both the organization and the employee. You can access your organization's privacy statement by clicking on the **View your organization's Privacy Statement** link. It will open a new window where you will be able to read the notice to end users:

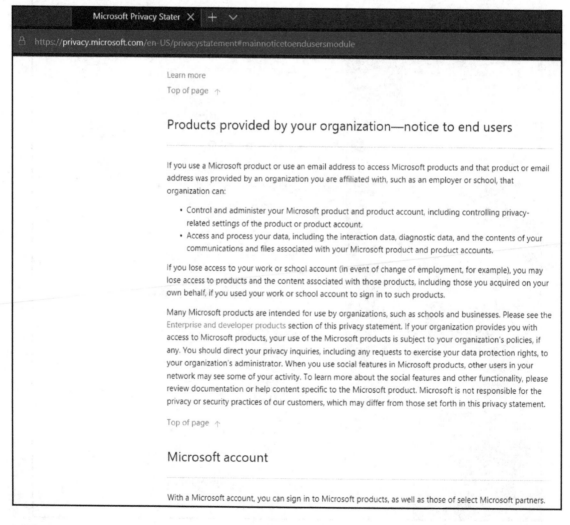

Make sure that you read this carefully and revisit it whenever you are notified that the privacy statement has been updated.

Additional security verification

When you click on this section, you will be able to update your phone numbers for account security and create or manage your app passwords:

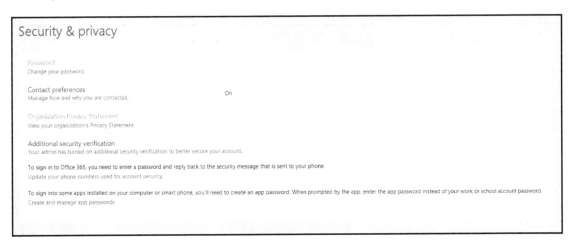

Let's begin by learning how to set and update security phone numbers for your account, which helps you add an additional layer of security, alongside traditional passwords.

Updating your account security phone numbers

Clicking on the **Update your phone numbers used for account security** link opens a new page and lands you in the **Additional security verification** tab. This is where you can set up security verification methods and choose your preferred method.

At a minimum, I highly suggest that you set up an authentication phone, preferably using your mobile (for text and voice message verification), and also set up an authenticator app. You can go to the Google Play Store or the Apple App Store and download your preferred authenticator app.

I highly suggest the Microsoft authenticator app. The authenticator app is more secure than text messaging your authentication phone, but you may need a backup method if your phone is lost, stolen, broken, or traded for a new phone and you need to set the app back up on a new phone, or if the app fails for some reason:

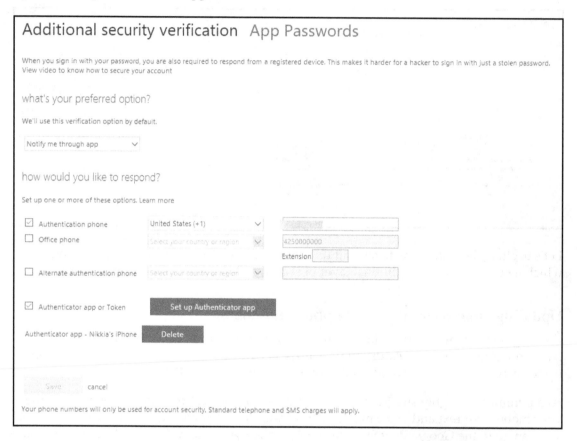

Remember to click on the **Save** button once you have finished adding or editing your options.

Managing app passwords

Clicking on the **Create and manage app passwords** link opens a new page and lands you on the **App password** tab. In this page, you can see the app passwords you have already created, delete any that you have previously created, and create new ones. When you create a new app password, remember to make note of it and keep it in a safe place.

You may find that you need an app password if your company has initiated **Multi-Factor Authentication** (**MFA**) and you find that your preferred authentication method doesn't fire you into certain applications, such as InfoPath:

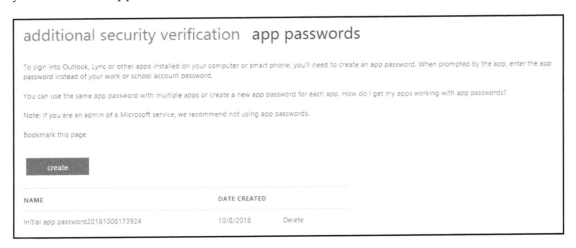

If you lose your app password, you cannot retrieve it from this page. You can only delete it and create a new one, so don't forget to note down your password when you create it and keep it in a safe place:

Click the up arrow on the bottom-right corner of **Settings** when you wish to collapse it.

App permissions

App permissions shows you how many app have permission to your Office 365 data and allows you to revoke permissions. You can see the number of apps that have permission in the **App permissions** block on the **My account** page. You can click on the **App permissions** link in the left navigation bar or click on the **Change app permissions** button in the **App permissions** block to get to its page:

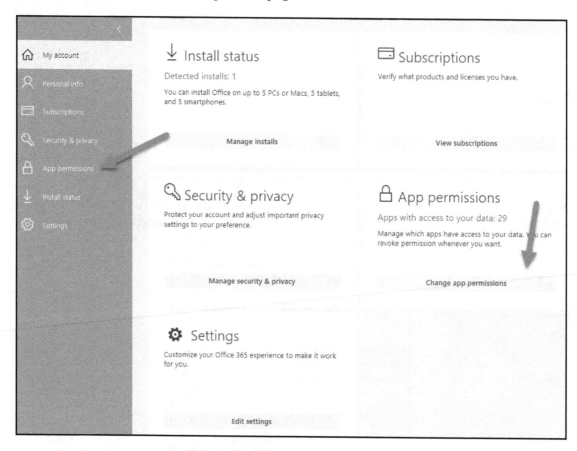

Once you're on this page, you can see the apps that are available to you. For some apps, you will be able to revoke permission and, for others, you will not be able to:

You will be able to see the **Details** for any of the apps, regardless of whether you can revoke permission.

Settings

Settings gives you the ability to customize parts of your user experience in Office 365. You can click on the **Settings** link in the left navigation bar or click on the **Edit settings** button in the **Settings** block to get to the **Settings** page:

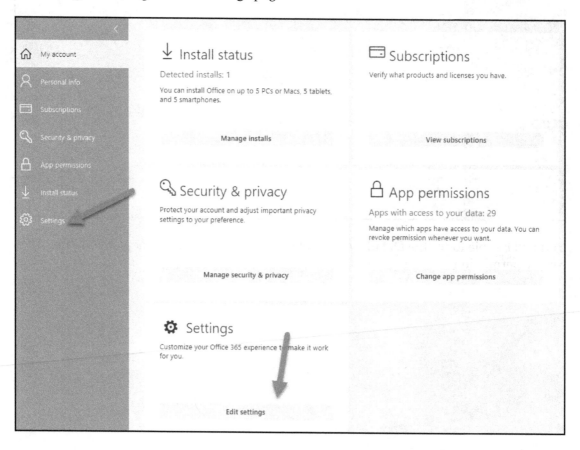

The settings that you can see on the **Settings** page are the same ones you can see under the gear icon, which is also a **Settings** menu:

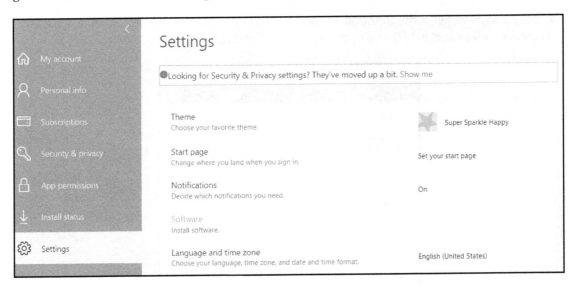

The gear has these and more options, so we will cover these options in the *Configuring your personal settings* section later in this chapter.

Profile picture for Microsoft Teams

When you click on your profile picture anywhere in Microsoft Teams, a side panel opens. On this panel, you get some of the same options that you do in Office 365, such as **Change picture**, as well as some different options, such as **Settings**:

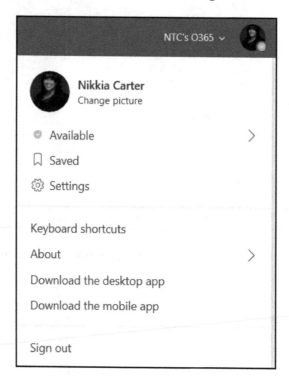

We will discuss these options for Microsoft Teams in `chapter 10`, *Using Microsoft Teams*.

Configuring your personal settings

The **Settings** we will look at in this section pertain to the settings you get when you click on the gear from the Office 365 Home page. The gear menu changes as your make your way through the different applications in Office 365:

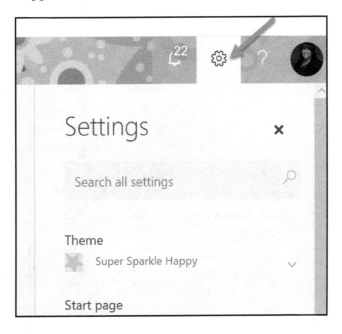

The following screenshot is just a portion of the **Settings** that you can configure for yourself as an end user. Let's walk through each of these options:

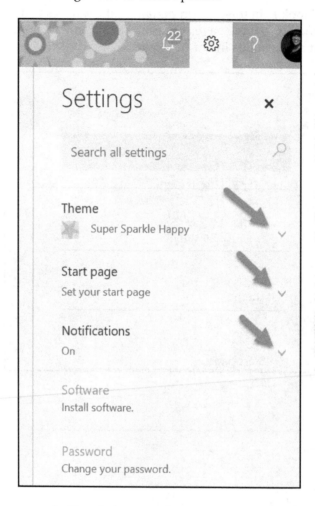

Some sections can be expanded by clicking on the down arrow to the right of them. For example, if you click the down arrow next to **Themes**, you will get a list of themes you can choose from. If you click on the down arrow next to the **Start page**, you will see a dropdown of start page options.

Some of the options that are available through the gear menu are redundant links to settings we have covered in the previous section; for example, we have already learned how to change our passwords and to view our organization's privacy statement. Since we've already learned these skills, we won't revisit them in this section.

The search box

You may not always know the exact option for a setting that you may be looking to configure. This box allows you to search the settings that are available to you:

As you start to type into the box, you will start getting options:

If you don't see the option that you are looking for, try using other words that describe the setting.

 You will get options that are in the **Settings**, as well as others. Some settings may not apply to you, depending on what software licenses you have available to you through your subscription.

Themes

You have the ability to choose a color theme that you would like to use to customize your Office 365's look. Simply click on the down arrow next to **Themes** and choose from the available themes.

New themes are added all the time. Some even have animation! Remember to click the **Save** button once you have chosen your theme or your theme will return to the previous one as soon as you close **Settings** or navigate away from the page:

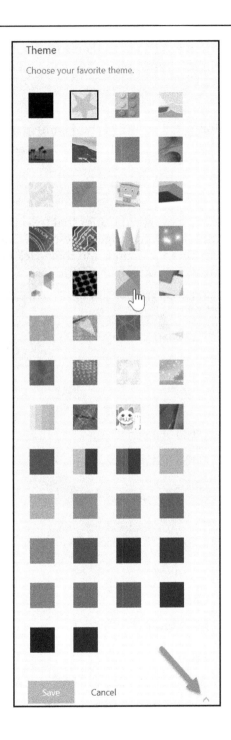

If your organization has created a theme for your organization and has chosen to make it an overriding theme, you will not be able to choose your own.

Click the up arrow in the bottom-right corner of the **Theme** page's **Settings** when you wish to collapse it.

Start page

When you first enter Office 365 and every time after that (except if you are an admin), Office 365 will start on the Office 365 Home page, unless you choose a different start page. Click on the down arrow to expand this section, and then click on the dropdown menu and choose where you want to start when you log into Office 365:

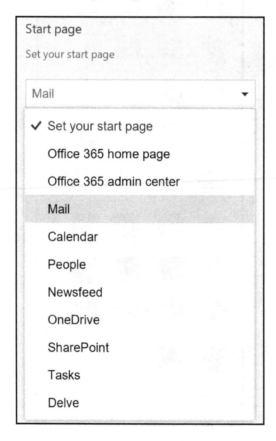

Remember to click the **Save** button after making your choice! Once saved, the next time you log into Office 365, you will land on the starting page that you chose:

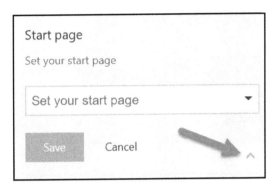

Click the up arrow in the bottom-right corner of the **Start** page's **Settings** when you wish to collapse it.

Software

In this section, you are able to access any software that you have available through your subscription:

Clicking on the **Software** link takes you to a page where you can download available software. If you don't have the desktop version of Office available in your subscription, you should have access to all of the tabs in the left navigation, besides the **Office** tab.

 For security reasons, you may be required to sign back in.

This page will automatically detect where you are on a Windows machine or on a Mac and give you access to the appropriate downloads:

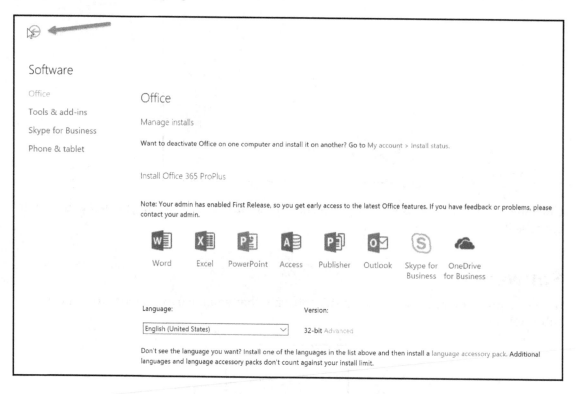

If you are on a Windows machine, you will need to determine whether you need to download a 32-bit or 64-bit version of Office. Most people use 32-bit, even if they are using a 64-bit machine.

To get back to the previous page, click on the back arrow in the upper left-hand corner.

Language and time zone

This section allows you to configure the language you want for Office 365 and to set the time zone, as well as set the formatting of the date and time. You have a choice of a few different standard and military formats:

For the current time zone, you should choose the one that you are in for accurate timestamps. The default is US Pacific Time.

Your app settings

In this section, you are able to open pages that will have settings for each area that the link is named after. For example, clicking on the **Office 365** link will take you to additional Office 365 settings. Let's look at the Office 365 app settings. We will explore the links and their settings in the following chapters:

When you click on the **Office 365** link in the **Your app settings** section, you are taken to a new page, where you will see a search box and some of the settings that we have previously gone over from the gear.

Licensing

There are many different full and add-on subscriptions available in Office 365. They give you access to different cloud software applications. Let's look at these options in more detail to see what the different subscriptions are and what they mean to you as an end user.

Office 365 consumer

The consumer version of Office 365 is generally referred to as Office 365 Home or Office 365 Personal.

The Personal and Home versions contain the following:

- Office Professional
- Cloud benefits, such as OneDrive cloud storage
- Apps for mobile devices
- 60 minutes of Skype calling

It is evergreen, which means that you will always have access to the most up-to-date version of Office and OneDrive, as long as you keep paying for your subscription. The key differentiating factor between Home and Personal is that Personal gives you a single license for PC/Mac for $6.99 monthly and Home gives you six licenses for $9.99 monthly, at the time of publishing this book. The Home licenses can be used by one person or shared among six people.

Office 365 commercial

This version of Office 365 is generally just referred to as Office 365 for Business or just Office 365, which tends to cause confusion for those who are not familiar with the different versions of Office 365.

Business plans

There are three levels on the Business side. Each includes integration for Active Directory, a 99.9% uptime guarantee, IT-level online support, and 24/7 support for critical issues by phone, as well as superior data security. The following is a breakdown of each Business subscription:

	Business Plan		
Services	**Business Essentials**	**Business**	**Business Premium**
Office desktop applications	No	Yes	Yes
Office mobile apps	Yes	Yes	Yes
Office web apps	Yes	Yes	Yes
Mailbox (50 GB)	Yes	No	Yes
OneDrive for Business (1 TB)	Yes	Yes	Yes

Skype for Business (not available for any new subscriptions since early this year)	Yes	No	Yes
Microsoft Teams for Business	Yes	No	Yes
SharePoint	Yes	No	Yes
Costs	$5 per user monthly or free for nonprofits at the time of publishing	$8.25 per month	$12.50 per user monthly or $3 per user monthly for nonprofits

These plans can cover a maximum of 300 users. You can see more details here: `https://products.office.com/en-US/compare-all-microsoft-office-products?activetab=tab:primaryr2`.

Enterprise plans

At the Enterprise level, there are also a few levels similar to the Business plans. The Enterprise plans include integration for Active Directory, a 99.9% uptime guarantee, IT-level online support, and 24/7 support for critical issues by phone, as well as superior data security. The following is a breakdown of each Enterprise subscription:

	Enterprise Plan			
	Pro Plus	**E1**	**E3**	**E5**
Services	This plan has a focus on Office Professional Plus	This plan also includes Enterprise-level benefits such as a Microsoft Stream corporate video portal, Compliance Center tools, and more	This plan blends E1 and Pro Plus and adds in unlimited email archiving and more	This is Microsoft's newest plan option that contains all of E3's features, plus analytics tools, advanced security, Skype for Business meeting PSTN conferencing, and Cloud PBX for cloud-based call management
Office desktop applications	Yes	No	Yes	Yes

Office mobile apps	Yes	No	Yes	Yes
Office web apps	Yes	Yes	Yes	Yes
Mailbox	No	Yes (50 GB)	Yes (100 GB)	Yes (100 GB)
OneDrive for Business (1 TB)	Yes	Yes	Yes	Yes
Skype for Business (not available for any new subscriptions since early this year)	Yes (will require purchase of a separate Skype for Business subscription for service)	Yes	Yes	Yes
Microsoft Teams for Business	No	Yes	Yes	Yes
SharePoint	No	Yes	Yes	Yes
Costs	$12 per user monthly	$8 per user monthly or free for nonprofits	$20 per user monthly or $4.50 per user monthly for nonprofits	$35 per user monthly or $15 per user monthly for nonprofits

These plans can cover unlimited users. You can see more details here: `https://products.office.com/en-us/business/compare-more-office-365-for-business-plans`.

In this book, we will cover the Business version of Office 365.

Summary

In this chapter, we discussed the Office 365 Home page, setting your personal settings, the available licensing, and what this all means.

You learned about the different options that are available on the Office 365 Home page and how to change your personal settings, such as changing the theme, changing the font, and making new folders in a personal email file. You also learned about the differences between the licensed version and the free web version of Office 365.

In `Chapter 3`, *Understanding Exchange,* you will learn about Exchange in general and how to make it useful.

Further reading

- For more details on the Office 365 Home, Personal, and Home and Student plans, check out the following link: `https://products.office.com/en-us/compare-microsoft-office-products`

- For more details on the Office 365 Business plan, check out the following link: `https://products.office.com/en-us/business/compare-office-365-for-business-plans`

Section 2: Managing Microsoft Exchange

2

In this section, readers will learn about Exchange in general as well as getting some specific information on making.

The following chapters will be covered:

- Chapter 3, *Understanding Exchange*
- Chapter 4, *Sending and Receiving Email*
- Chapter 5, *Using the Exchange Calendar*
- Chapter 6, *Using Contacts in Exchange*
- Chapter 7, *Getting Familiar with Other Exchange Settings*

3
Understanding Exchange

Microsoft Exchange is the engine behind your email client. Most people think of Exchange as Outlook since that is the mail client that they use to view the email served up from Exchange. Others use **Outlook Web Access** (**OWA**) to access their email from Exchange and may think of their Exchange service as OWA.

In this chapter, you will learn about Exchange in general. We will look at the background and history of Exchange, how you can get into Exchange Online, and parts of Exchange Online.

The following topics will be covered in this chapter:

- Background and History of Exchange
- History of Exchange
- Getting into Exchange Online
- Parts of Exchange Online

Background and History of Exchange

Microsoft's Exchange is more than just email. Although most people only think of it in those terms, it is actually a collection of multiple applications that coalesce into a platform used for digital messaging. Those applications include services for mail, contacts, a calendar, tasks, notes, and journaling (which no longer exists). We will discuss these in more detail later in this chapter.

Traditionally, this platform has also been used for collaborating with coworkers and colleagues, such as partners, vendors, and volunteers. With the advent of collaborative platforms, such as SharePoint, BaseCamp, Lotus, WebEx, Google Apps, and Zoho, email applications such as Exchange have been relied on a little bit less but still form an integral part of the collaborative process. With the release of Office 365 and its more intricate collaborative platform, Microsoft Teams, use of email for collaboration is on a slow decline.

History of Exchange

Microsoft first released Exchange to the public in March 1996. This first version was named Exchange Server 4.0 and it was released as the replacement for Microsoft Mail 3.5. There have been 10 releases of new versions of Exchange, starting with 4.0 and continuing through to the present-day version of Exchange Server 2019, which was released in October 2018. Here is a brief timeline of the Exchange releases:

- **1996**: The first version of Microsoft Exchange, Exchange Server 4.0, is released as a replacement for Microsoft Mail 3.5:

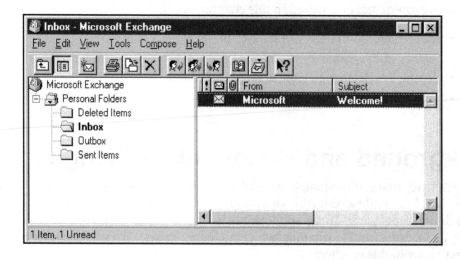

- **1997**: Exchange 5.0 is released with an admin console and SMTP network access. Also released was Microsoft Exchange Client 5.0.
- **1997**: Later 1997, Exchange Server 5.5 is released in Standard and Enterprise versions. Also released is Microsoft Outlook, as a replacement for Microsoft Exchange Client, and OWA.
- **2000**: Exchange Server 2000, otherwise known as Exchange Server 6.0, was released as the first version to be fully reliant on Microsoft's Active Directory. This release also had support for an instant-messaging utility, which later became Microsoft Office Live Communications server:

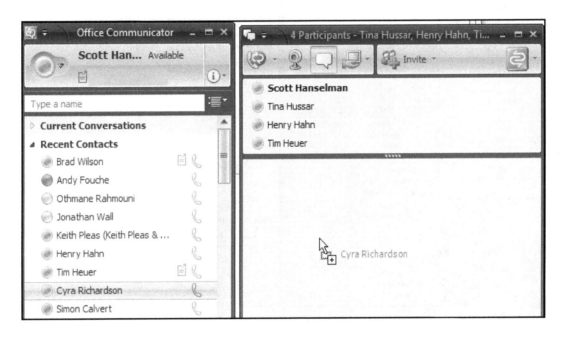

- **2003**: Exchange Server 2003, otherwise known as Exchange Server 6.5, was released with features such as multiple filtering methods and improved disaster recovery:

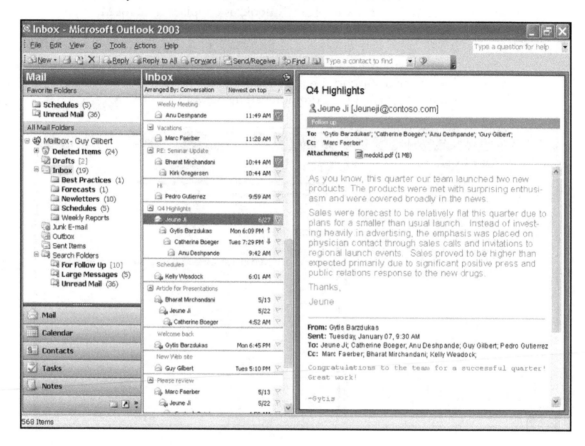

The **Outlook Web App** 2003 looks as follows:

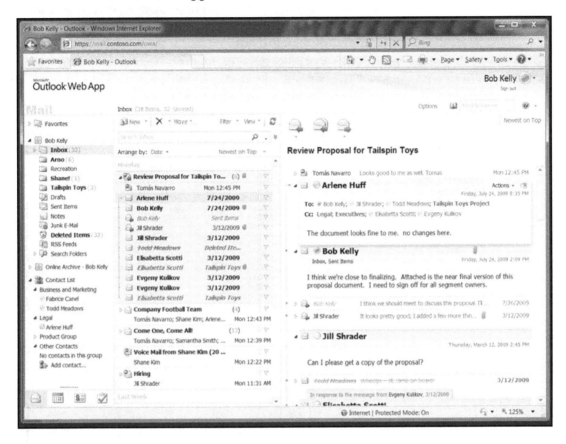

- **2006**: Exchange server 2007 released Standard and Enterprise editions with new features, such as voice mail integration, more filtering capabilities, and a new OWA interface. Standard and Enterprise editions began to be released with every version of Exchange from this point forward.

- **2009**: Exchange Server 2010 was released, with features such as support for multi-tenancy personal archiving, moderated distribution groups, administration delegation, boosted compliance and legal search, and OWA enhancements:

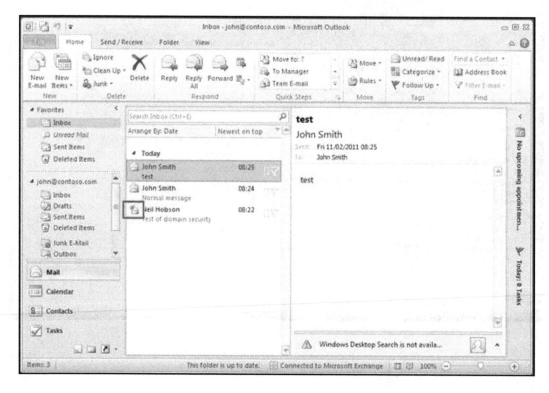

The first version of Outlook in Office 365 looks as follows:

- **2011**: Office 365 was released with a version of Exchange called Exchange Online.
- **2012**: Exchange Server 2013 was released with features such as offline support for OWA, public folders, site mailboxes (bringing together mail and SharePoint), data-loss prevention, fast search, and the Outlook Web App for desktop, tablet, and mobile. The following screenshot shows the Outlook desktop application:

The Outlook Web App is as follows:

- **2013**: An updated version of Office 365 with an updated version of Exchange Online was released.
- **2015**: Exchange Server 2016 was released with features such as the ability for hybrid deployment with Office 365 through a configuration wizard and changes to OWA, which was renamed Outlook on the Web.
- **2018**: This is the release of present-day Exchange Server 2019 with new features for security and performance. The feature of unified messaging has been removed from this version.
- **2018**: Later 2018, the newest version of Outlook on the Web was released. This version is available via an opt-in toggle. A simplified ribbon as well as new colors and icons are just a few of the improvements made. Here's Outlook 2019:

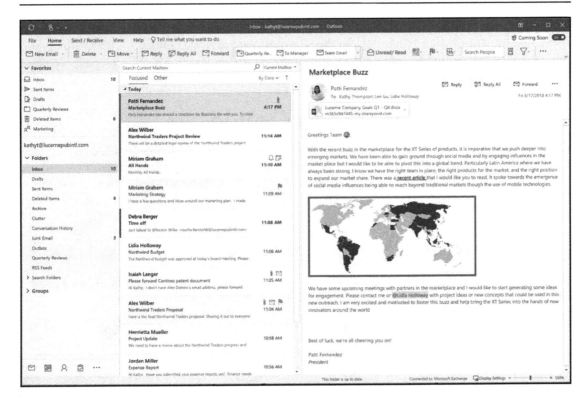

The newest version of Outlook on the Web, formally known as Outlook Web App, is as follows:

With each new release, Microsoft added more and more features and capabilities to make Exchange the application it is today. In this chapter, we will focus on Exchange Online, which is the offering for Exchange via Office 365.

Getting into Exchange Online

Once you log in to Office 365, you can get to Exchange Online, which is denoted as Outlook, in one of two ways: via the Office 365 Home or via the app launcher. Of course, you can also get access to Exchange Online via the Outlook desktop application or via the Outlook mobile app on your phone or tablet.

Outlook via the Office 365 Home

When you log in to Office 365, you will be able see all of the applications that are included in your subscription plan.

From the **Office 365 Home**, you can click on the **Outlook** icon to go to **Outlook**:

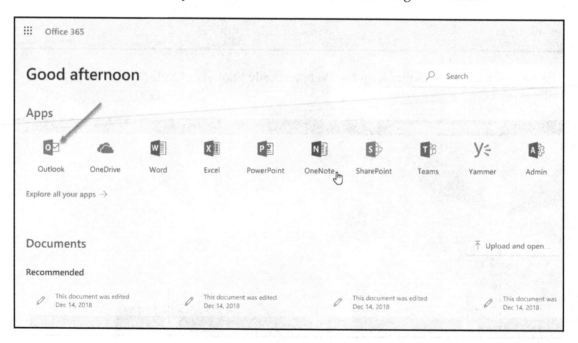

You can also right-click on the **Outlook** icon and choose **Open in new tab**, **Open in new window**, or **Open in new InPrivate window** from the drop-down:

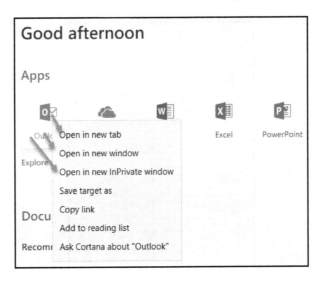

In IE, Chrome, Firefox, and Edge, you should at least have the choice to **Open in a new tab**. If you do not have this choice, you may want to check with your admin. The other choices may depend on your browser.

Outlook via the app launcher

Outlook can also be opened through the app launcher, which includes all of the applications in your plan.

From any area of Office 365, go to the upper-left corner and click on the app launcher. Once the app launcher ⠿ is open, you can click on **Outlook** to open the application:

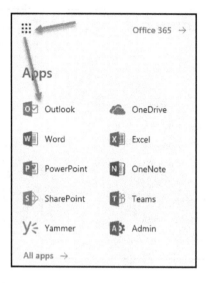

You can also hover over Outlook on the app launcher, then click on the open menu ⠿ that appears:

On the menu, choose **Open in new tab** to open **Outlook** in a new tab.

Parts of Exchange Online

Exchange is a platform made up of many different applications, and the online version of Exchange is no different. Unlike **Exchange Online** via the **Outlook** desktop application, **Exchange Online** via **Outlook for the web** has only four applications available, but rest assured that they are the ones most people use every day. Those applications can be easily accessed once in **Outlook** via the icons on the bottom-right:

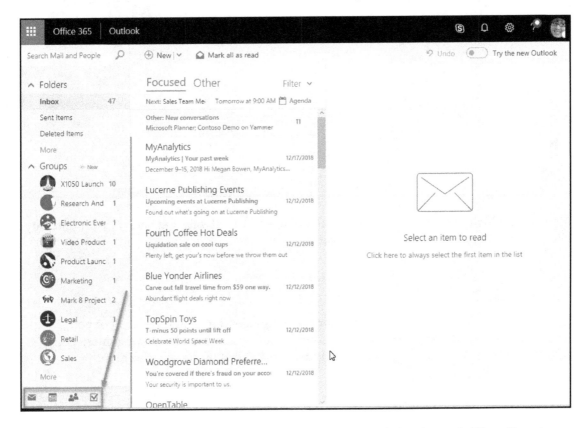

Here is a brief synopsis of each of the applications in **Outlook for the web**. We will go into more detail later in this section of this book.

Email

When you first enter **Outlook**, you land in the email application. This is where you can see all of your emails and create new ones. The Outlook inbox is shown in the following screenshot:

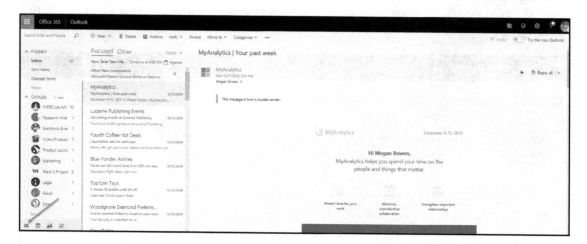

No matter which **Outlook** application you are in, you can always get back to your email by clicking on the mail icon on the bottom-left.

Calendar

This portion of Outlook allows you to manage your calendar. You can see all of your calendar events and invitations, as well as create new ones and edit existing ones. The following screenshot shows you the events and invitations of the selected month:

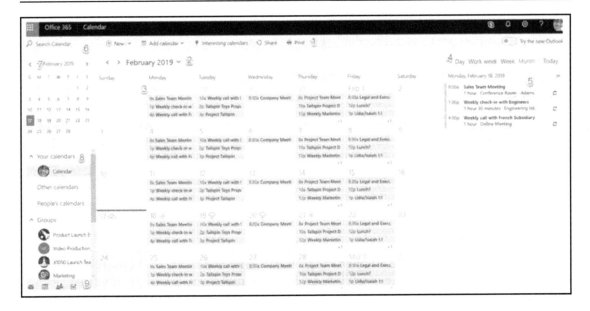

No matter which Outlook application you are in, you can always get back to your calendar by clicking on the calendar icon on the bottom-left.

Contacts

This portion of Outlook allows you to manage your contacts as well as see your company's global address book and contacts for the company. You can see all of your contacts and create new ones:

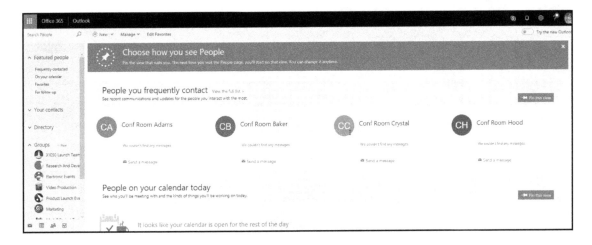

No matter which **Outlook** application you are in, you can always get back to your contacts by clicking on the contacts icon on the bottom-left.

Tasks

This portion of Outlook allows you to manage your personal tasks as well as assign tasks to others. You can see all of your tasks as well as create new ones and edit existing ones. No matter which **Outlook** application you are in, you can always get back to your tasks by clicking on the tasks icon on the bottom-left.

Summary

In this chapter, we discussed Exchange in general. We looked at the background and history of Exchange, how you can get into Exchange Online, and the parts of Exchange Online.

You learned about the background of Exchange and to how to get into Exchange via OWA and Outlook. You also learned about email, calendar, contacts, and tasks, which are the different parts of Exchange.

In Chapter 4, *Sending and Receiving Email*, you will learn about communicating using mail in Exchange.

Sending and Receiving Email

4

Exchange, the engine that serves your email and other functionalities, such as calendar, contacts, and tasks, can be accessed through your browser, through the Outlook desktop application, and through Outlook mobile apps. Most of the functionality is the same via both platforms, but there are some differences for each as well.

In this chapter, we will look at the parts of mail in OWA and the parts of mail in Outlook on your desktop.

The following topics will be covered in the chapter:

- Parts of Mail in OWA
- Parts of Mail in Outlook

Parts of Mail in OWA

Accessing email using OWA, renamed Outlook on the web, is done through your web browser. You will need to log in to Office 365 and click on the **Outlook** block on Office 365 Home or in the app launcher:

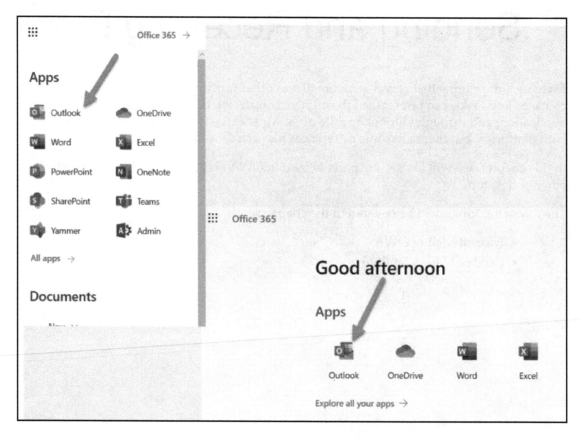

Once you get into Outlook on the web, you will have access to your email. Here are the parts of the interface:

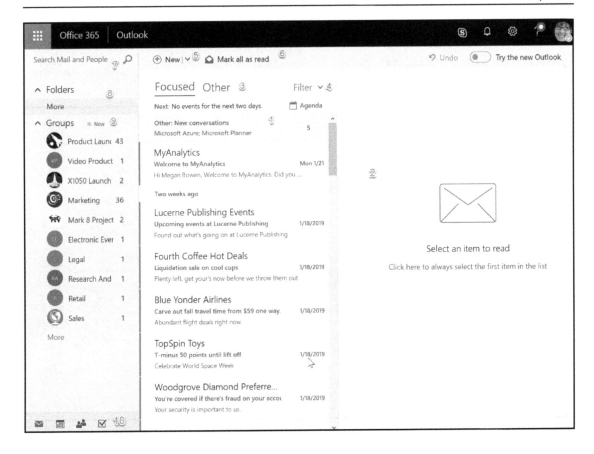

#1 The list of your emails

In this section, you can see your emails based on the way you filtered them (see #4 in the preceding screenshot).

#2 Displaying an email message

When you click on an email, it displays in this section so that you can read it. Once open, you will have some other options available via the **Reply all** menu:

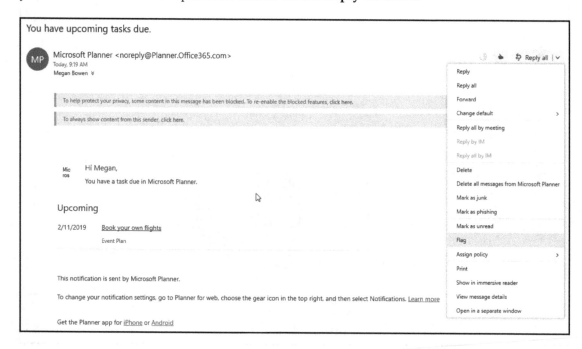

You will also have the ability to **Like** the selected email and, depending on your subscription, may have also have access to **MyAnalytics**:

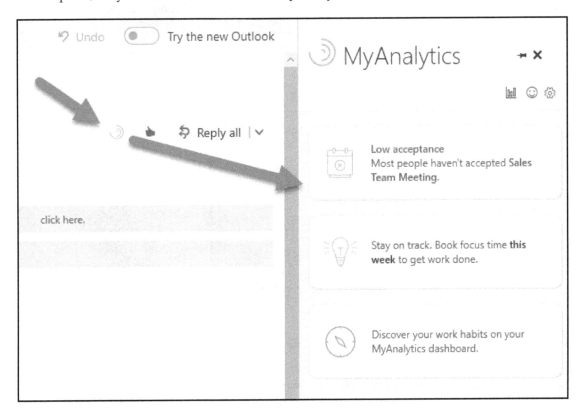

#3 Focused and other filters

The **Focused** filter shows you emails that you read and respond to the most. The **Other** filter shows emails that aren't labeled as junk but that you don't read and respond to often, if at all. The system learns, as time goes on, which emails should be focused on or not focused on.

#4 Filter

The **Filter** gives you the ability to filter and sort your email in different ways:

#5 Action bar

The action bar starts with the **New** menu when no email is selected (see the following screenshot). Once an email or multiple emails are chosen, the action bar adds more options for **Delete**, **Archive**, the **Junk** menu, the **Move to** menu, the **Categories** menu, and the open menu (**...**):

 Having trouble keeping your inbox clean? Use the **Sweep** option on the action bar to sweep away emails from the same sender as the email you selected.

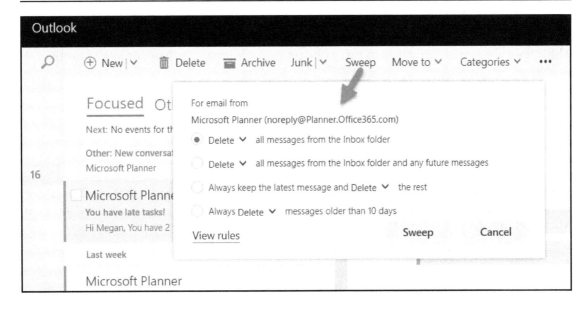

This **Sweep** option is not available in the desktop version of Outlook.

We'll now look at the different menus in the action bar.

The New menu

The **New** menu gives you the ability to create a new **Email Message**, but you also get the ability to create a new **Calendar event** or a new Office 365 **Group** (depending on configuration and permissions):

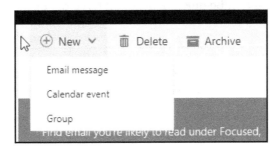

You can create the new event or Group without leaving your email. Side panels will open for each and you will be returned to your email once closed.

The Junk menu

The options here will allow you to mark one or multiple emails as **Junk** or as **Phishing**:

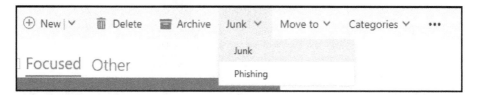

Junk email will be moved to the **Junk** email folder now and emails from that sender will be routed to the **Junk** folder automatically thereafter. You can also chose to report the email to Microsoft to help to improve the system's ability to catch this sort of mail as junk:

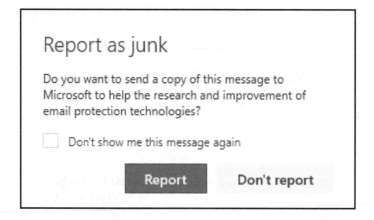

Emails marked as phishing will be deleted, and you have the option to report them to Microsoft:

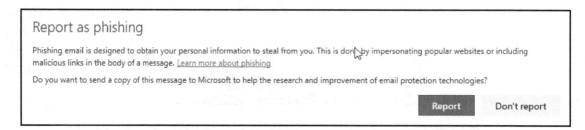

The Move to menu

This menu gives you option to move selected email(s) to any folder you desire:

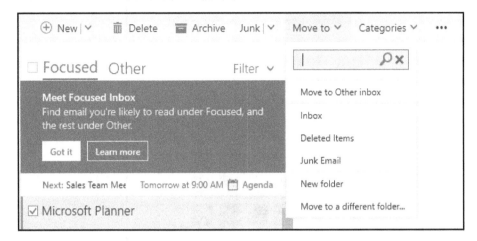

The Categories menu

This menu allows you to categorize your selected email(s) into categories with names and color indicators. You can create new ones as well as manage them:

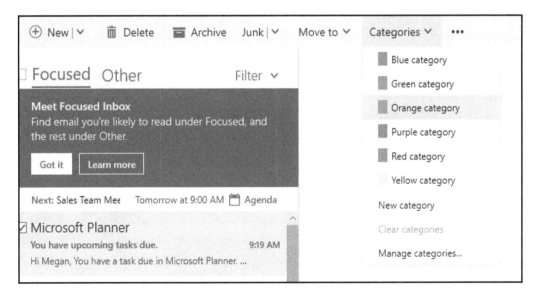

When managing them, you can change the color of an existing one. Since you cannot rename them, you can delete one and add a new one to replace it:

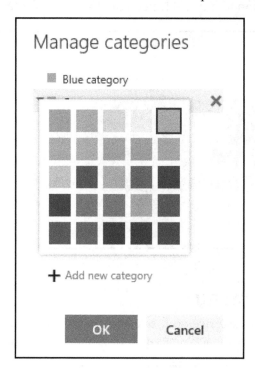

The open menu

This menu, denoted as **...**, gives you a lot of other options for your selected email(s). When you click on **...**, you'll get the following list of options:

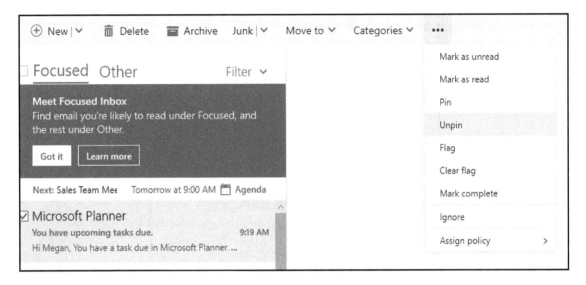

#6 Mark all as read

Clicking this button will mark all of your messages as read in the **Focused** filter or in the **Other** filter, depending on which you happen to be in. Once clicked, you can revert one or multiple emails to a non-read state by selecting the read email(s), opening the email's options menu by right-clicking on the selected email(s), and choosing **Mark as unread**:

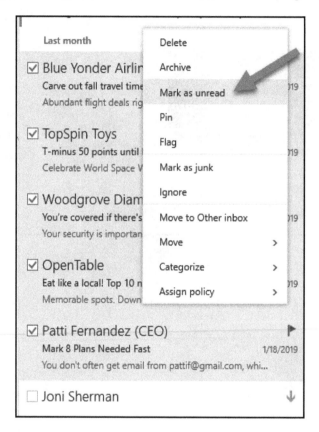

You can also change email(s) back to unread, clicking on the open menu (**...**) on the action bar, and choosing **Mark as unread** or clicking on **Mark as unread** in the section where emails are displayed:

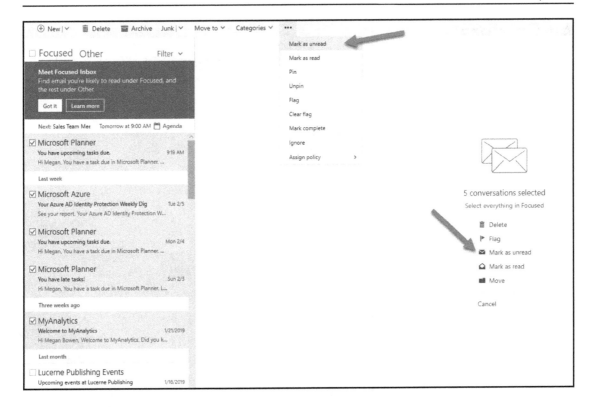

#7 Search

This allows you to search by mail or people so you can search by keywords in the email, subject line, the person who sent the email, and so on.

#8 Folders

This section allows you to see the folders that come with your email out of the box and any custom folders you may have created. To see your folders, click on **More** to expand the section:

To collapse the section, click on the back arrow:

#9 Groups

In this section, you can see all of the Office 365 Groups you have access to. You may even have the ability to create Groups, depending on how your environment is set up and the permissions you have.

#10 Outlook apps

The buttons in this bar give you the ability to switch back and forth between the Outlook applications of mail, calendar, people, and tasks.

Email options

Email option is not numbered in the screenshot provided at the beginning of this chapter, but you can see it in the following screenshot. Here are the options you get when you right-click on an email:

Parts of Mail in Outlook

You can access your Office 365 email through Outlook on your desktop. This is the most popular method of interacting with email. If your subscription has the download of Office available, you may want to take advantage of it. One way you can tell whether you have the Office licenses is by logging in to the Office 365 portal, going to **Office 365 Home**, and clicking on the **Office installs** drop-down menu:

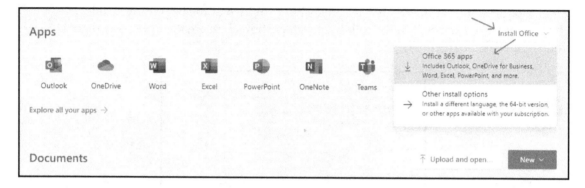

The other way is to click on your profile | **My account** | **Install status** | **Install desktop applications**:

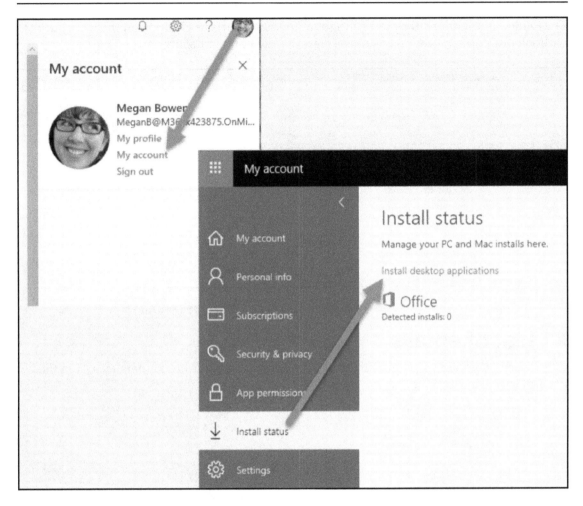

If you need more help, cannot download Office, or need to add Office, talk to your company administrator.

The Outlook desktop application has a lot of the same parts as Outlook on the web, but the Outlook desktop application has more. Here are the parts of its interface:

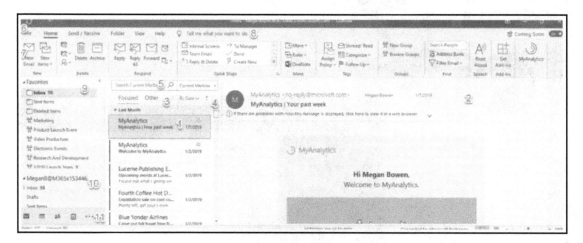

#1 List of emails

In this section, you can see your emails based on the way you filtered them (see #4 in the preceding screenshot).

#2 Display of email

The email you select will be displayed here.

#3 Focused and other filters

The **Focused** filter shows you the emails that you read and respond to the most. The **Other** filter shows emails that aren't labeled as junk but that you don't read and respond to as often, if at all. The system learns, as time goes on, which emails should be focused on or not focused on.

If you don't have these filters (you are seeing **All** and **Unread** instead), you can turn them on via the **View** ribbon:

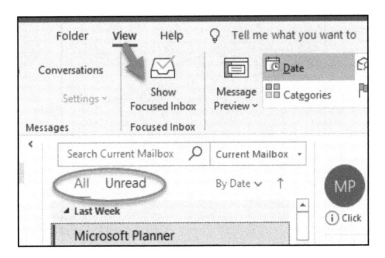

#4 Filters

The **Filter** gives you the ability to filter and sort your email in different ways:

#5 Search

You can use this to search your email by keywords or phrases, by people's names, or a combination of all of these. You can also choose where you search, such as in the current mailbox, current folder, or all mailboxes:

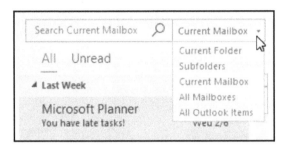

#6 The tabs

There are six tabs that are always present in Outlook, and they each have their associated ribbon (with the exception of **File**). When you click on **File**, you are taken to what is referred to as the backstage of this Office program. We will look at the ribbons in *The ribbons* section. As for the backstage of **File**, let's look at that now.

 It is important to note that, depending on other portions of Outlook that you may have clicked on, there may be additional contextual ribbons that appear.

The Outlook backstage

When you click on the **File** tab, you are taken to the backstage instead of opening a ribbon. This reaction to clicking on the **File** tab is the same for all Office applications. For the most part, the options in Outlook are the same for all Office applications. Here are the options available in Outlook's backstage.

Info

This is the tab you start on when you go to the backstage. On this tab, you can see your accounts and add new ones, manage account and mailbox settings, set automatic replies, manage your rules and alerts, and manage add-ins:

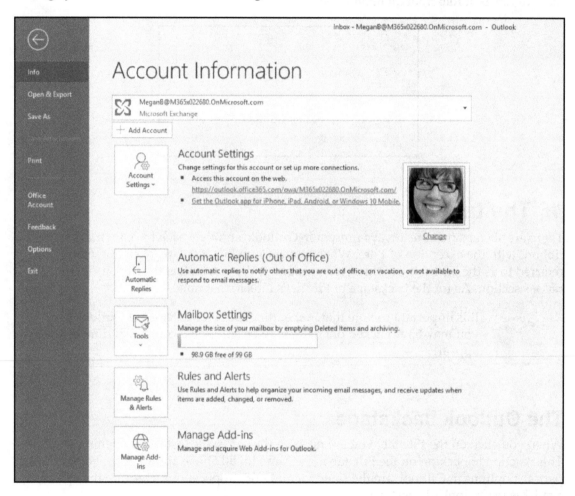

Open & Export

Via this tab, you can open a calendar file (`.ics`or `.vcs`), a `.pst` file, or a `user` folder shared with you. This is also the place you would go to export a `.pst` or other files from Outlook:

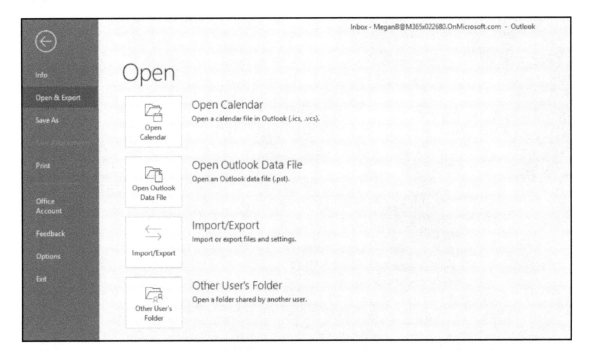

Save As

Clicking on this tab opens the **Save As** dialog box in order to save the message you were in when you clicked on **File** and then **Save As**:

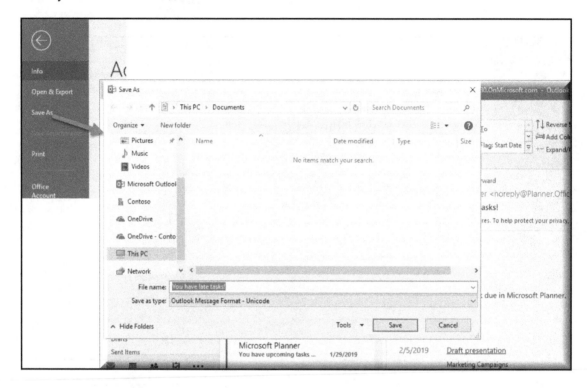

Save Attachments

Clicking on this tab gives the ability to save any and all attachments attached to the message you were in when you clicked on **File** and then **Save Attachments**:

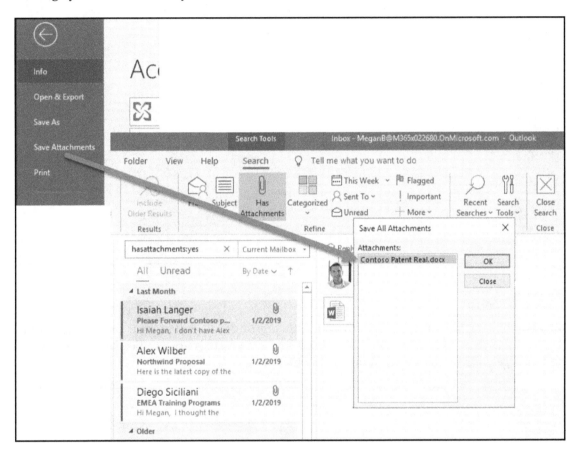

Print

Clicking on this tab gives you the ability to print the message you were in when you clicked on **File** and then **Print**. You can send it to a printer that your computer is connected to, either directly or via a network, or to file formats such as PDF and OneNote:

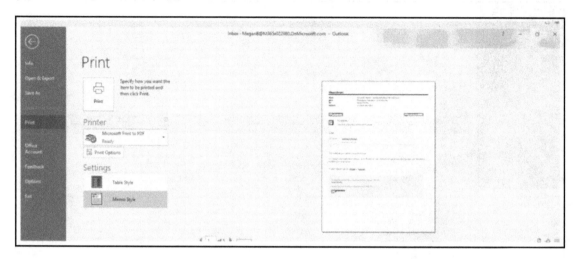

Office Account

On this tab, you can see details about your Office product as well as your user information. You can switch accounts, see your connected services (such as your Office 365 account), and change your Office background and theme:

You can also use *Add a service* here. This gives you the ability to add in another Office 365 or OneDrive-Personal account. Adding a connected service gives your Office the ability to access the services and information in that account with respect to the Office application. For example, adding a connect service through Word will give Word the ability to access Word files in those connected accounts.

In Outlook, this function is not as obvious as in the other Office applications, but it gives you the ability to more easily access files from your OneDrive—personal and Office 365 accounts to be added as attachments into an email message:

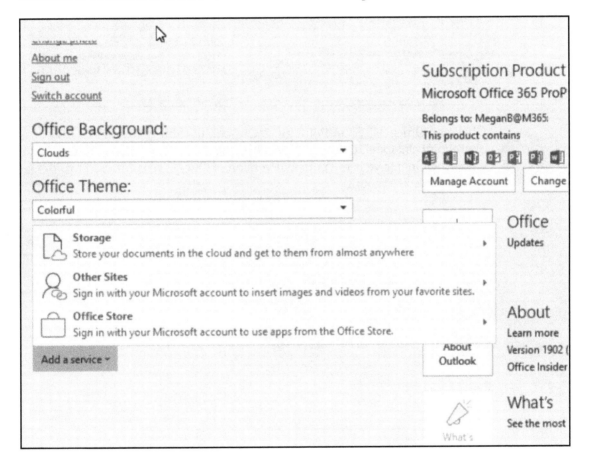

To add an Office 365 account or a OneDrive - Personal account to your Outlook, click on **Add a service**, followed by **Storage**, and then on either **Office 365 SharePoint** or **OneDrive**:

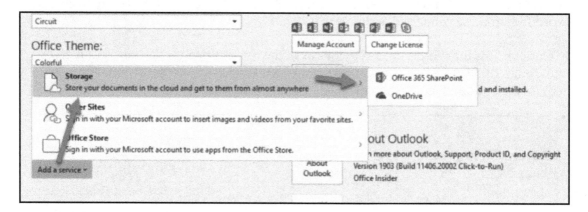

 Choosing Office 365 SharePoint gives Outlook the ability to access SharePoint *and* OneDrive *for Business* files via that Office 365 account. Choosing OneDrive is the personal version of OneDrive connected to your Microsoft account.

Feedback

Clicking on this tab gives you the ability to submit feedback to Microsoft and to get the latest news about Outlook:

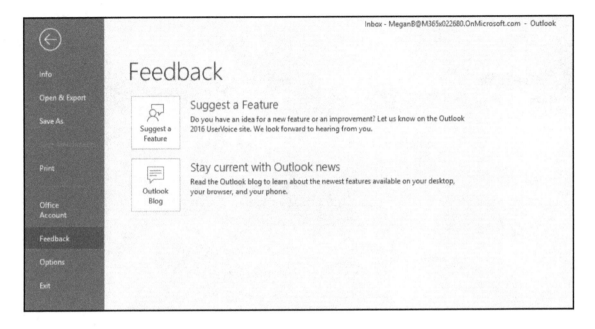

Options

Clicking on **Options** opens the **Outlook Options** window, where you can configure lots of options:

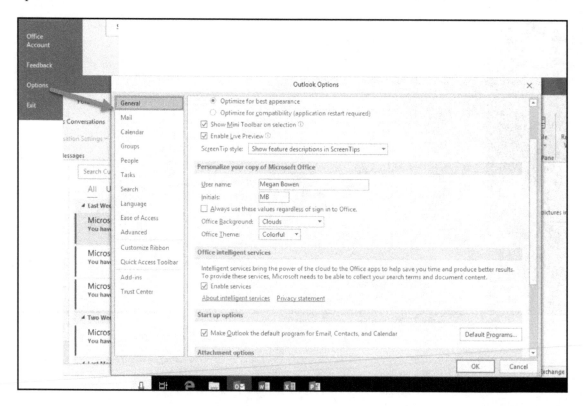

Exit

This will close Outlook as soon as you click on it:

#7 The ribbons

There are five main ribbons that are associated with tabs. Let's take a look at these in the following subsections.

 Sometimes you may encounter contextual tabs and ribbons that pop up when needed. You may also notice that your ribbon has more, less, or different buttons than the ones shown here. The ribbons may vary depending on the subscription, add-ins, or other factors.

Home

On this tab's ribbon, there are lots of functions that most people use every day. You have options for creating, deleting, and archiving email as well as for responding to, moving, tagging, and finding email. You also have options for browsing Office 365 Groups and contacts, and for creating Quick Steps for managing your email:

Using the **New Items** drop-down button, you can create other Outlook items without leaving email:

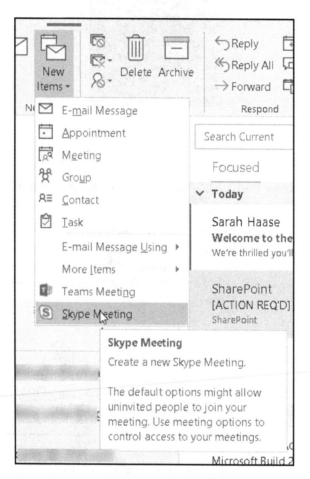

 If you have Skype for Business and/or Microsoft Teams turned on in your organization but you don't see them in this list, you or your administrator will need to turn the add-in on in your Outlook **Options** (in the **File** backstage).

Did you know that you can change any email into a meeting or appointment? Just select the email you want, then click on the **Reply with Meeting** button in the **Respond** section of the **Home** tab and a meeting invite is created. You will then have the option to change the meeting to an appointment by clicking the **Cancel Invitation** button or prevent forwarding the meeting using the **Response Options** button. Both are in the **Attendees** section of the **Meeting** tab:

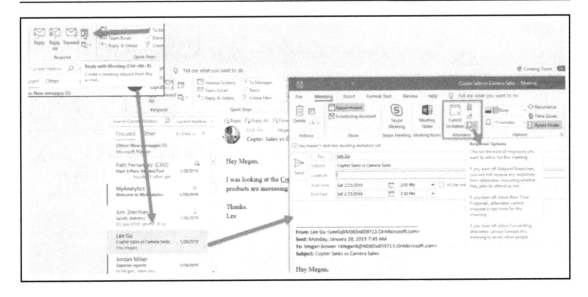

Send/receive

This ribbon has options for manually forcing Outlook to send and receive email and update folders:

Have you had an issue with Outlook not connecting? If so, sometimes clicking the **Work Offline** button in the **Preferences** section to force Outlook to go offline and then clicking it again to go back online can prompt Outlook to refresh the connection.

Folder

The options on this ribbon can help you to create, manage, and search folders:

View

The options on this ribbon help you to manage your view of Outlook:

If you prefer to show your emails as **Conversations** (emails from the same person with the same subject line are grouped together), you can turn it on by clicking on the **Show as Conversations** checkbox in the **Messages** section. The first time you click it, you will have an open prompt to apply this setting to all mailboxes or just this folder:

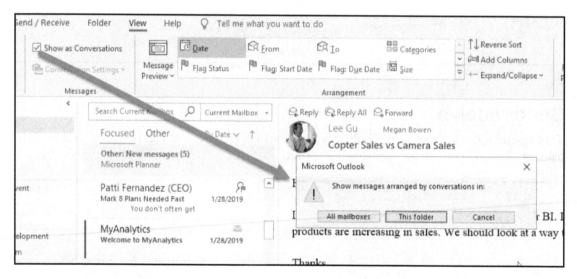

Help

On this ribbon, you have multiple help options, such as getting self-serve support, contacting support, and running diagnostics:

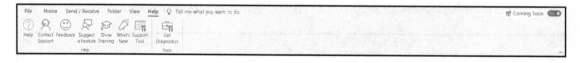

Tell me what you want to do

If you have ever wondered whether there was a command for something you wanted to do, or were having trouble finding the button for the command, this box is for you! Simply type what you want and get options:

You even get some suggested options by simply clicking in the box:

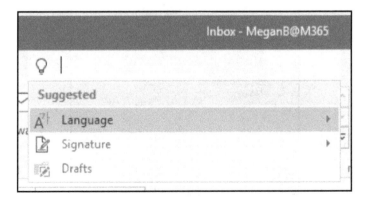

Favorites

This section starts with the **Inbox**, **Sent Items**, and **Deleted Items** of your main mailbox. You may also see Office 365 Groups that you are a member of. You can add to the **Favorites** section by dragging and dropping from anywhere, such as the Inbox of other mailboxes or Office 365 Groups, if any, listed in the **List of email accounts** (*#10*) section:

You can also remove a portion of a mailbox by right-clicking on it and choosing **Remove from Favorites**:

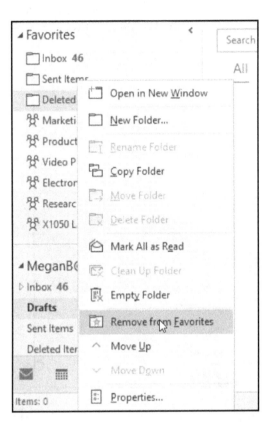

The line between this section and the list of emails section can be dragged to give more or less space to the viewable portion of the section.

List of email accounts

This is the list of all of your mailboxes and Office 365 Groups. You can see the parts of your mailboxes by clicking on the down arrow beside it in this list:

The line between this section and the **Favorite** section can be dragged to give more or less space to the visible portion of the section.

Outlook apps

This is the section where you can move between the applications inside of Outlook. You can also set which ones you see, hide the ones you don't want to see, and arrange them in the order you like:

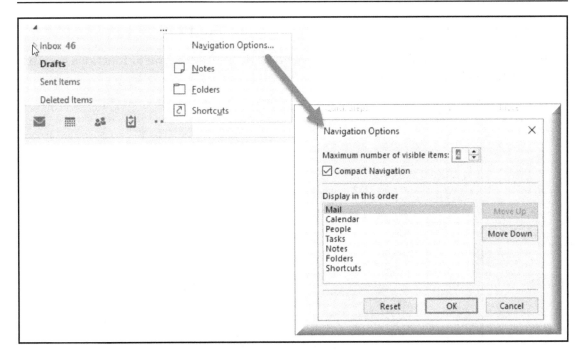

Depending on how many items you want to be visible, you may need to adjust the width of the section by dragging the line between the side panel and the email list:

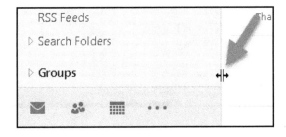

Email options

Right-clicking on any email message will give you a drop-down menu of functions that can be performed on that specific email:

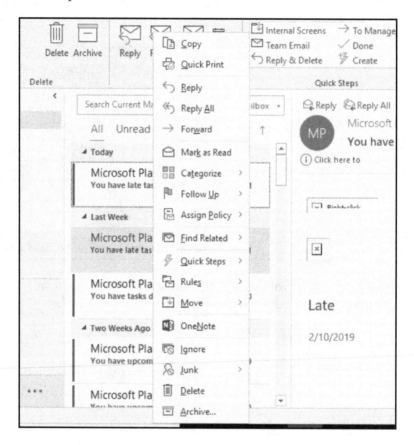

Summary

In this chapter, we explored Outlook for the web and the desktop Outlook application from the email perspective. We looked at the different parts of each and their functions. You can learn more about each of these by going to `https://support.office.com` and clicking on Outlook. From there, you will be able to choose Outlook for the web or on the desktop.

In Chapter 5, *Using the Exchange Calendar*, we will look at using the Exchange calendar via Outlook for the web and via the desktop Outlook application.

Using the Exchange Calendar 5

The calendar in Exchange is another part that most users use. This and all parts of Exchange can be accessed through your browser and through the Outlook desktop application. Most of the functionality is the same via both platforms but there are some differences for each as well.

In this chapter, the following topics will be covered:

- Parts of the calendar in OWA
- Parts of the calendar in Outlook

Parts of the calendar in OWA

Accessing your calendar using Outlook on the web is done through your web browser. You will need to log into the Office 365 portal and click on the **Outlook** block on the Office 365 Home or in the app launcher:

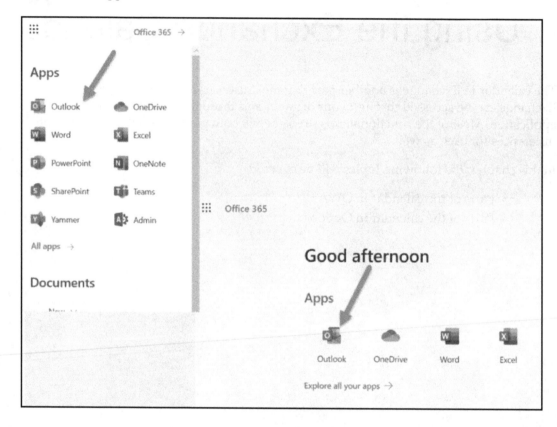

Once you get into Outlook on the web, you first land in your email. You can access your calendar by clicking on the calendar icon:

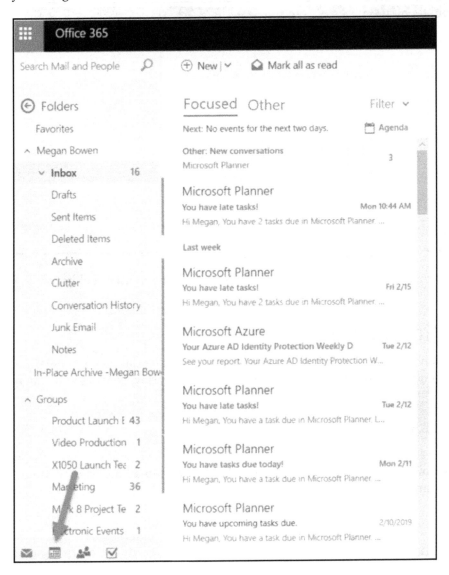

Let's look at the parts of this interface:

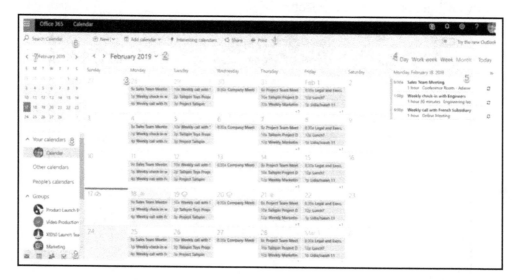

In the previous screenshot, you can see the events for the month of February.

#1 Action bar

On the action bar, you have options for creating a new calendar event or email, adding another calendar, configuring an interesting calendar overlay, sharing your calendar, or printing it.

New

This option allows you to create a new calendar event or email message without leaving your calendar:

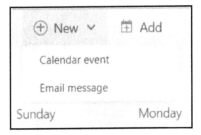

When creating a new event or an appointment, you have all the usual suspects. You can also add a Skype for Business meeting:

Although the **Add Skype meeting** button says **Skype**, it is really Skype for Business and not the consumer version of Skype.

Add calendar

With this option, you can add many different calendar types as overlays on your main calendar:

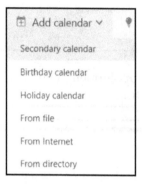

Once you add a calendar, the events in it will be shown alongside any previous calendars you have added.

Interesting calendars

As the title suggests, this is an interesting option indeed. This gives you the ability to add one of many **Bing calendars** as an overlay. Click on interesting calendars and a side panel opens:

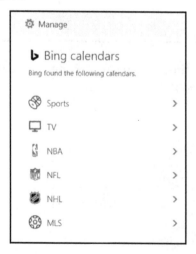

Using the example of **Football**, you can click on it or one of your own choice:

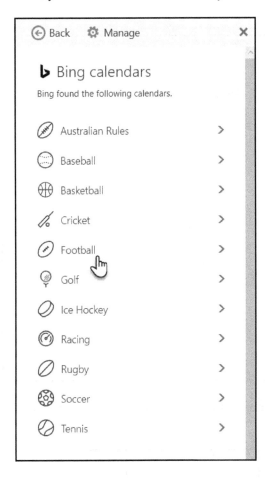

You can then drill down to the team you want. I would choose the **NFL** team, the **Baltimore Ravens**:

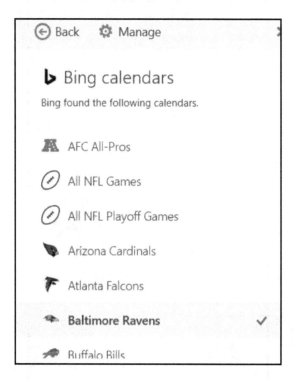

Once the choice is made an overlay is added and all events related to that calendar will be colored to match the tab:

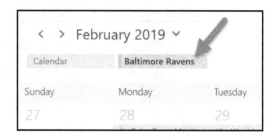

To remove any interesting calendar(s) that are no longer wanted, click on **Manage** then click the **X** next to the unwanted calendar(s):

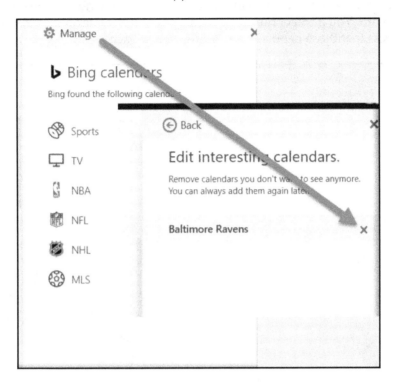

Share

Clicking on this option opens a side panel where you can see who you are currently sharing your calendar with. You also get the ability to share your calendar with new people, change the level of access that those people have, and/or remove access:

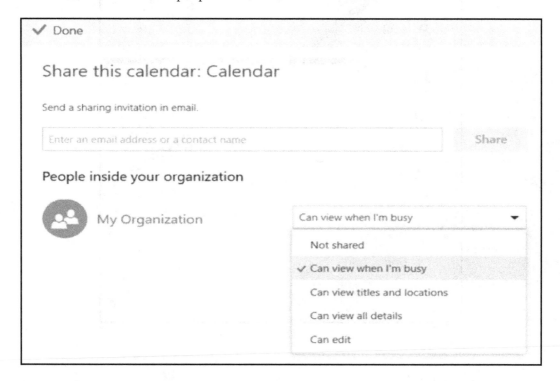

 Everyone in your organization gets access to your calendar by default to be able to see when you are busy. This is so that, when trying to schedule a meeting the Scheduling Assistant and other capabilities are able to see when you and others may be available. I highly recommend that you do not turn this access off.

You can share your calendar by entering a name or email in the **Send a sharing invitation in email** box. As you start typing, the system will start suggesting people and places:

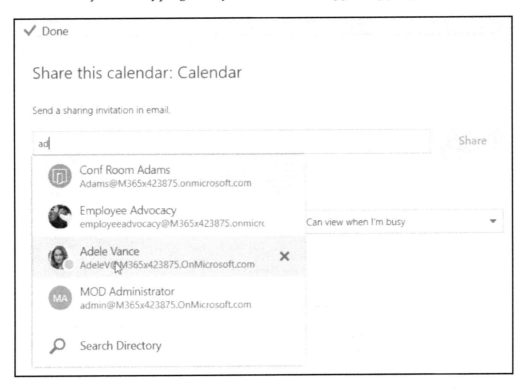

Once the person or place is chosen, you will be able to choose the level of access you wish to grant and then click the **Share** button or abort the operation by clicking on the trash can icon:

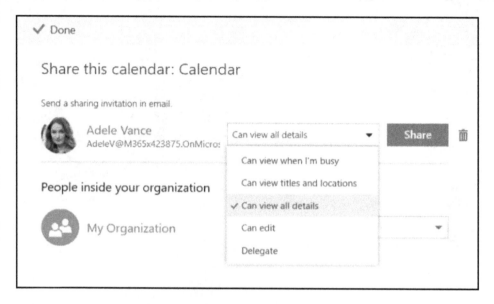

Any time you wish, you can come to this panel and choose to change the level of access or delete access for any in your list that you wish:

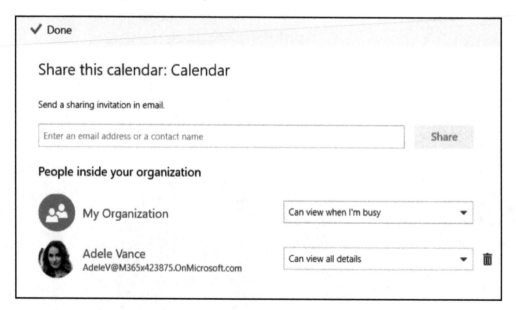

Clicking the **Done** button closes the panel.

Print

Clicking on this button opens a wide side panel where you can preview what you have selected to print, configure your print options such as which calendar or calendar view you would like to print, and choose to print or cancel the operation:

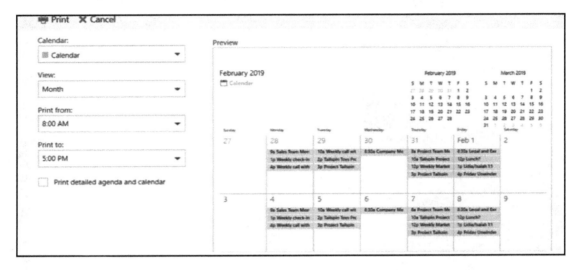

Clicking the **Print** button from here opens your computer's **Print** dialog box with all of the normal options:

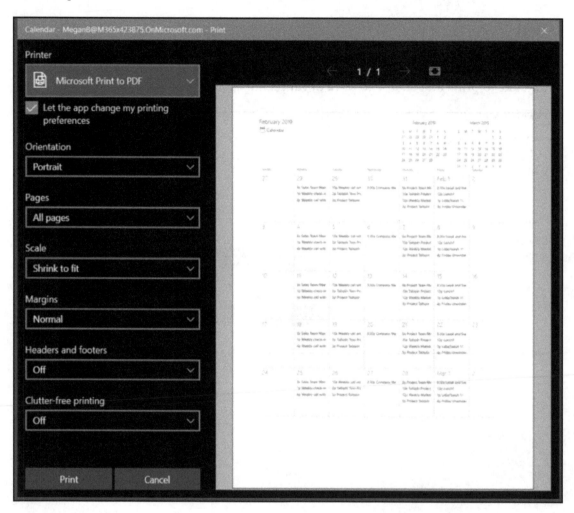

#2 Month/year navigation

This navigation gives you the ability to use the < and > buttons to move backward and forward through the months, respectively. You can also click on the down arrow near the month and year to get a dropdown for navigating through the years as well as the months:

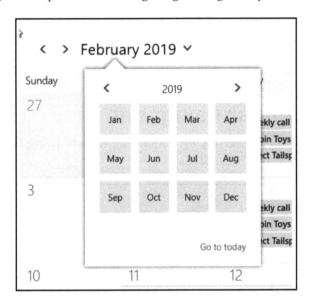

This navigation changes based on the view your calendar is in (see the *#4 Calendar views* section for more on views).

#3 Calendar

This section shows your calendar as well as any other calendar overlays that may have been chosen.

#4 Calendar views

These options allow you to change the view of your calendar to the **Month**, which is usually the default, or to the **Week**, the **Work Week**, or the **Day**.

#5 Selected day's events

This section is only visible in the **Month** view. In this section, you can see all of the events for any date you click on.

#6 Search

The search helps you to search events on your calendar.

#7 Month calendar navigation

This navigation allows you to navigate by clicking on days or using the < and > buttons to move backward and forward by month:

You can also click on the month/year to open the navigation by months and years.

#8 Calendars and groups

In this section, you can see all of your calendars and calendars you have been given access to as well as any Office 365 groups that you may be a member of:

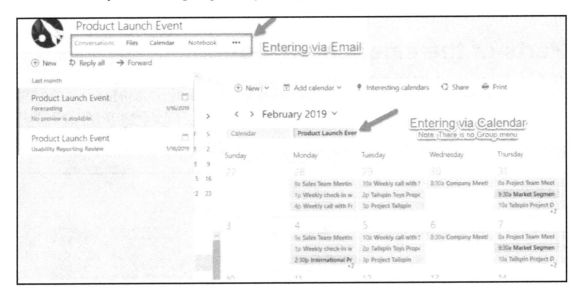

Getting into a group through the calendar can be confusing because the group calendar comes in as an overlay and you don't have access to the menu that you would have if you go through email or people. I recommend that you enter a group through email or people.

#9 Outlook apps

The buttons in this bar give you the ability to switch back and forth between the Outlook applications of mail, calendar, people, and tasks.

Parts of the calendar in Outlook

You can also access your Office 365 calendar through Outlook on your desktop. This is the most popular method of interacting with the calendar. If your subscription has the download of Office available, you may want to take advantage of it. One way you can tell if you have the Office licenses available to you is by logging into the Office 365 portal and going to the Office 365 Home and clicking on the **Install Office** dropdown:

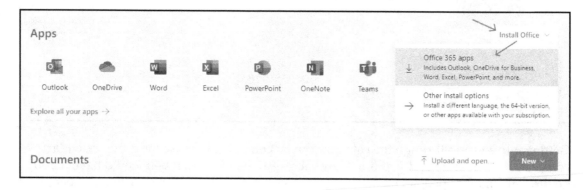

The other way to get to your desktop installs is to click on your persona, then on **My account**, then on **Install status**, then on **Install desktop applications**:

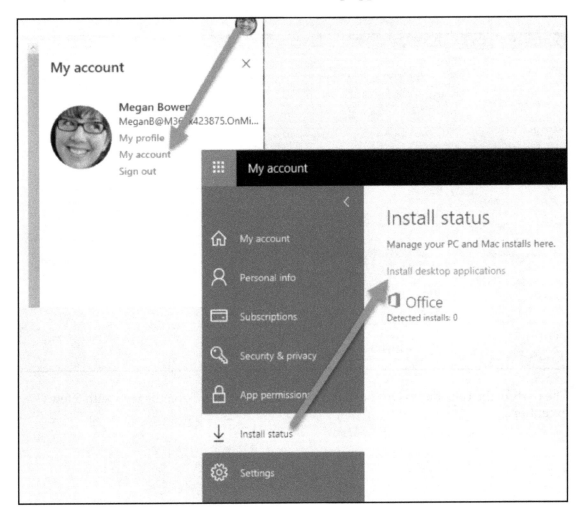

If you need more help, cannot download Office, or need to add Office, talk to your company admin.

The Outlook desktop application has a lot of the parts that Outlook on the web has and more. To get to Contacts in Outlook, open Outlook on your desktop and click on the calendar icon:

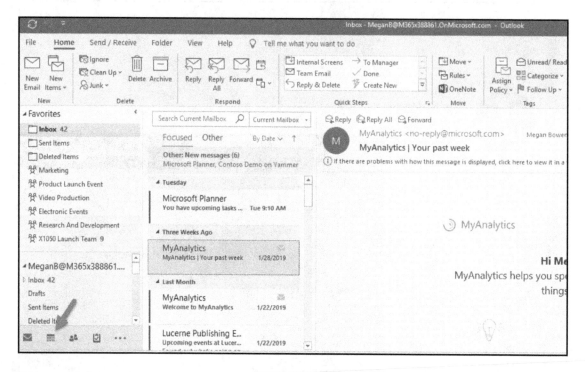

The parts of the calendar in Outlook are very similar to Outlook on the web with a few exceptions:

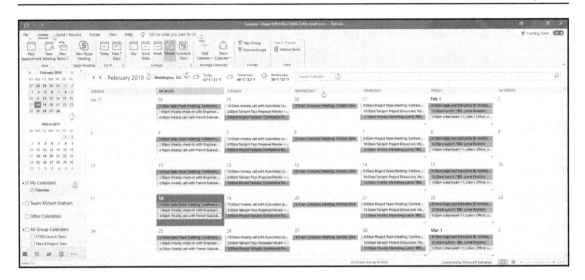

Let's explore this version of your calendar.

#1 The tabs

There are six tabs that are always present in Outlook and they each have their associated ribbons with the exception of **File**. When you click on **File**, you are taken to what is referred to as the backstage of this Office program. We will look at the ribbons in the following section. As for the backstage of **File**, let's look at that now:

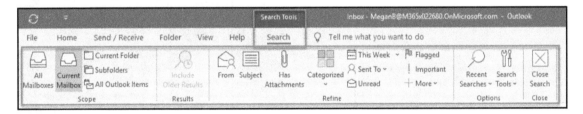

It is important to note that, depending on other portions of Outlook that you may have clicked on, there may be additional contextual ribbons that appear.

The Outlook backstage

When you click on the **File** tab, you are taken to the backstage instead of opening a ribbon. For more details on the backstage, see *#6 The tabs* in `Chapter 4`, *Sending and Receiving Email*.

Home

On this ribbon, you can create a new meeting or appointment, arrange the view, browse Office 365 groups, add and share calendars, and search the address book:

If you have Skype for Business and/or Microsoft Teams turned on in your organization but you don't see them in this list, you or your admin will need to turn the add-in on in your Outlook's **Options** (in the **File** backstage):

Using the **New Items** dropdown button, you can create other Outlook items without leaving email.

Send/receive

This ribbon has options for manually forcing Outlook to send and receive emails and update folders:

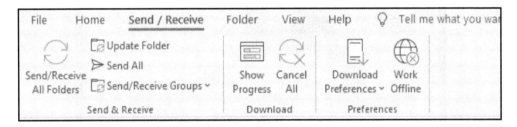

Have you had an issue with Outlook not connecting? If so, sometimes clicking the **Work Offline** button in the **Preferences** section forces Outlook to go offline; clicking it again to go back online can prompt Outlook to refresh the connection.

Folder

The options in this ribbon allow you to create a new calendar, share and add calendars, copy, rename, and view the properties of a selected calendar:

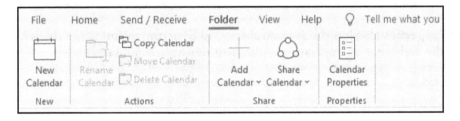

Under your calendar's properties is where you can add, edit, and revoke permissions to your calendar:

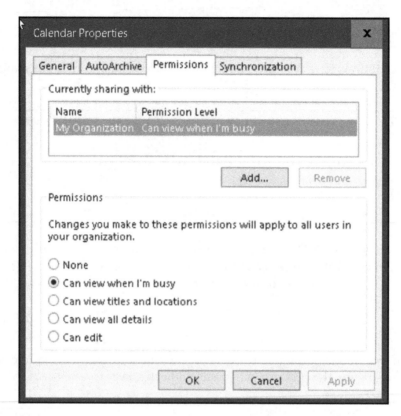

Calendar Properties also has the **AutoArchive** and **Syncronization** tabs, which allow you to modify the archiving and synchronization settings for a calendar.

View

On this tab's ribbon, change the view and view its settings, color code the calendar events, and add various panes such as the **People** pane:

Help

On this ribbon, you have multiple help options such as getting self-service support, contacting support, and running diagnostics:

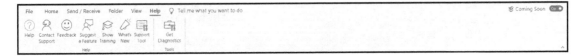

#2 Tell me what you want to do

If you have ever wondered if there was a command for something or were having trouble finding the button for the command, this box is for you! Simply type what you want and get options:

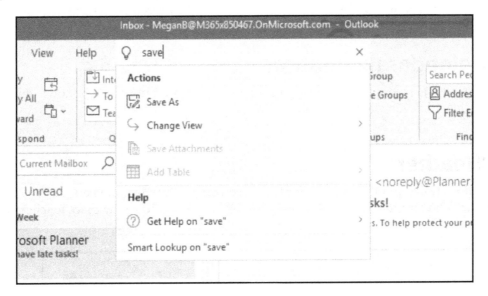

You even get some suggested options by simply clicking in the box:

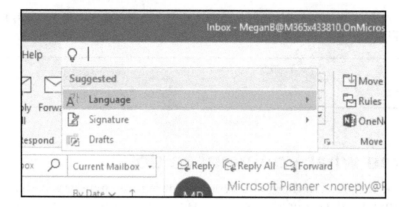

These options include some commonly used actions and frequently searched options, such as **Language**, **Signature**, and **Drafts**, as can be seen in the preceding screenshot.

#3 Calendar navigation

You can navigate through the months, weeks, or days using the < and > buttons, depending on your calendar's view at that moment.

#4 Weather

This section shows you the weather for the place you set. The default is normally **Redmond**, **Washington** (Microsoft headquarters). You can add a new place by clicking on the dropdown next to the current place:

Type in the place you want to add and hit *Enter* or the magnifying glass that will appear in the box:

The weather will switch to the place you added but all your locations will be available under the dropdown as well as the ability to add another location.

#5 Search

You can use this box to search your calendar's events.

#6 Calendar

This is the area for your calendar. The view of your calendar will be based on the one you choose from the **Arrange** section of the **Home** tab:

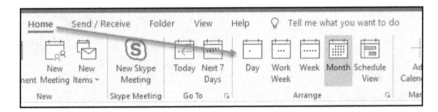

You can choose from **Day**, **Work Week**, **Week**, **Month** (usually the default), and **Schedule View.**

#7 Another calendar navigation

You can navigate through the months, weeks, or days using the < and > buttons as well as the days showing on the current and next month's calendars. You can also skip ahead in the months by clicking and holding down the left mouse button on the first calendar's month/year.

#8 List of calendars

This section has a list of your calendar and any other calendars shared with you. Office 365 group calendars also show up here.

#9 Outlook apps

This is the section where you can move between the applications inside of Outlook. You can also set which ones you see or hide and arrange them in the order you would like:

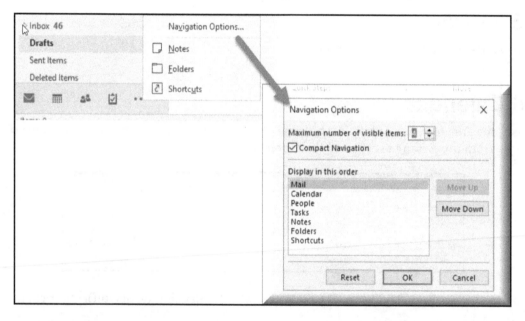

You can determine the visible and invisible items in **Navigation Options**.

Summary

In this chapter, we explored Outlook on the web and Outlook, the desktop application, from the calendar perspective. We looked at the different parts of each and their functions. You can learn more details about each of these by going to `https://support.office.com` and clicking on Outlook. From there, you will be able to choose Outlook on the web or on the Outlook desktop application.

In `Chapter 6`, *Using Contacts in Exchange*, we will look at using exchange contacts via Outlook on the web and Outlook, the desktop application.

Using Contacts in Exchange

6

Exchange, the engine that serves your contacts as well as your email, calendar, and tasks, can be accessed through your browser and through the Outlook desktop application. Most of the functionality is the same via both platforms but there are some differences for each as well.

In this chapter, we will cover the following topics:

- Parts of people (contacts) in OWA
- Parts of contacts in Outlook

Parts of people (contacts) in OWA

Accessing your contacts using Outlook for the Web is done through your web browser. You will need to log in to the Office 365 portal and click on the **Outlook** block in Office 365 Home or in the app launcher:

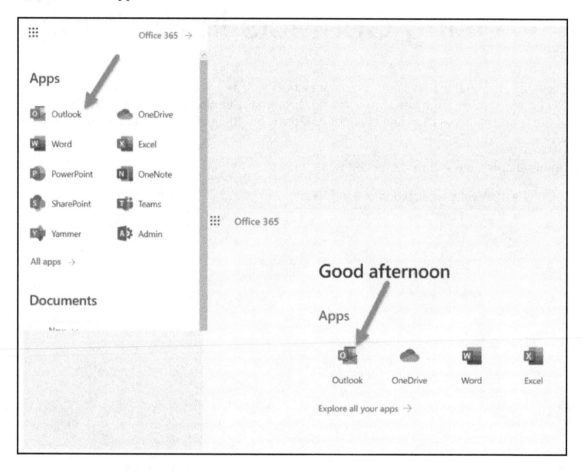

Once you are in Outlook, click on the people icon:

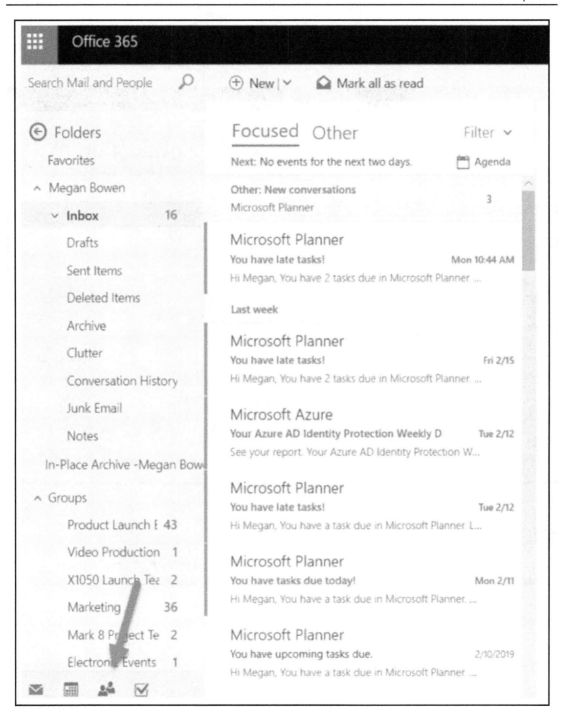

The following is a screenshot of people, otherwise known as contacts, where you will first land. You can think of this page as a home page whose main section (#2) changes based on things you click on. Let's take a closer look:

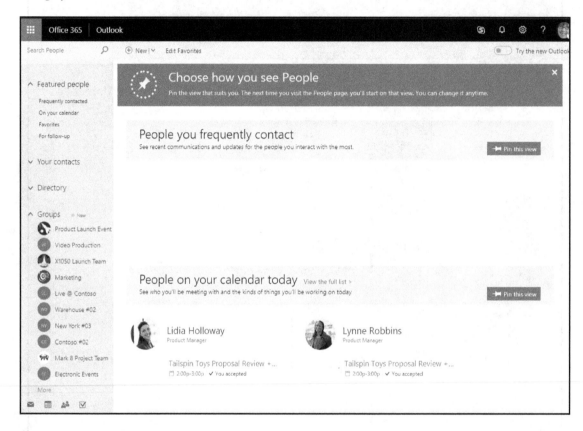

#1 The action bar

This bar starts with drop-down menus for **New** and **Manage** and an option for **Edit Favorites** when on the home page for people, but these options change when you select things from the left navigation:

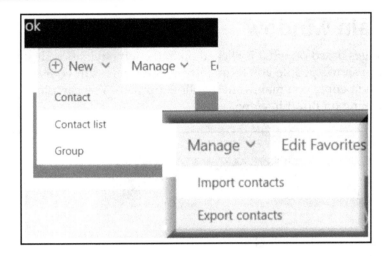

The following is an example of the action bar when you click on **Your contacts** and then click on one of the **Contacts** from the list. At this point, you get actions that correspond with what is chosen:

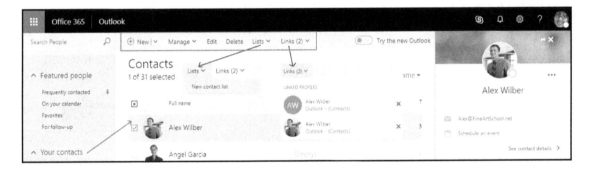

#2 The main window

This section changes based on what is clicked on in the left navigation. It starts with the home page, which shows people you frequently contact, events in your calendar today, your favorites, and people you may want to follow up with. You can pin any of them to your page by clicking on **Pin this view**:

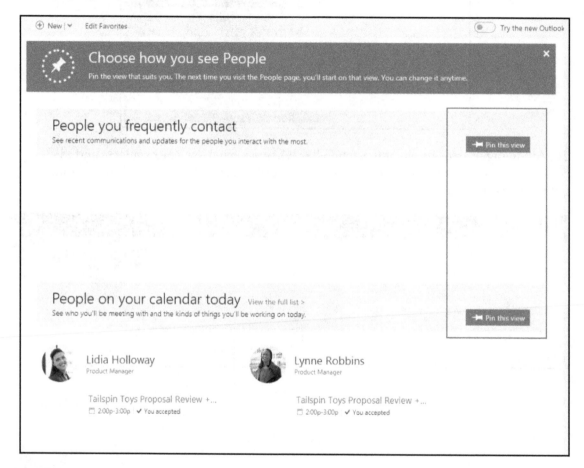

#3 Search

You can use this box to search people, whether by contacts, rooms, equipment, or an Office 365 Group.

#4 Left navigation

On the left navigation, you can navigate to **Featured people**, **Your contacts**, **Directory**, and **Groups**:

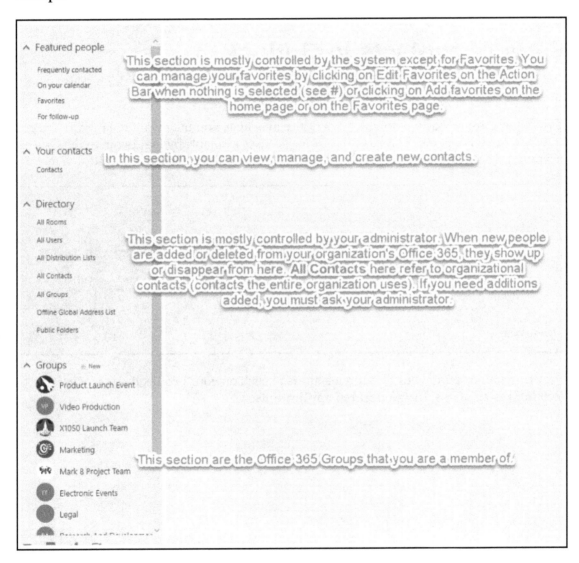

#5 Outlook apps

The buttons in this bar give you the ability to switch back and forth between the Outlook applications for mail, calendar, people, and tasks.

Parts of contacts in Outlook

You can also access your Office 365 contacts through Outlook on your desktop. This is the most popular method of interacting with contacts.

If your subscription has the download of Office available, you may want to take advantage of it. You can tell whether you have the Office licenses available by logging in to the Office 365 portal, going to Office 365 Home, and clicking on the **Office installs** drop-down menu:

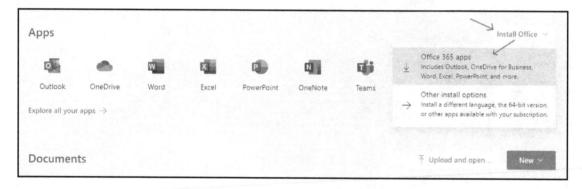

The other way to get to your desktop installs is to click on your profile, then on **My account**, **Install status**, **Install desktop applications**:

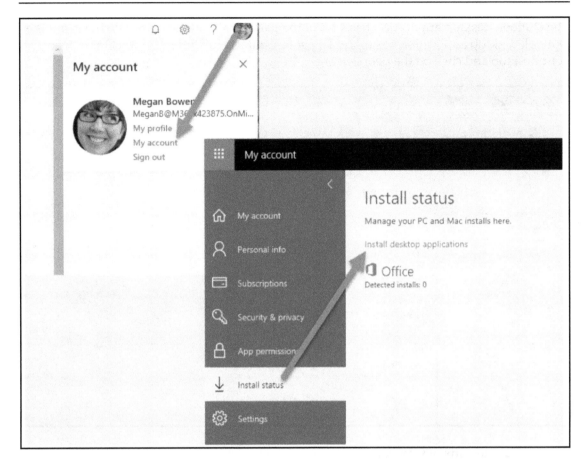

If you need more help, cannot download Office, or need to add Office, talk to your company admin.

The Outlook desktop application has a lot of the parts that Outlook on the Web has but the Outlook desktop application has more. To get to **Contacts** in Outlook, open Outlook on your desktop and click on the people icon:

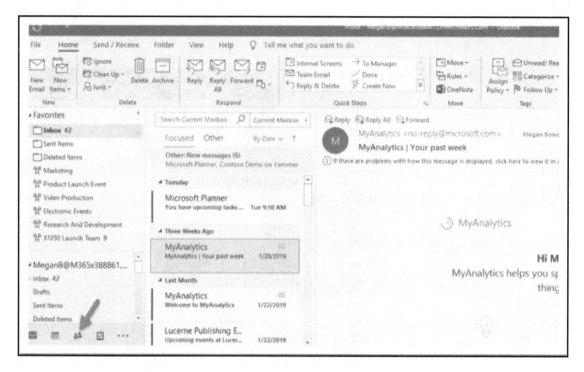

Let's look at the parts of **Contacts**.

#1 The tabs

There are six tabs that are always present in Outlook, and they each have their associated ribbon (with the exception of **File**). When you click on **File**, you are taken to what is referred to as the backstage of this Office program. We will look at the ribbons next. As for the backstage of **File**, let's look at that now:

 Depending on other portions of Outlook that you may have clicked on, additional contextual ribbons may appear.

The Outlook backstage

When you click on the **File** tab, you are taken to the backstage instead of opening a ribbon. For more details on the backstage, see *#6 The tabs* section in `Chapter 4`, *Sending and Receiving Email*.

Home

On the **Home** tab, you have the option to create new items, delete items, share, tag, and more:

One of the most popular functions is creating new emails, calendar items, contacts, and so on. Using the **New Items** drop-down button, you can create other Outlook items without leaving email:

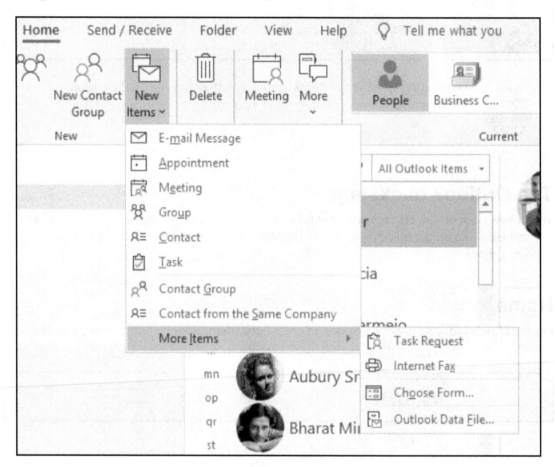

Send/receive

This ribbon has options for manually forcing Outlook to send and receive email and to update folders:

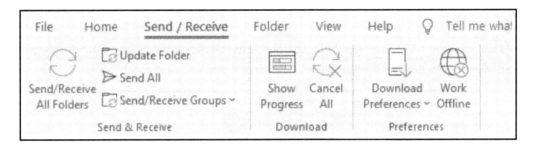

 Have you had an issue with Outlook not connecting? If so, sometimes clicking the **Work Offline** button in the **Preferences** section, to force Outlook to go offline, then clicking it again, to go back online, can prompt Outlook to refresh the connection.

Folder

This tab's ribbon has options for creating new, renaming, and copying folders, sharing and opening shared contacts, and viewing folder permissions and properties:

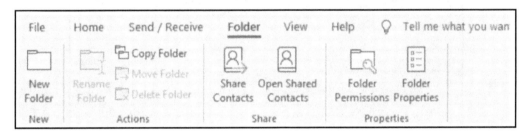

View

The options on this ribbon help you to manage how Outlook looks:

Help

On this ribbon, you have multiple help options, such as getting self-serve support, contacting support, and running diagnostics:

#2 Tell me what you want to do

If you have ever wonder whether there was a command for something, or you were having trouble finding the button for the command, this box is for you! Simply type what you want and get options:

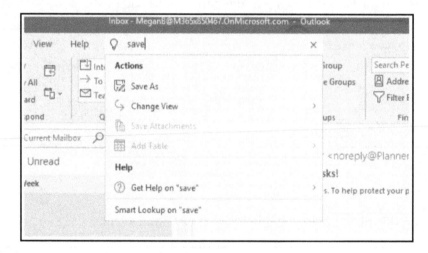

You even get some suggested options by clicking in the box.

#3 Left navigation

This portion of the interface helps you to navigate to your contact lists. When you start, you may only have one, but if you add other email accounts, you will have their contact lists show up here as well.

#4 Search and filtering

You can use the search box to search your contacts. The filter drop-down menu lets you control the scope of your search:

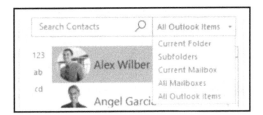

#5 List of contacts

This is the list of contacts contained in the contact list you have clicked on. You can use its navigation to quickly get to subsets of contacts:

You can also right-click on a contact to get a drop-down list of operations you can perform on the contact:

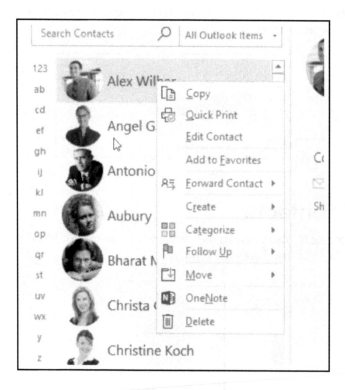

#6 Contact details pane

Once you choose a contact by clicking on it, the details of that contact will be shown in this pane. You will be able to show more details, email the contact, instant message them, and use other options via the open menu (...):

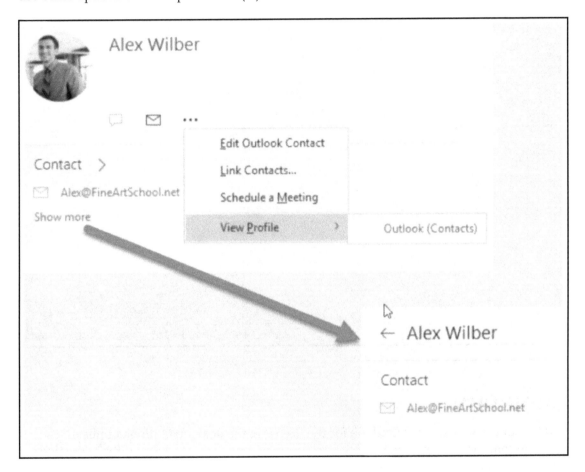

#7 Outlook apps

This is the section where you can move between the applications inside of Outlook. You can also set which ones you see and hide the ones you don't want to, and arrange them in the order you like:

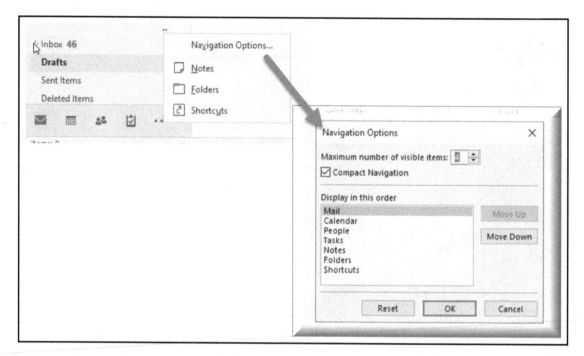

Summary

In this chapter, we explored Outlook for the Web and the desktop Outlook applications from the contacts perspective. We looked at the different parts of each and their functions. You can learn more about each of these by going to `https://support.office.com` and clicking on Outlook. From there, you will be able to choose Outlook for the Web or the desktop.

In `Chapter 7`, *Getting Familiar with Other Exchange Settings*, we will look at other settings in Outlook for the Web and the desktop Outlook application.

7
Getting Familiar with Other Exchange Settings

In this chapter, you will learn about the other settings that you can set in Exchange. You will learn how to set up an auto-forward setting in Office 365. You will also learn how to input a signature in the outline app and the web version so that it will display at the end of every email that's sent to the receiver. There are lots more options in Outlook, but we'll cover a few that you need to know about as an end user.

In this chapter, we will cover the following topics:

- Creating an email signature
- Setting an out of office reply
- Creating email rules
- Setting a forwarding email

Creating an email signature

Your organization may have a standard email signature they would like you to use, or you may wish to set up your own. Let's look at where we can get to this setting.

Creating an email signature via Outlook on the web

To get to this option on the web, click on **Settings** (the gear icon), and then on **Email signature** in the **Mail | Layout** section of the left navigation:

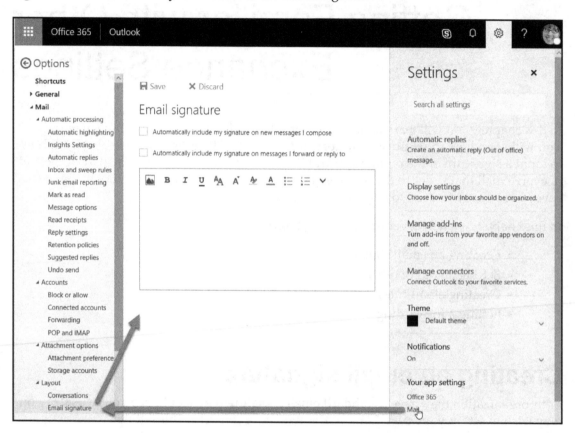

Creating an email signature via Outlook

There are two ways you can get to this option. We will look at both.

Option 1 – creating an email signature in Outlook via a new, forward, or reply email

Create a new email, or reply or forward to an email. Then, on the **Message** tab in the **Include** section, click on the **Signatures** drop-down button. This will open the **Signatures and Stationary** window, where you can then create, edit, and delete signatures, as well as assign them to any email account:

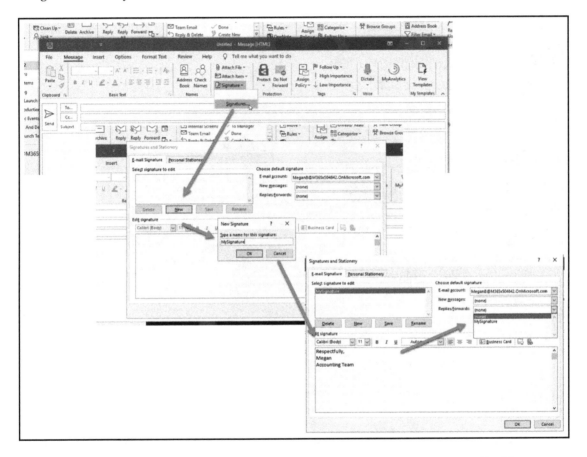

 You may have noticed the **Stationary** tab. The options there will add a background color, pattern, or image to your email. This is not recommended and is is not designed well for accessibility.

Option 2 – creating an email signature in Outlook via the file backstage

Click on **File** to get to the backstage and then click on **Options**. This will open the **Options** window. From there, click on the **Mail** tab and then on the **Signatures** button, which will open the **Signatures and Stationary** window (see the screenshot in the Option 1 – creating an email signature in Outlook via a new, forward, or reply email section):

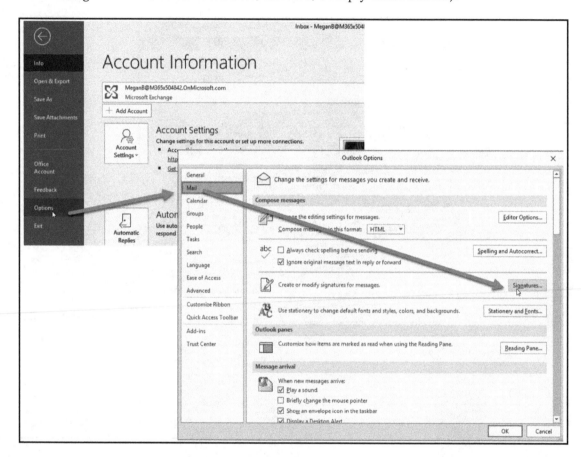

Setting the out of office reply

When you are out of the office, you may want to set an automatic reply to notify people that you are out and possibly give them additional instructions. Let's look at where we can get to this setting.

Setting an out of office reply via Outlook on the web

To get to this option on the web, click on **Settings** (the gear icon) and then on **Automatic Replies**, where you will have the option to configure the automatic replies for emails you receive from internal and external people:

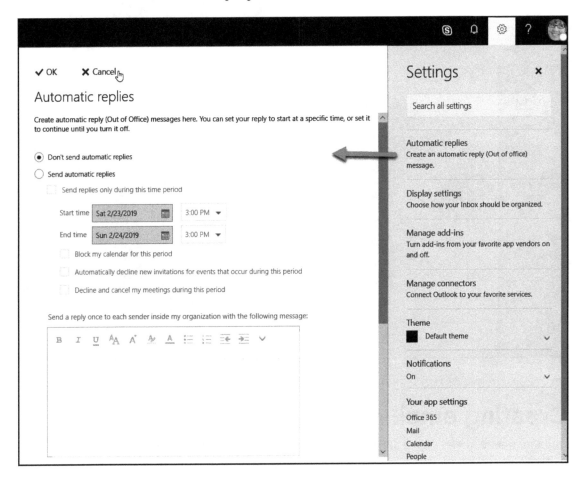

Setting the out of office reply via Outlook

To set the **Out of Office (OOO)** reply in Outlook, go to the **File** backstage. This option is on the **Info** tab and labeled **Automatic Replies (Out of Office)**. Click on the **Automatic Replies** button and the **Automatic Replies** window will open. Here, you will have the option to configure the automatic replies for emails you receive from internal and external people:

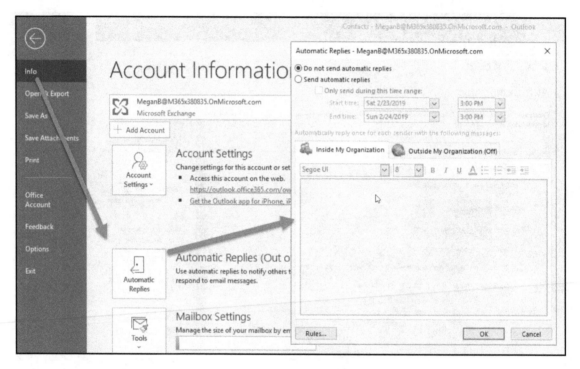

Creating email rules

In Exchange, you can create alerts and rules to do things such as route emails from a certain person to a certain place. Let's look at where we can get to this setting.

Creating email rules via Outlook for the web

To get to this option on the web, click on **Settings** (the gear icon) and then click on **Inbox and sweep rules** in the **Mail** | **Automatic processing** section of the left navigation:

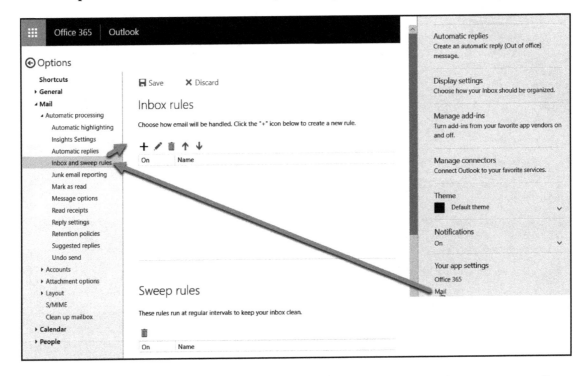

You also can delete sweeping rules that you've created from the action bar in your email.

Creating email rules via Outlook

In the **Move** section on the **Home** tab in your email, you will find the option to create new rules and alerts, as well as manage them:

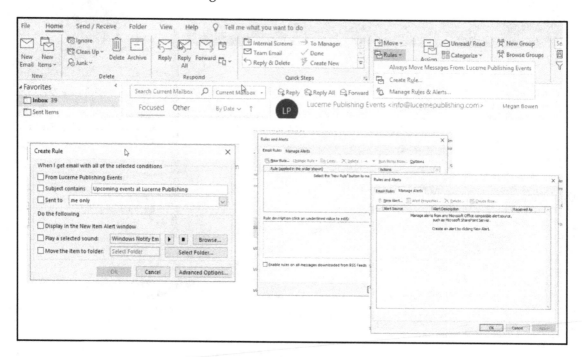

Setting a forwarding email

You may need to forward emails to another mail box, especially if you have more than one. Let's look at where we can get to this setting.

Setting a forward email via Outlook on the web

To get to this option on the web, click on **Settings** (the gear icon) and then on **Forwarding** in the **Mail** | **Accounts** section of the left navigation bar. Along with forwarding the email, you can choose to keep a copy of the email in the original inbox by checking the box:

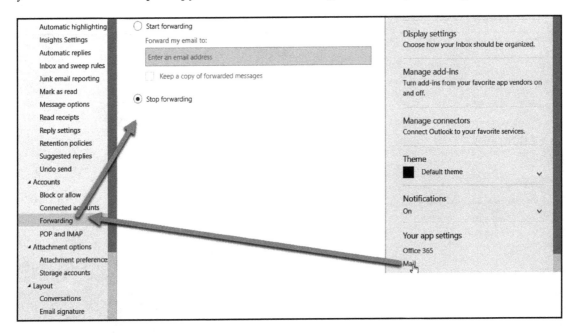

You can only set one forwarding email address.

Setting a forward email via Outlook

In order to set a forwarding email address in this version of Outlook, you will need to create a rule (see *Creating email rules* section). On the **Create Rules** window, click the **Advanced Options...** button and then choose a condition for what emails are to be forwarded from the **Rules Wizard** window:

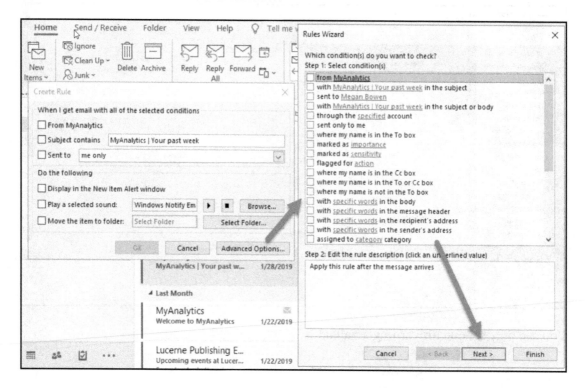

If you want all emails to be forwarded, do not check any conditions and click **Next**. You will be asked to verify your choice to not select any conditions:

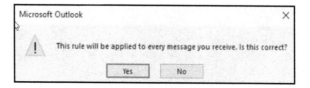

Check the box next to **forward it to people or public group** or **forward it to people or distribution list**. In the **Step 2** pane, click on the **people or public group** or **people or distribution** list:

In the **Rule Address** window, you can choose people from the address book by double-clicking on each, and/or typing in addresses on the **To** line, and then clicking the **OK** button. Remember to separate each address with a semicolon (;) if you are typing addresses in:

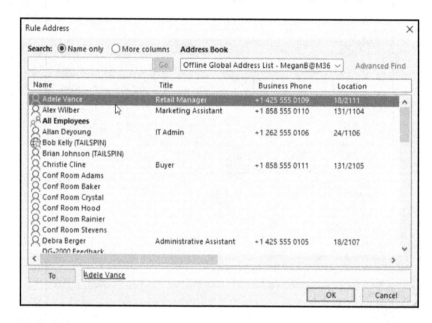

Once the **Rule Address** window closes, click the **Next** button if you want to add any exceptions, or the **Finish** button to set the rule:

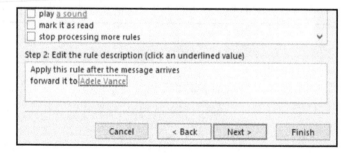

Summary

In this chapter, we explored the other settings that are available in Outlook for the web and the desktop Outlook application. We looked at the different parts of each and their functions. You can learn more about each of these by going to `https://support.office.com` and clicking on **Outlook**. From there, you will be able to choose Outlook for the web or desktop.

In `Chapter 8`, *Understanding Skype for Business and Microsoft Teams*, we will look at using the Exchange calendar with Outlook for the web and the desktop Outlook application.

3
Section 3: Skype for Business and Microsoft Teams

In this section, readers will learn about Skype for Business and Microsoft Teams in general and will be given some specific information on how to make it useful.

The following chapters will be covered:

- Chapter 8, *Understanding Skype for Business and Microsoft Teams*
- Chapter 9, *Using Skype for Business*
- Chapter 10, *Using Microsoft Teams*

8
Understanding Skype for Business and Microsoft Teams

Skype for Business and Microsoft Teams are great platforms for communication. Microsoft Teams takes things a step further and adds in the power of collaboration. In this chapter, we will learn about what Skype for Business and Microsoft Teams are and how they're related. We will start with the history and background of Skype for Business and the history and background of Microsoft Teams. Then, we will look at the parts of Skype for Business and of Teams and how to get into each. Finally, we will look at the way forward as Microsoft Teams takes the place of Skype for Business.

We will cover the following topics in this chapter:

- History and Background of Skype for Business
- History and Background of Microsoft Teams
- The parts of Skype for Business
- The Parts of Teams
- How to get into Skype for Business
- How to get into Teams
- The Way Forward with Teams

History and Background of Skype for Business

When Office 365 first came on the scene, it made its debut with Lync, which was the successor of Office Communicator. Lync was an online communicator that gave users the ability to instant message, see your contacts' online presence and share your presence, audio and video call, and transfer files, as well as hold online meetings where you could share screens, whiteboards, specific files, polls, and surveys.

In November 2014, Microsoft announced that Skype for Business would replace Lync. Skype for Business was a great improvement on connectivity and reliability. It was built on the backbone of Skype. Skype has been around for many years, has been used by people around the world, and has consistently been a reliable platform.

History and Background of Microsoft Teams

The next generation of Skype for Business is **Microsoft Teams**. Teams will be the replacement for Skype for Business but, as of writing this book, it is not yet a full replacement. Most users will still need to use Skype for Business as well. We will explore this further in *The Parts of Skype for Business* section.

Before the development of Teams, Microsoft had seriously considered buying Slack, which is now the direct competitor to Microsoft Teams. The news broke on March 4th 2016 about Microsoft's consideration, which was opposed by Bill Gates. He thought that Microsoft should focus on improving Skype for Business instead. The **Executive Vice President** (**EVP**) of Applications and Services at the time, who wanted to purchase Slack, left Microsoft later that year and Teams was born. Teams was announced on November 2nd 2016 and launched worldwide on March 14th 2017.

The parts of Skype for Business

In this section, we will look at the parts of Skype for Business. In the following screenshot, you can see that I have numbered different parts, such as calendar and settings:

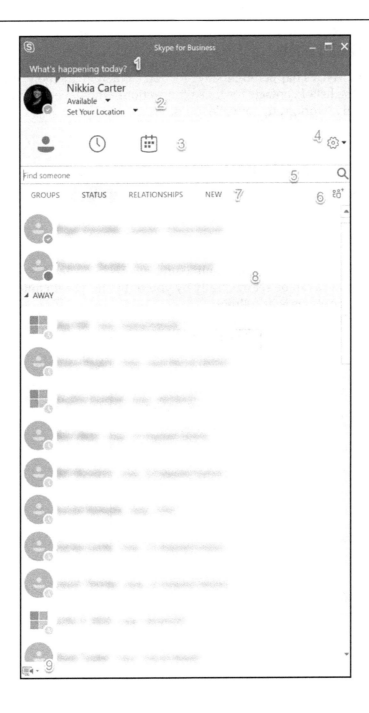

Let's explore!

#1 Personal note

When a note in the What's happening today? section is filled in, the note appears under the person's name in the list of contacts for those connections who have a **Privacy Relationship** of friends and family, workgroup, or colleagues.

#2 Presence, location, and photo

This section consists of three parts. Let's look at each in detail.

Presence

Presence, the colored indicators of your online presence, is indicated by color and text. In general, these indicators can be set manually by you or by the system automatically. The list of your presence options is as follows:

Let's now explore the description of each.

Green/available

This indicator shows that a person is online and available to contact.

Red/busy

This indicator shows that you are online but not available to contact. This presence does not prevent people from contacting you. It only tells people that you are busy and probably should not be disturbed. This indicator can also be red/in a meeting or red/in a call.

The red/in a meeting is automatically set for you when your Office 365 calendar in Exchange says you are in a meeting. The red/in a call shows automatically when you are in an audio or video call via Skype for Business. All automatically-set indicators will unset once the trigger is over. For example, once your meeting time is over, your presence will go to green/available or to one of the yellow indicators, such as yellow/away.

Red with dash/do not disturb

This indicator doesn't just let people know that you are unreachable, it actually *prevents* people from contacting you, unless the **Privacy Relationship** is set to **Workgroup**, until the indicator is changed to something else. It can be set for you when you start presenting your screen during an online meeting. As soon as you stop presenting, your presence will be changed to something else.

If you set yourself to this presence, you must remember to set yourself to something else when you are ready to be contacted again.

Yellow/be right back

This indicator shows people that you are away but should be back shortly. When you set this for yourself, your presence will revert to the previous presence or your automatically-set presence once you move your mouse or type on the keyboard.

Yellow/off work

When you set this presence, it lets people know that you are not working and not available for contacting.

Yellow/appear away

When you set this presence, people see yellow/away which indicates that you are away from your computer. This indicator can also be automatically set for you when you stop moving the mouse and typing. First, the indicator will get set to yellow/inactive, and then it will set to yellow/away after five minutes or more, depending on your settings.

Reset status

When you chose this option, your presence will be reset to green/available.

Sign out

Signs you out of Skype for Business but does not close the application.

Exit

Signs you out of Skype for Business and closes the application.

White with question mark/unknown

This indicator is not shown in the list of presences that you can choose for yourself, but can be automatically chosen for you. This presence that is shown when your organization prevents your presence from being seen by others, you no longer have a license for Skype for Business, or you no longer have your account.

White/offline

This indicator is not shown in the list of presences that you can choose for yourself, but can be automatically chosen for you. This is a presence that is shown when you are offline, signed out, or have exited from the application.

Location

This section allows you to set your location. To set or edit your location, simply click on the area and a textbox will open where you can type in or edit your location. Some examples you may want to set are working remotely, building 1, or Office 3:

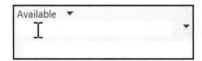

You can choose whether others will see your location by clicking the dropdown and checking or unchecking **Show Others My Location**:

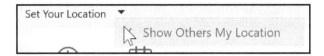

When you set a location, the system will remember your location and automatically reset it based on the IP address of the internet you are connected to. For example, if you are working at home and set your location to Teleworking, the next time you are at your home, your location will be automatically set as Teleworking.

Photo

If you don't have a picture or want to change your picture, click on your picture or the picture icon to be taken to the page in Office 365 where you can add a picture or modify your picture.

 You may have to sign in to change your picture.

#3 The contacts, conversations, and meetings tabs

These are the three main tabs, which may have sub-tabs. Let's look at these tabs and what you get by clicking them.

 For more details, see the *#7 Sub-tabs* section.

Contacts

On this tab, you can see all of your contacts. You can add contacts via the **Find someone** box and/or the people, or use the sub-tabs to see your contacts categorized in different ways:

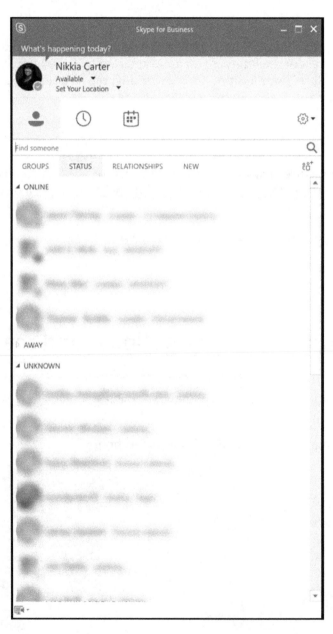

You will also be able to see unknown contacts under your contacts.

Conversations

In this tab, you can see the conversations you have had via Skype for Business:

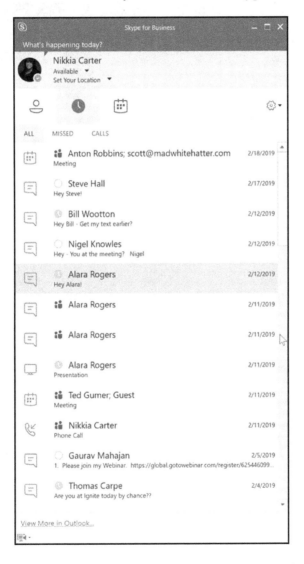

Through the sub-tabs, you can see all of your recent conversations, missed conversations, and audio/video calls.

Meetings

On this tab, you can see all of your upcoming meetings for today. Skype for Business reads your Outlook calendar and displays all of your events for today. Any Skype for Business and Microsoft Teams meetings will include a button for joining the meeting:

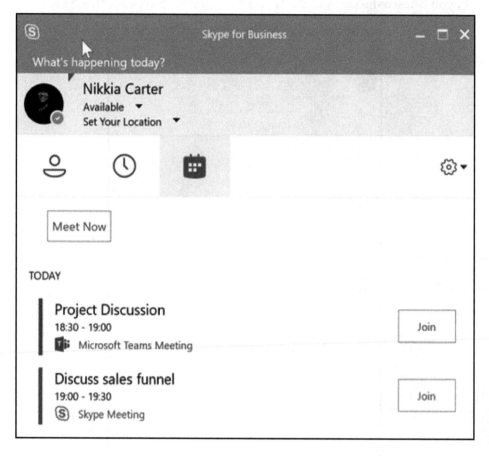

The events you see will be your events that are upcoming for today only.

#4 Settings

This button will open a dropdown of setting options for Skype for Business. You can do things such as access **File**, **Tools**, and **Help** as well as being able to start an online meeting immediately via **Meet Now**. Under **File**, you can do things such as **Sign Out**, change your status, **View Received Files**, and **Exit** Skype for Business:

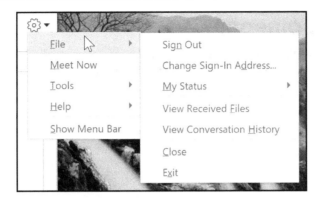

Under Tools, you can do things such as open the **Recording Manager** and go to specific settings for audio, video, and dial-in conferencing calls:

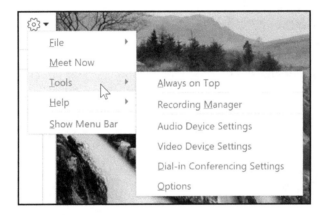

Under **Help**, you can access help, the **Privacy Statement**, and the about section:

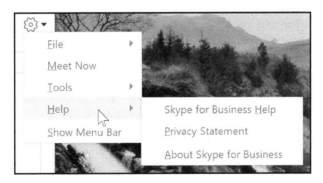

Let's now learn how to find your business friends and colleagues on Skype.

#5 Finding someone

You can find contacts to add to your Skype for Business contacts list by clicking in the find someone box and typing in a name or email address. Once you press *Enter*, Skype for Business will search your Outlook contacts and all of the Skype and Skype for Business users:

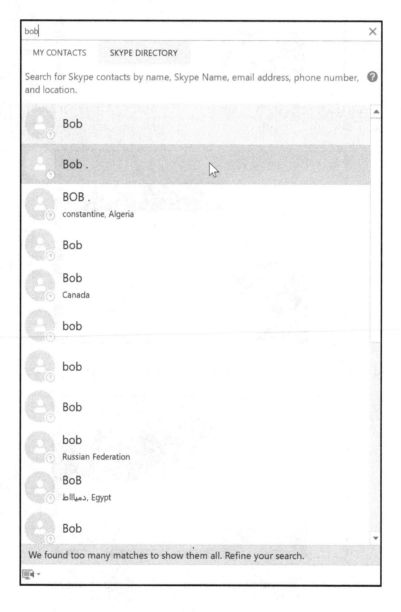

It is OK to use a name for a person in your organization or in your Outlook contacts, but it is best to use email addresses to look up people outside of your organization due to the sheer number of results you may get.

#6 The add people button

You can use this button to clarify your search to contacts that are internal or external to your organization, allow you to create a group to categorize your contacts, or display your contacts options:

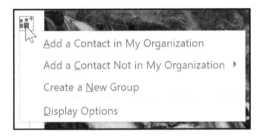

Here are the display options for your contacts:

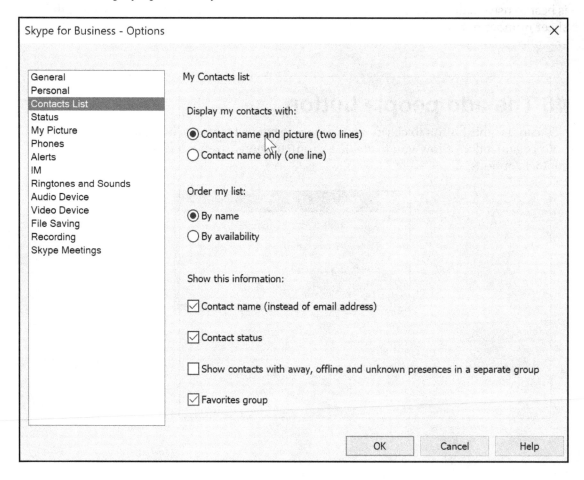

Click on **OK** to complete the setup.

#7 Sub-tabs

These are the tabs that are described in *#3 The Contacts, conversations, and meetings tabs*.

Contacts

These sub-tabs allow you to see your contacts categorized in different ways: by groups, status (which is presence), and relationship. You can choose whether to add these people to your contacts or to block them:

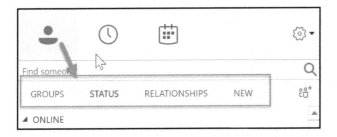

You can also see any potential contacts, that is, people who have added you as a contact in their Skype for Business, under **New**.

Conversations

These sub-tabs allow you to see all recent conversations, any missed conversations, and all calls, whether video or audio. You can re-enter any conversation by double clicking on it. From there, you can read what was typed and/or re-initiate the conversation:

You can double-click on any calls but be aware that this may re-call the person or people, or may just open the IM window with all people attached. I have seen it happen both ways over the years:

A record of all of your conversations via Skype for Business is retrievable by your organization as well as by you. If you are looking for a conversation that is not showing under the **Conversations** tab or you need to search your conversations, you can click on **View More in Outlook...** at the bottom of the Conversations tab, then Skype for Business will attempt to open the Conversation History folder in your desktop Outlook application.

#8 The main section

What you see in this section will be which tab, and possibly sub-tab, you are in. For example, if you are in the Contacts tab and the Status sub-tab, you will see your contacts categorized by their current presence.

#9 Selecting primary device

Clicking on this button will open a dropdown where you can see your default setup, set your audio settings, and check your call quality if you have a license that allows you to make calls:

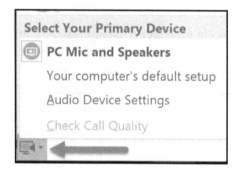

Clicking on the your computer's default setup will open the audio options:

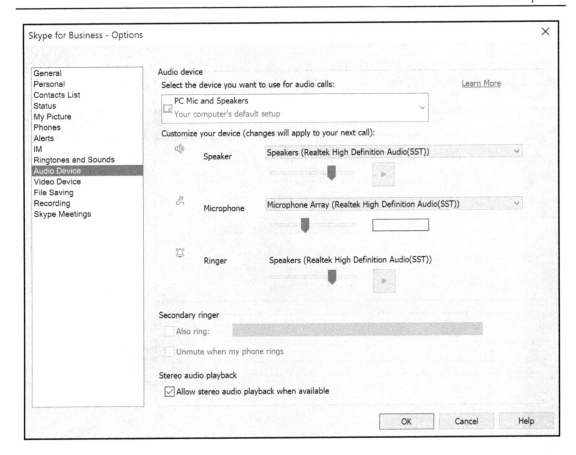

Click on **OK** to complete the setup.

The Parts of Teams

In this section, we will look at the parts of Microsoft Teams. As you can see, I have marked some important parts of Teams that you should learn about in the following screenshot:

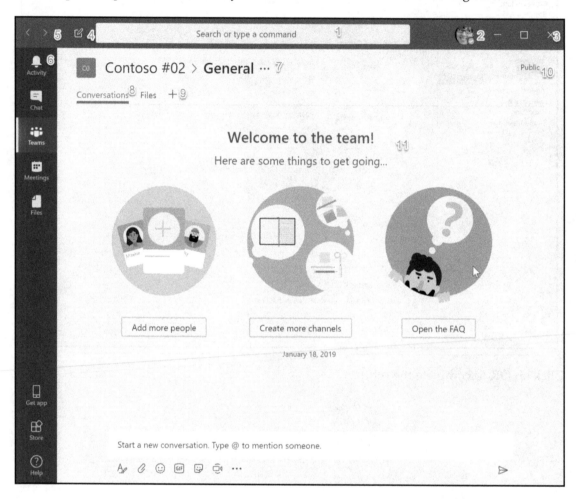

Let's explore different parts of Microsoft Teams.

#1 Search box

This search box lets you search all the Teams data you have access to. It also allows you to execute the Teams commands. For a list of commands, type in @, as in the following screenshot:

You can get a list of different options even if you don't type @.

#2 Your profile picture

Click on your picture and a dropdown opens with options for changing your presence, changing your settings, and signing out:

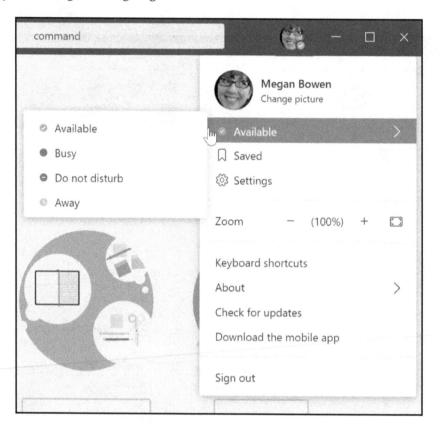

#3 The minimize, maximize, and close buttons

These buttons allow you to minimize, maximize, and close the desktop application.

#4 New chat button

By clicking this button, you can initiate a chat message:

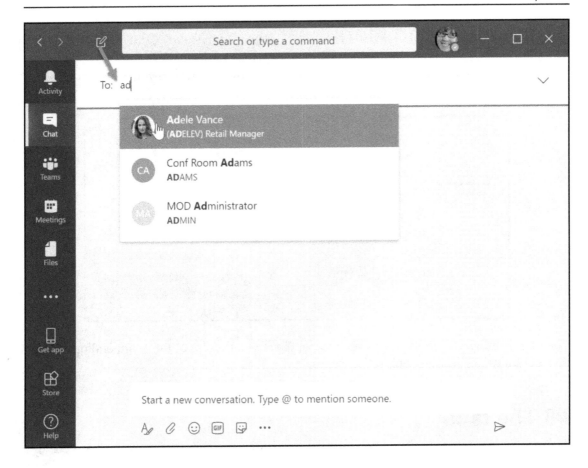

#5 Back and forward buttons

Once you have navigated around in Teams, you can use these buttons to move back to a previous page and move forward to pages you have moved back from.

#6 Left navigation

The upper half of the left navigation has buttons to help you see any new activity, initiate new chats, and see your contacts, see all Teams you are a member of, view all meetings on a daily basis, and view all files you have access to. Depending on your subscription, you may also have a button to make calls via Teams. The lower half of the left navigation has buttons to download the app (desktop if via the online Teams and mobile if via the desktop), to access the Store, and to get help.

#7 Location and menu

These items show when you are in a Team and they show you where you are in the Team, which Team you're in, and which channel you're in:

The menu allows you to do things such as get the email address of the Team and open the SharePoint site collection behind the scenes.

#8 The tabs

These tabs help you to navigate between the applications within the Team, such as getting to files.

#9 Adding a tab

You may be able to add more applications to the Team, if you are an owner. Simply click on the + and then search for or navigate to the app you want to add. You can see more apps by clicking the **More apps** button at the bottom of the screen:

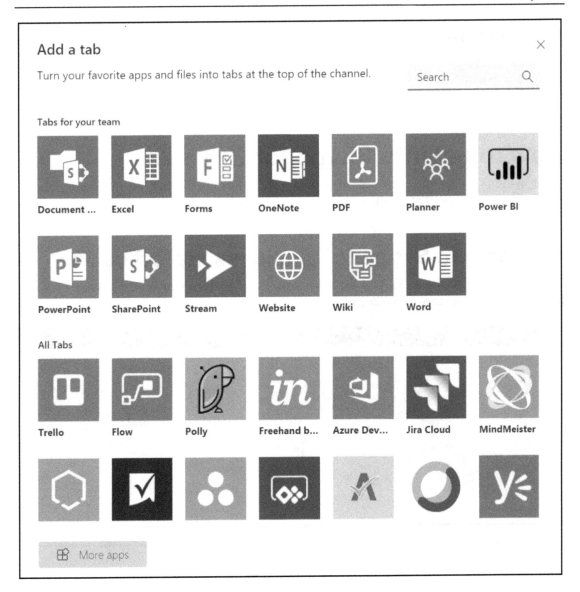

You may need to set some settings and/or give the chosen app a title.

#10 Public/private indicator

This indicator lets you know whether the Team is a private or a public Team.

#11 The main app screen

This main screen of the app will show items based on what is chosen from the left navigation panel. Choose **Meetings**, and you will see the meeting for today plus the details of the default selected meeting.

How to get into Skype for Business

You can get into Skype for Business in two ways: via the Office 365 or via the Skype for Business desktop app. Let's look at both ways in detail.

Getting into Skype for Business via Office 365

When you log into Office 365, you are automatically logged into the online version of Skype for Business. People can see your presence and contact you:

 It may take a minute or so before your presence updates. There may be times where you are signed out and will need to sign in. Click on your persona to log in and/or change your presence.

You can see your contacts and IM them when you go to **Outlook** and click on **Skype for Business** in the suite bar.

Getting into Skype for Business via the app

Once you download the app, you can sign in. Once you sign in, until you have to change your password, the application will remember your credentials and log you in automatically. If you log out and attempt to log back in with the same email, you will only need to enter your email:

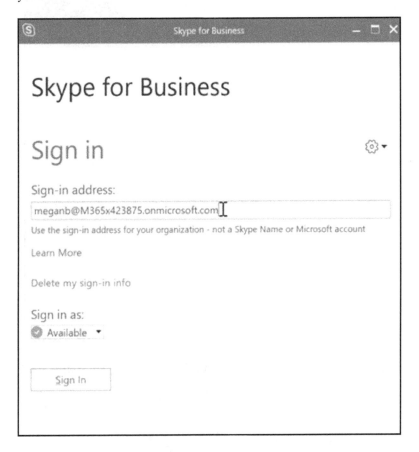

The system will remember your password and sign you in the rest of the way.

How to get into Teams

You can get into Microsoft Teams in two ways: via the Office 365 or via the Microsoft Teams desktop app. Let's look at both ways in detail.

Getting into Teams via Office 365

When you log into Office 365, you are automatically logged into the online version of Microsoft Teams. Others can see your presence and contact you:

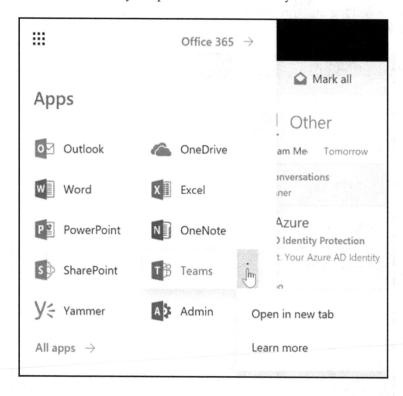

You can see your contacts and IM them when you go to Microsoft Teams via the app launcher, or on Office 365 Home.

Getting into Teams via the app

Once you download the app, you can sign in. You can download the app from Microsoft Teams online from the left navigation panel:

Once you sign in, until you have to change your password, the application will remember your credentials and log you in automatically. If you log out and attempt to log back in with the same email, you will only need to enter your email:

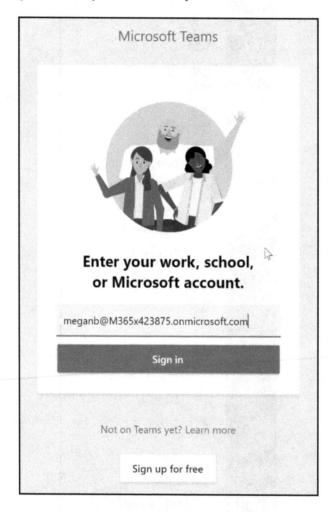

There have been times where automatic logging in has not worked for everyone. You may have to enter your password.

The system will remember your password and sign you in the rest of the way.

The Way Forward with Teams

Microsoft Teams will be the replacement for Skype for Business eventually, but the time frame for that is not clear. The Microsoft Teams team is working on achieving feature parity with Skype for Business but, as of writing of this book, they still have a ways to go. Just know that Microsoft Teams will fully replace Skype for Business one day, and be the way of future unified communications in Office 365.

Summary

In this chapter, we learned about Skype for Business and Microsoft Teams and how they're related. You learned about the background and parts of Skype for Business and Teams. You should now be able to easily get into Skype for Business and Teams.

In Chapter 9, *Using Skype for Business*, we will dive deeper into Skype for Business, and you will learn how to use Skype for Business to facilitate communication.

Using Skype for Business

9

When using Skype for Business, there are a number of things that you should know about. In this chapter, you will learn about presence and how to update the Skype for Business contact list for users who are not in the same organization. You will also learn how to use Skype for Business to set up and work in meetings with other users.

In this chapter, the following topics are covered:

- Knowing the presence settings
- Working with contacts
- Instant messaging
- Initiating calls
- Working in meetings
- Sending a meeting invite

Knowing the presence settings

Presence is an indicator color that lets you know if the contacts in your list are online, or busy, or doing something else. The same applies to contacts that have added you to their list. They can see your presence:

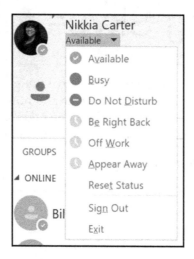

These presences can be set by you manually by clicking on the dropdown under your name or they may be set automatically by the system. Since, everything in Office 365 is tied together, Skype for Business can read your Outlook calendar and know when you are in a meeting and it will change your presence for you when the time comes as well as when the meeting is over. It will also change your presence when you start and end an audio or video call and when you start and stop sharing your screen.

 When you set your presence manually, it will stay that way unless an automatic change happens such as a meeting time.

It is important that you understand what presence is and what the indicator lights mean. Let's explore them.

Available

This presence is the green indicator. It means *"I'm online and available"*.

Busy

This presence is the red indicator. It means "*I'm busy. Please do not disturb me.*" This presence does not prevent people from being able to ping you. It is just an indicator. If you set it, the description, that is, the words following the color indicator, will say **Busy** but if it is set automatically, the description will describe what you are doing. If you are in an audio or video call, it will say **In a Call**. If you are in a meeting according to your calendar, it will say **In a Meeting**.

Do not disturb

This is the red indicator with the dash through it. It means exactly as it says and will prevent people from being able to ping you unless that person has a privacy relationship of workgroup. If you are sharing your screen, your presence will be auto-set and the description will say **Presenting**.

 If you set this presence manually, you need to remember to set it back to something else when you are ready for your contacts to be able to ping you again. Otherwise, they will have to try to reach you some other way.

The aways

There are three different types of away and each one of them is yellow. Even though they all share the same color, they react a little differently.

Be right back

When you set this one, you will return to your previous presence or automatic presence when you wake your computer or move your mouse. It can be set for you automatically when you have not touched the mouse in a while or when you lock your computer. The description in this case will say **Inactive**.

Off work

This is one that you set manually and lets your contacts know that you are gone for the day.

Appear away

This is one that you can set when you want to look like you are away but it will also be set for you when you have been inactive for a longer period of time.

Offline

This isn't a setting that can be set under the presence dropdown but it is automatically set when you are offline. The indicator color is white.

Unknown

This isn't a setting that can be set under the presence dropdown, but it is one that is seen when your contact has either lost their license (for example, if they left the organization they were with) or the organization has blocked presence to others outside of their organization for the entire organization or maybe just for that one individual. The indicator color is gray.

Working with contacts

When working with your contacts, you have some options you need to be aware of. You can get options in two ways: through the dropdown and by hovering over the person's picture icon.

Options by hovering

When you hover over the person's picture icon, you get options for instant messaging and audio or video calling that person:

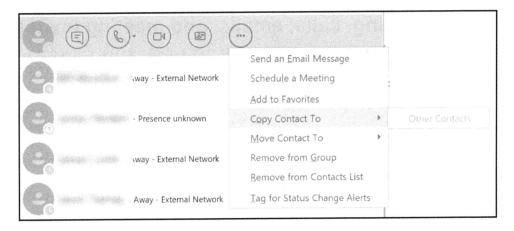

You can see their contact card and get to more options like those on the more options dropdown (see the *Options by dropdown* section that follows).

Options by dropdown

When you right-click on one of the contacts in your list, you will get a dropdown menu of options you can perform on that contact:

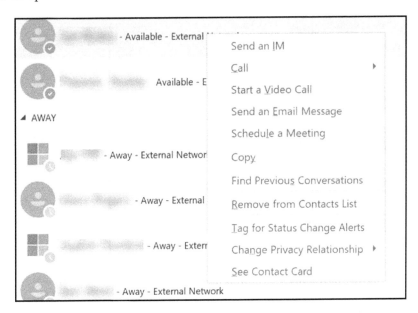

Most of these options are obvious but we will look at the ones you are most likely to use.

Instant messaging, calls, emails, and meeting invites

You can **Send an IM** (instant message) or start a video or audio call. You can send an email or set up a meeting with that person via your default mail application such as Outlook or Microsoft Mail.

Removing a contact

Using **Remove from Contacts List** will remove the contact from your Skype for Business. If you are on the **GROUPS** sub-tab, under either the **FAVORITES** group or any other group, you will have more removal options such as adding to or removing from the **FAVORITES** group or any other group:

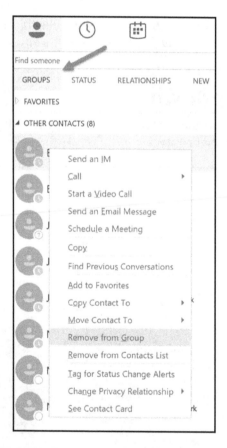

This removal will not remove the contact from Skype for Business although, if they were only in a group, you will not be able to see that person anymore.

Copying and moving contacts

These options allow you to copy and move contacts to different groups in your list:

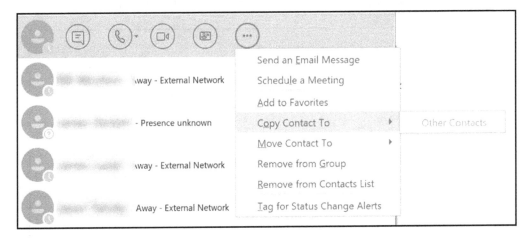

Copying means that the contact will be in its original place as well as copied to the other group you choose. Moving means that the contact will be removed from the original place and placed in the group you choose.

Tag for status change alerts

When you click on this option, you will get a popup notification that will appear in the bottom right-hand corner of your screen that will let you know when that person goes on and offline. This effectively ties a bell around their neck.

Change privacy relationship

The privacy relationship you set for each contact affects what info of yours they can see as well as whether they can ping you when you are in **Do not disturb** mode:

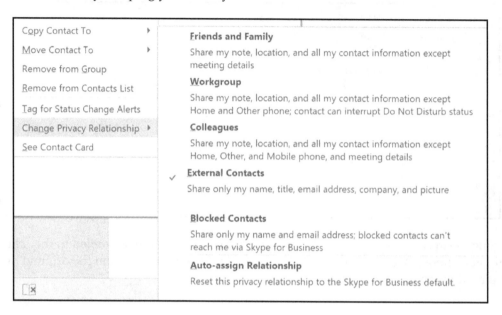

You can also block people through this setting.

 By default, people internal to your organization are added as **Colleagues** and people outside are added as **External Contacts**.

Working with groups

You can create, move up or down, and rename groups by going to the **GROUPS** sub-tab and right-clicking on one of the groups:

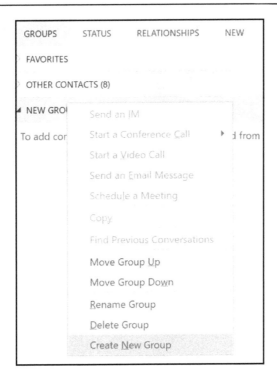

You will also see the option for deleting a group if the group you click on is empty.

Instant messaging

To instant message any of your contacts, you can either hover over your contact's picture and click on the IM button (see the following screenshot) or simply double-click on your contact:

Either way, an instant message window will open and you will have lots of options including instant messaging:

Let's cover the functionalities of each option.

#1 Text box

In this area (**1**), you can type your message.

#2 Message area

In this area (**2**), you can see all messages for all participants.

#3 Message options

Here (**3**) you have options for adding an attachment, a link, and/or emoticons to your message. You can also denote your message as important by clicking on the !. Normally, you can type your message and hit *Enter* to send your message but sometimes you may find that doesn't happen. In that case, you can use the blue button with the paper airplane to send the message.

#4 IM button

Clicking this button (*#4*) toggles open/closed the instant message text box (*#1*).

#5 Call buttons

Click on the button with the video camera on it to initiate a video call or click on the button with the phone on it to initiate an audio call (**5**).

#6 Presentation button

There are a lot of cool options available via this button (**6**)! You can choose to share a PowerPoint file, a certain window, or your entire desktop (or multiple desktops if you have them and would like that). You can add attachments, share notes, or take notes of your own via OneNote, and/or co-author a Microsoft Office document:

Under **More...**, there are options for creating a poll, a **Q&A** board, or starting a whiteboard. Once these options are used, there is an option to save them via the **Manage Content** option as follows:

Clicking the **Manage Content** option opens the **Content** window where you can see the content you loaded up in your presentation session. Through this window, you can switch which piece of content you want the participants to see. You can set the permission on the content or remove any piece of content. You can also see other options under the more options icon depending on the content's type:

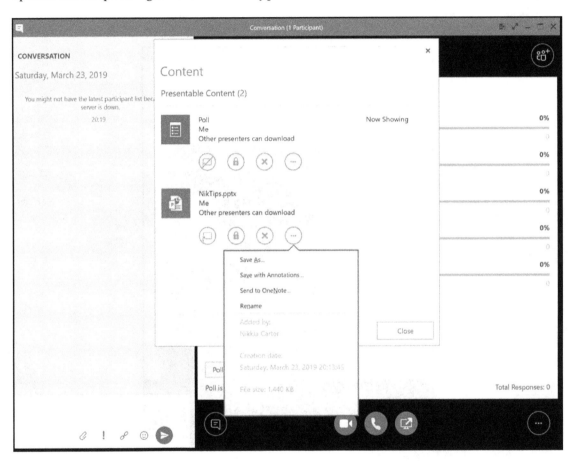

When you are presenting your screen, you can click on the more options button in the lower right hand of the window. This will give you options such as recording the session.

If you record the session, make sure you follow the laws for recording in your state.

You can see all the participants by clicking on the people icon. It opens the **PARTICIPANTS** list where you can right-click on a participant to promote them to becoming a presenter or demote a presenter to being an attendee:

Clicking on the **Participant Actions** button pops open a window with options such as preventing attendee video:

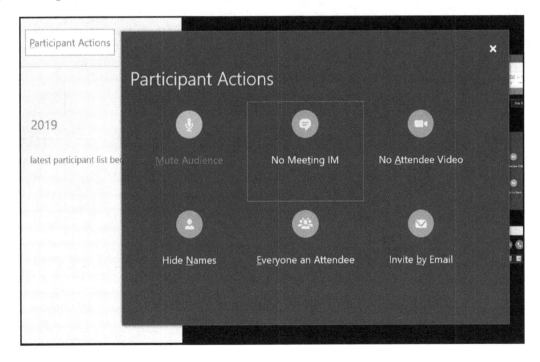

Clicking on the **Invite More People** button opens a window where you can choose other people to join the meeting.

Inviting a potential attendee this way brings them into the conversation immediately. The intended additional participants must already be in your contacts list.

When you are presenting, you will have the button to **Stop Sharing** at the top of the window:

If you are presenting your desktop, you will also have one on a dropdown bar on the top of your screen.

#7 More options button

If you click this button when you aren't presenting your screen, you get the options seen in the following screenshot:

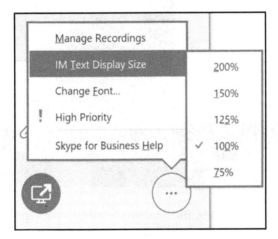

If you are presenting your screen, you will have more options:

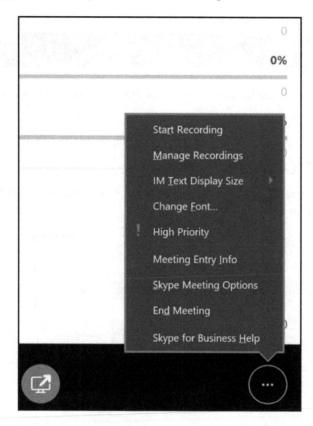

When you're presenting your screen, the **Start Recording**, **Manage Recordings**, **Meeting Entry Info**, **Skype Meeting Options**, and **End Meeting** options are available, which help you manage recordings and meetings.

#8 Participants list

Clicking on this button will open the list of participants where you can right-click on a participant to promote a participant to becoming a presenter or demote a presenter to being an attendee.

#9 Add more participants button

Clicking on this button opens a window where you can choose other people to join the conversation:

Inviting a potential attendee this way brings them into the conversation immediately. The intended additional participants must already be in your contacts list.

Initiating calls

You can initiate a call by hovering over the contact's picture and choosing the audio or video call button:

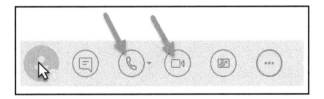

If you are already in an instant message with the contact you want to call, click on the audio or video call button at the bottom of the window:

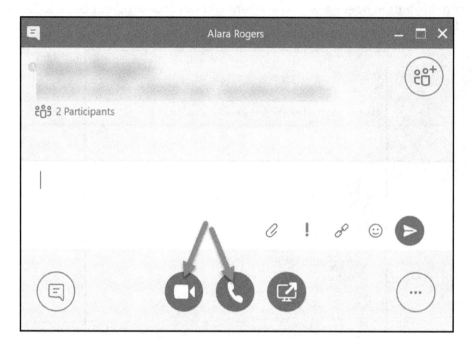

Working in meetings

You can initiate a meeting in two ways: on demand or via invitation. When you are in an instant message with someone, you can easily turn that instant message into a meeting by sharing and/or adding audio or video conferencing.

 For more details, see the *#6 Presentation button* section earlier in this chapter.

You can also set up a meeting in a more formal way by sending an invitation. For more details, see the *Sending a meeting invite* section next.

Sending a meeting invite

You can send a meeting invite in two ways. One way is via the calendar in Outlook online or on your desktop.

Sending via Outlook online

If you choose online, click on the **Add Skype meeting** button to add it to your meeting:

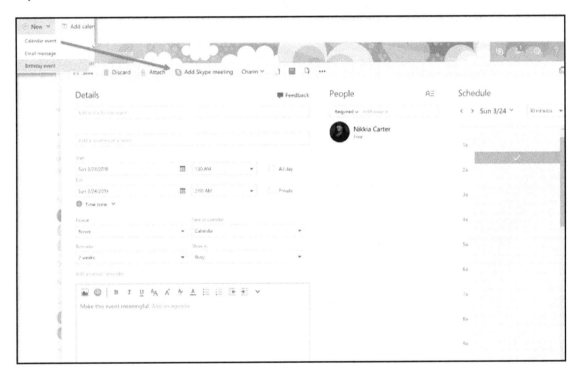

The link will not be added so you can see it, but it will be there once sent:

> Your Skype meeting has been created. We'll add joining details after the invitation is sent.

Send via Outlook on your desktop

In Outlook on your desktop, click on the **New Items** button on the **Home** tab and then click on **Skype Meeting**:

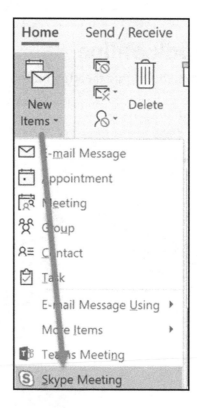

When the meeting invite window opens, fill out the invite with the pertinent information and attendees and send as you would any other meeting invite via Outlook:

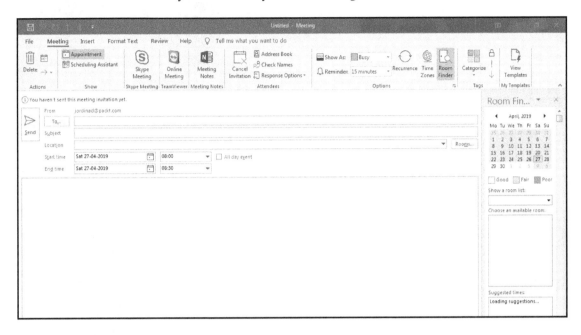

Summary

Skype for Business is very reliable when it comes to having a conversation within the same organizations. In this chapter, we discussed how to use Skype for Business to facilitate communication. You learned about the presence settings and working with contacts. You also learned about the things you can do in a meeting and how to send a meeting invite.

In Chapter 10, *Using Microsoft Teams*, you will learn how to use Microsoft Teams to facilitate communication.

10
Using Microsoft Teams

Microsoft Teams is one of Microsoft's newest additions. It is a great collaboration and unified communication platform that will take the place of Skype for Business. Teams is similar to Slack. When using Microsoft Teams for Business, there are several things that you should know about.

In this chapter, you will learn to understand the presence settings and how they work, how to work with your contacts, how to initiate instant messaging and meetings, and how to set up a meeting with other users.

In this chapter, the following topics will be covered:

- Exploring presence settings
- Working with contacts
- Instant messaging
- Initiating calls
- Working in your Teams
- Working in meetings
- Sending a meeting invite

Exploring presence settings

These presence settings are like those in Skype for Business. Presence is an indicator color that lets you know if the contacts in your list are online, busy, in a meeting, and so on. This applies to contacts that have added you to their list. They can see your presence status, as well:

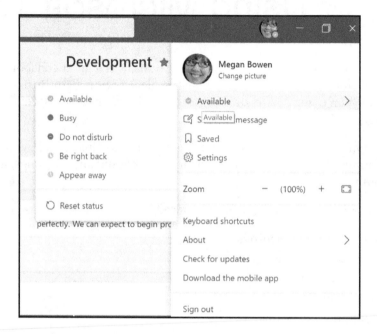

These presences can be set by you manually, by clicking on the drop-down menu under your name, or automatically by the system. Since everything in Office 365 is tied together, Teams can read your Outlook calendar and know when you are in a meeting, and will change your presence for you when the time comes, as well as when the meeting is over. It will also change your presence when you start and end an audio or video call and when you start and stop sharing your screen.

 When you manually set your presence, it will stay that way unless an automatic change happens, such as for a meeting.

It is important that you understand what presence is and what the indicator light means. Let's explore them.

Available

This presence is the green indicator with a tick mark. It means *I'm online and available.* By default, Teams will display this presence when you are not in a meeting or on an audio or video call.

Busy

This presence is the red indicator. It means *I'm busy. Please do not disturb me.* This presence is just an indicator and does <u>not</u> prevent people from being able to ping you. If you set it, the description – the words following the color indicator – will say **Busy**, but if it is set automatically, the description will describe what you are doing. If you are in an audio or video call, it will say **In a Call**. If, according to your calendar, you are in a meeting, it will say **In a Meeting**.

If you have desktop notifications enabled on Teams, you will not receive any while your presence is set to busy. This helps keep away the distraction of receiving messages, especially if you are using your computer in a meeting.

Do not disturb

This is the red indicator with the dash through it. It lets people know that you do not want to be disturbed and will prevent people from being able to ping you. If you are sharing your screen, your presence will be auto-set and the description under the indicator will say **Presenting**.

 If you manually set this presence, you need to remember to set it back to something else when you are ready for your contacts to be able to ping you again. Otherwise, they will have to try to reach you some other way.

The aways

There are three different types of presences to reflect being away and each is demarcated with yellow. Even though they all share the same color, they each react a little differently.

Be right back

When you set this one, you will return to your previous presence or automatic presence when you wake your computer or move your mouse. It can be set to activate automatically when you have not touched the mouse in a while or when you lock your computer. The description in this case will say **Inactive**.

Appear away

This is one that you can set when you want to look like you are away, but it will also be set for you when you have been inactive a longer period of time.

Offline

This isn't a setting that can be set under the presence drop-down menu, but it is automatically set when you are offline. The indicator is white.

Unknown

This isn't a setting that can be set using the presence drop-down menu, but is one that is seen when your contact has either lost their license (for example, if they left the organization they were with) or the organization has blocked presence appearing to others outside of their organization. This could be policy for the entire organization, or maybe for just that one individual. The indicator is gray.

Working with contacts

Before you can message anyone, you need to know how to access them. As with all messaging services, each user becomes a contact that you can message depending on the settings in your organization. You can get to your contacts in two ways: through the **Chat** button or through the **Calls** button. Both are on the left-hand navigation pane:

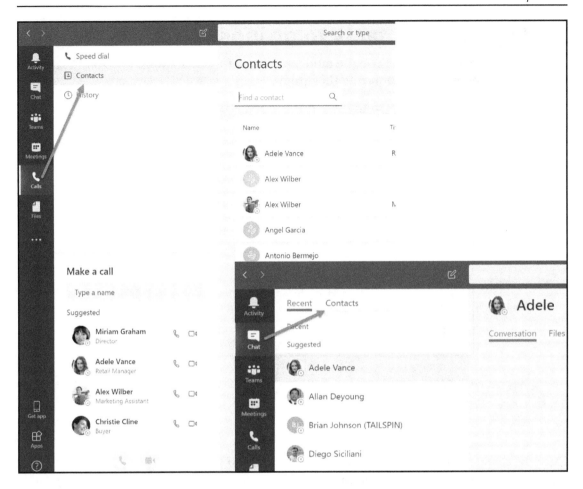

 Depending on your license, you may also have **Make a call** section, where you can initiate video or audio calls to your contacts.

Depending on what you want to do, you can locate your contact here and call them or initiate a text-based chat.

Adding chat contacts to groups

To add a new chat contact, click on the more options menu of the group you want to add them to, then choose **Add a contact to this group**:

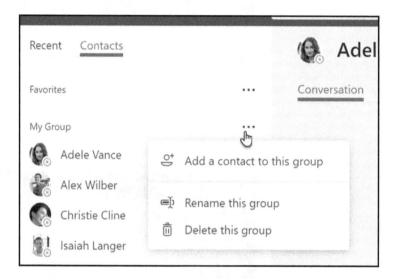

 Add people from inside your organization using their name and people outside using their email address.

Once the contact is added, you will have some options. If the person is in your organization, you will be able to do the following:

- Remove them from the group
- Get notified when they are online
- See information related to them, such as conversations and files
- Be able to chat with them or start a call or meeting where you could also invite more people

You can see some of these options in the following screenshot:

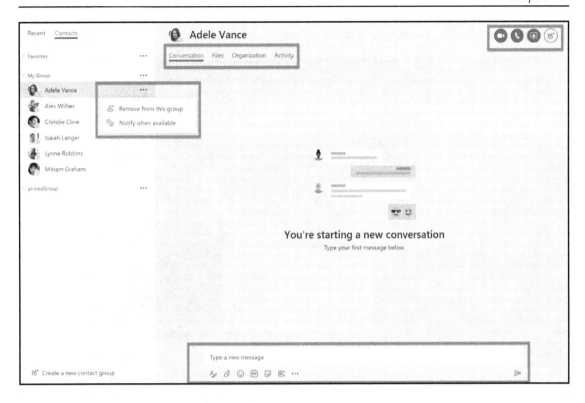

If the person is not in your organization, you will be able to remove them from the group and chat or call with them:

However, all other options will not be available to you.

Adding call contacts

To add a call contact, click **Contacts** then the **Add Contact** button, then fill in the pop-up box with a name. The **Add** button will light up. Click on it, then you will get another popup, where you can add more information to the contact. Click the **Add** button to add them to your list:

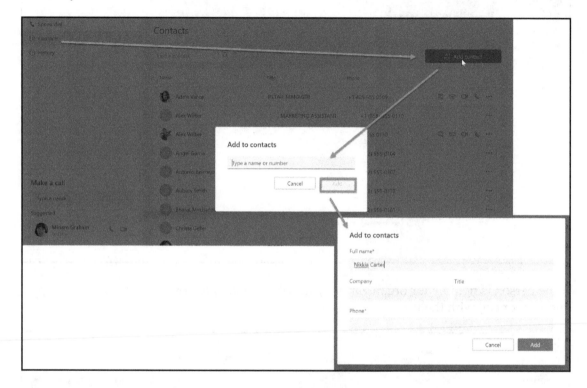

If the person is not in your organization, you may see a message that there are no matches in your organization. Simply click elsewhere on the box and you will see the **Add** button:

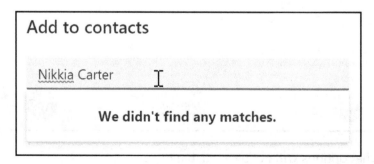

When you add a chat contact, they will appear under **Contacts** and under **Speed dial** with some options:

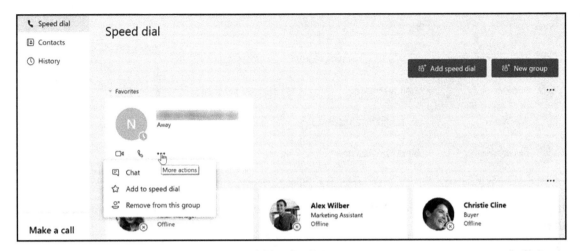

If the person is in your organization, you will be able to see their contact info and contact them with chat, email, or audio or video call. You will also be able to remove the contact, add that person to speed dial, and search for contacts:

If the person is not in your organization, you will be able to see their contact info. You will also be able to add them to speed dial, edit or remove the contact, and block the contact:

If you added the person via **Chat**, you will also have some contact and other options for that contact:

You will also have contact card options depending on the type of contact:

Just double-click on the contact to open the contact card and see the available options.

Instant messaging

To instant message, otherwise known as chat, with your contacts or others in your organization, you can use the **Chat** button or choose a contact via your **Chat Contacts** or **Call Contacts** where you will see the option (see the **Working with Contacts** portion of this chapter).

The **Chat** button is at the upper-center portion of the Teams window, right next to the search box. Clicking on it opens a chat window where you can type the names of the people you want to chat with:

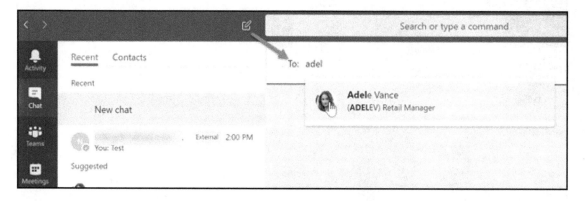

If the person you want to chat with isn't in your organization, you must use their email address. You can only chat with one external person at a time and not with any internal people, but you can send a meeting invite where you can chat with more than one external person along with internal people.

Initiating calls

To call your contacts or others in your organization, use **Chat Contacts** or **Call Contacts**, where you will see the options for video and audio calls (see the *Working with contacts* section of this chapter).

Working in your Teams

When you click on **Teams** on the left-hand navigation bar, you will see all of the Teams you have access to:

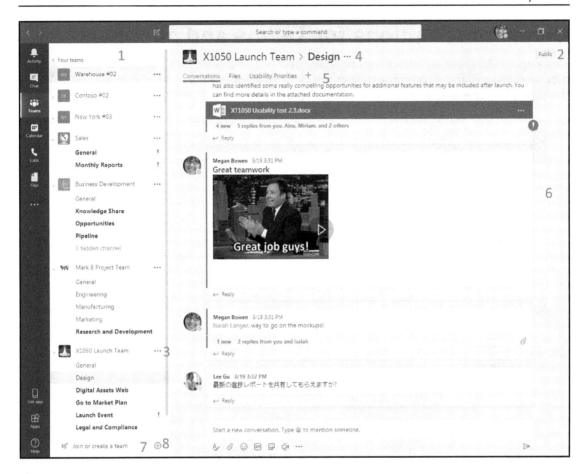

Let's look at Teams in some detail.

The Teams and channels panel

In this section, you can see all of the Teams you have access to. In order to expand the Team to see the channels or collapse to hide the channels, simply click on the **Team**. You can favorite any of your teams by clicking on more options (see the *Using more options for Teams and channels* sections).

Privacy indicator

This indicator lets you know if the Team is a **Private** or **Public** Team.

Using more options for Teams and channels

Clicking on the more options menu for the Team or the channel will give you a drop-down menu of options. If you own the group, you will have options to add a channel and manage, edit, and delete the Team, and add connectors to a channel:

Connectors are services you can add in to bring in pertinent information and capability into your Team's channel:

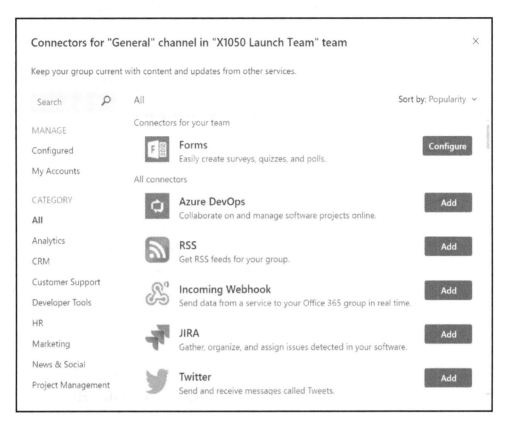

Besides other Office 365 applications, connectors lets you connect third-party apps as well.

More options for the selected Team's channel

There is a more options menu next to the Teams' channel in the main window:

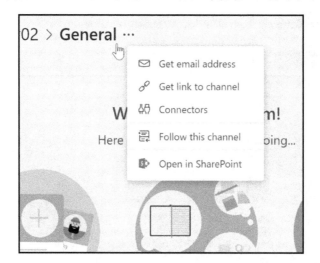

You get a few options here; for example, if you need to get the SharePoint site collection behind the Team, click on **Open in SharePoint**.

The tabs

Each Team's channels automatically come with **Conversations** and **Files** tabs when created. Others can be added if you are an owner:

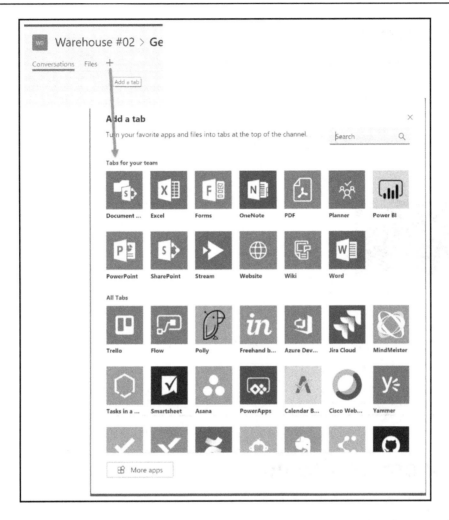

Click on the + to add tabs that can bring in additional information and/or functionality into your Team.

The main window

This window shows whatever tab is clicked on:

Join or create a Team

Click on this button to create a new Team or join an existing one by searching for it or using a Teams code:

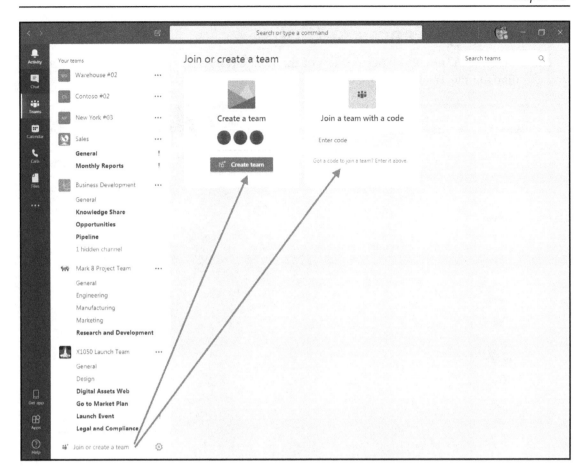

 Team creation may be restricted by your organization's Office 365 administrator.

If you do not have a code for the Team that you want to join, you should ask for one from the Team's creator.

The manage Teams settings

Clicking the gear button at the bottom-left of the window opens settings through which you can manage the Teams you own:

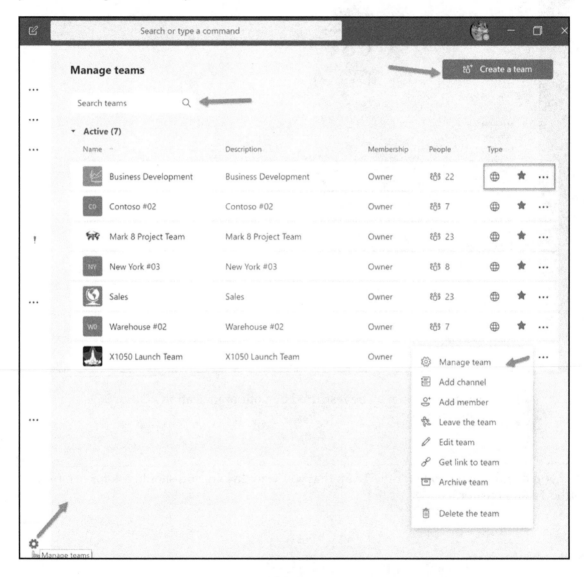

You can search for Teams, create Teams, see information about each Team, mark the Team as a favorite for easier access, and use other options.

Working in meetings

When it's meeting time, click on the link in the invite or in your calendar and the online meeting window will open.

Once you click on the link, a browser window using your default browser will open and you will be given the option to join on the web or via the Teams desktop application. If you plan to use the browser option, you should have your default browser set to anything other than Chrome. This browser has been historically problematic with Office 365 at random times in the past:

You will have options to turn on your camera and mic. If you turn on your camera, you will also have the option to blur your background:

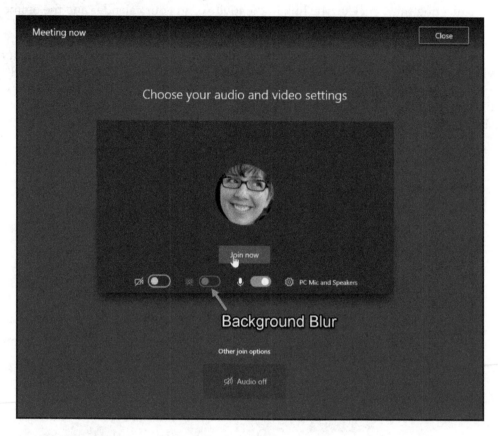

Once you click on the **Join now** button and you are in the meeting, you can hover your mouse over the screen to see your meeting options. The main options you will use are at the bottom. You can toggle your camera and mic on or off, or start recording:

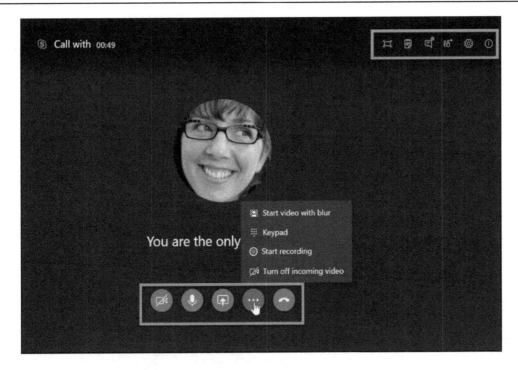

 If you record the meeting, remember to follow the recording laws in your country and state.

To share your screen or other items, click on the **Share Tray** button to open the tray and choose what you want to share. Click on the button again to close the tray:

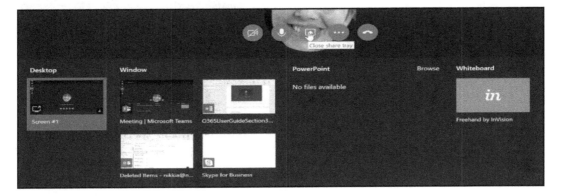

The upper options allow you to go into fullscreen, open the notes area, open the chat window, open the settings pane, or get information about the meeting. Clicking on the gear opens the settings pane where you can do things such as change your audio or video device:

You have the ability to take notes directly in your Teams meeting. Start by clicking on the note icon, then click on the **Take notes** button:

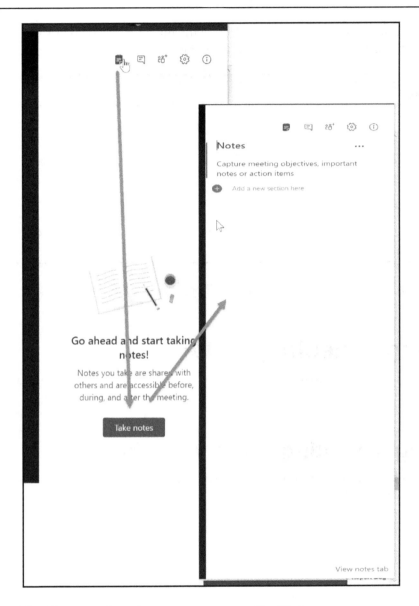

 The **Notes** options does not connect to OneNote.

When the meeting ends, you will be able to rate the meeting's call quality. This rating is shared anonymously with Microsoft's Teams team:

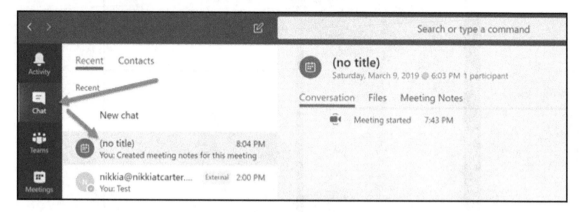

The notes, chat, and files from the meeting will be kept in **Chat**.

Sending a meeting invite

You can send an invite via Teams or Outlook on your desktop. Let's look at how we can send one using Teams.

Sending a meeting invite via Teams

Go to **Meetings** on the left-hand navigation bar, click on the **Schedule a meeting button** on the bottom-left, then fill out the popup:

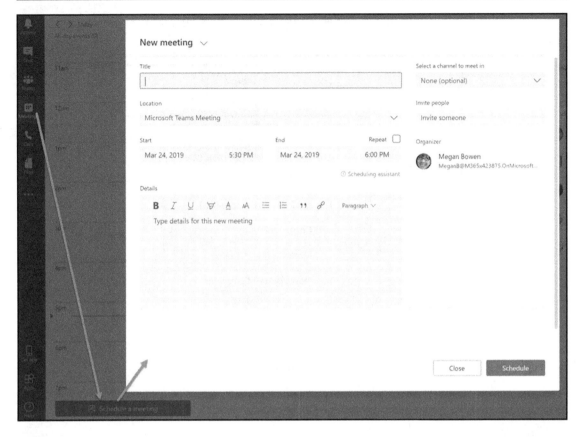

If any of your invitees are not in your organization, use their email address. Also, make sure you click on the drop-down menu in order to add the person:

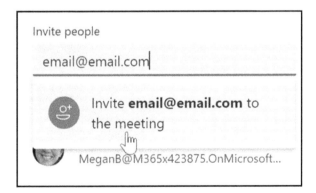

You will have the ability to use the **Scheduling assistant** and can assign the meeting to a specific group or channel:

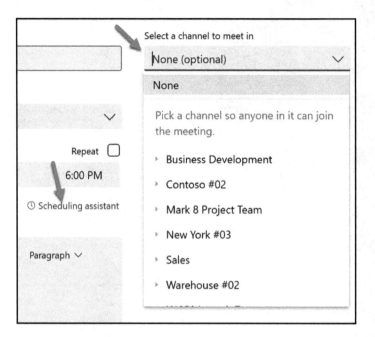

 You can only assign the meeting to a Team or channel when all of the invitees are participants in the Team.

You will be able to cancel meetings where you are the organizer:

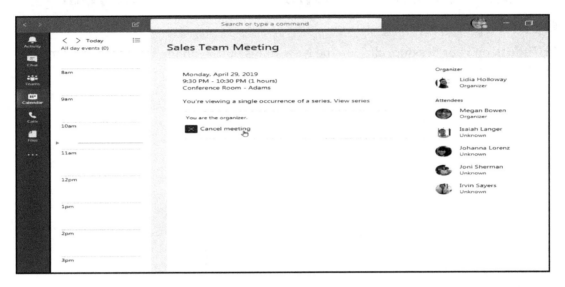

Once the meeting is cancelled, the people you invited will receive a cancellation notification via email that is similar to the one they would get for cancellation of Outlook meetings.

Sending a meeting invite via Outlook on your desktop

In Outlook on your desktop, click on the **New Items** button on the **Home** tab and then on **Teams Meeting**:

When the **Meeting Invite** window opens, fill out the invite with the pertinent information and attendees and send it as you would any other meeting invite via Outlook:

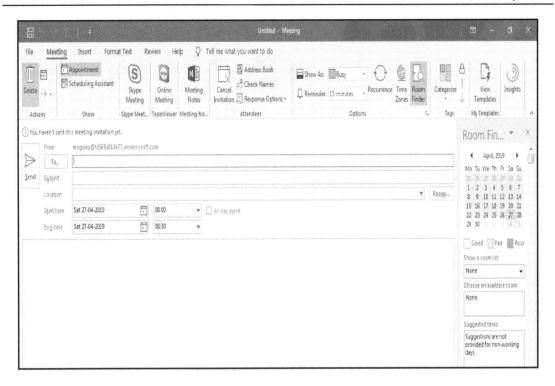

Accordingly, you can still use your Teams on Outlook to send a meeting invite.

Summary

In this chapter, you learned about using Microsoft Teams to facilitate communication. You can now add and chat with or call people within and outside of your organization. You learned how to create and manage teams and how to use various options to enhance the Teams experience. Finally, you can invite people in your Team to meetings via Teams and Outlook. You can now efficiently use Teams to ensure effective communication within your team and with external stakeholders.

In Chapter 11, *Understanding OneDrive For Business*, you will learn about OneDrive for Business: what it is, some history about it, and how it is different from OneDrive.

4
Section 4: OneDrive for Business

In this section, readers will learn about OneDrive for Business in general and will be given specific information on how to make it useful.

The following chapters will be covered:

- Chapter 11, *Understanding OneDrive For Business*
- Chapter 12, *Working with Files in Your OneDrive for Business*

11
Understanding OneDrive For Business

OneDrive for Business is the main place that individual users can store their personal work files. To reiterate, these are the work files that you work on as an individual in your organization. It is important to remember that these files belong to your organization and your organization will have access to them. Do not save your personal documents and files here; use OneDrive for that. In this chapter, you will learn about the history and background of OneDrive for Business, how to get to it, and its parts.

The topics covered in this chapter are as follows:

- History and background of OneDrive for Business
- Getting into OneDrive for Business
- Parts of OneDrive for Business
- How is OneDrive for Business different from OneDrive

History and background of OneDrive for Business

OneDrive for Business, not to be confused with OneDrive, is the business version of OneDrive that is connected to or purchased via Office 365. It is the replacement for Microsoft's SharePoint Workspace. It was released in the first version of Office 365 and has continued to evolve like the rest of Office 365.

Like OneDrive, OneDrive for Business is a file-hosting and sync service created by and hosted by Microsoft. Both have a sync app that allows you to sync your documents to your computers and a mobile app for accessing your files on your mobile device. Unlike OneDrive, OneDrive for Business can only be accessed online via the Office 365 portal. OneDrive is accessed via the consumer portal of `https://www.msn.com/en-in/`, `https://outlook.live.com/owa/`, `https://outlook.live.com/owa/`, and so on. Both were formally named SkyDrive and SkyDrive for Business until a lawsuit forced a renaming to OneDrive and OneDrive for Business in 2014.

Getting into OneDrive for Business

Once you are logged into the Office 365 portal, you can get to OneDrive for Business. You have two options for accessing it: via the Office 365 Home or via the app launcher.

On the Office 365 Home, locate and click on the **OneDrive** button. I know it says **OneDrive** but it is really OneDrive for Business:

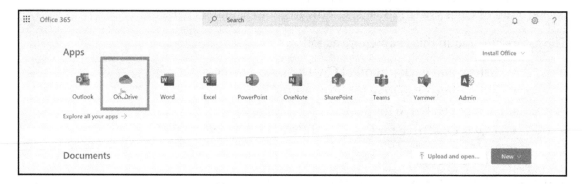

If you happen to be in a different part of Office 365, you can click on the app launcher then on the **OneDrive** button. You can open it in a new tab, instead of the current tab, by hovering over the **OneDrive** button, clicking on the open menu, then on **Open in new tab**:

Either way you go, you will land in your **Files** in your OneDrive for Business:

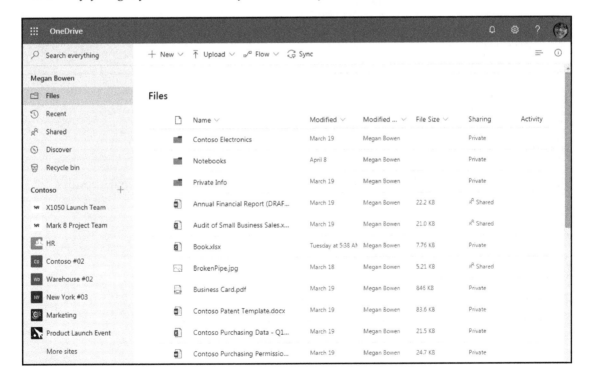

Parts of OneDrive for Business

Just like every other part of Office 365, each application has a few parts:

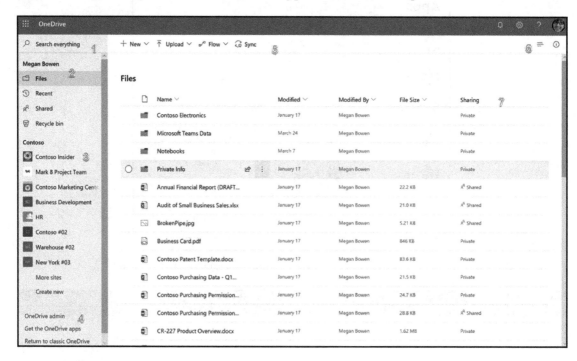

Let's look at those parts in detail.

#1 Search box

Start typing in the box and the system will start offering you some preliminary results:

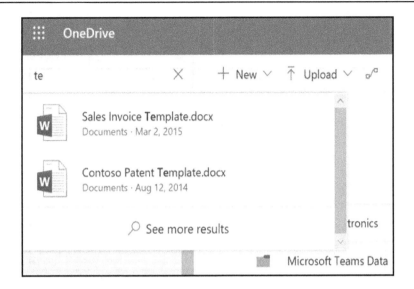

Click on the **See more results** link at the bottom of the preliminary results dropdown and the main window portion of the page will show more results. The **Filters** pane will also open on the right side with options for filtering down your search results by the modified date, the file types, and/or by author(s)/contributor(s). If you want to search in SharePoint, there is a link at the very bottom of the main window that will allow you to do just that!

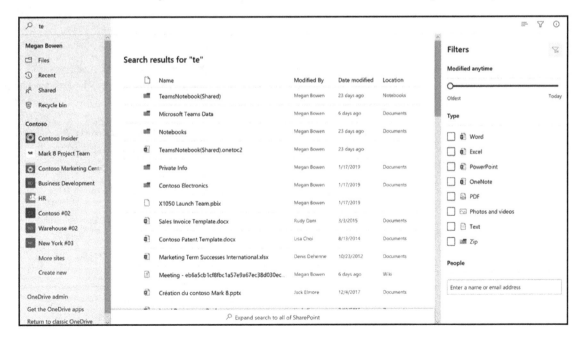

To clear the search box, click in the search box then on the **X** on the right-hand side of the box:

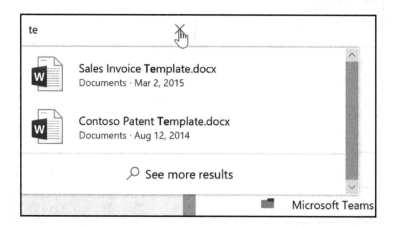

Before you click on the search box, there is text in it that says **Search everything**. Everything means all of your files and folders. This does not include results from SharePoint:

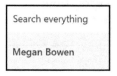

The search capability is very powerful. So powerful, in fact, that you may get back too many results. The search will search the title of the file, web page, or site, the URL, the text contained within, and any attached metadata.

To help with getting more precise results when searching, you can use phrases and the logical operators, AND, OR, and NOT, to search just like you can with a search on the web. For example, you can search `test in sequence not January`, which would return results containing `test in sequence` but will exclude any results with the word `January`. There are query syntaxes you can use that are more advanced. For more information, see `https://docs.microsoft.com/en-us/sharepoint/dev/general-development/keyword-query-language-kql-syntax-reference`.

#2 Your OneDrive navigation

Clicking on these opens the selected option in the main window. **Files** shows all your files and folders and is the default landing location when you enter OneDrive for Business.

Recent

Recent shows all your recent file activity:

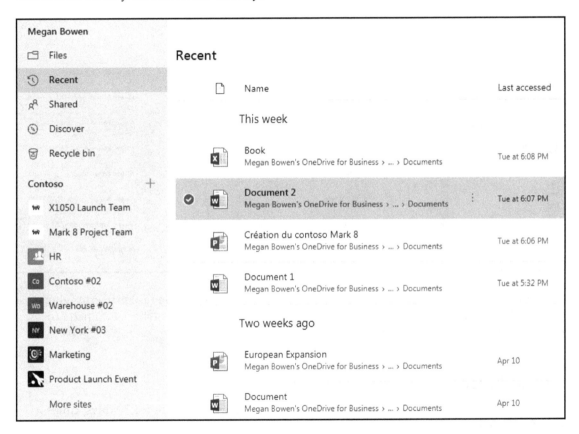

You don't need to search a document you were recently working on. You can go to it using the **Recent** tab.

Shared

Shared shows files shared with you and by you. Files that were shared with you (see the **Shared with me** tab) will not show in your **Files**:

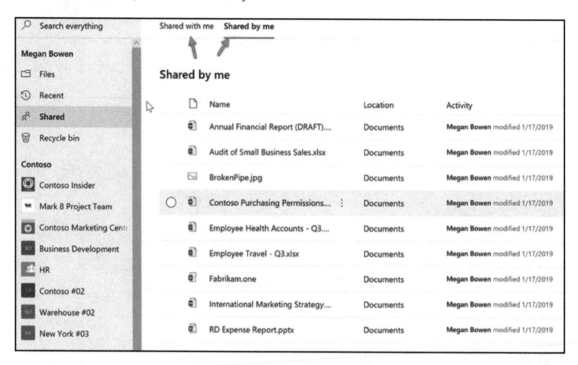

Seeing files called out as being shared by you (see the **Shared by me** tab) is useful when you need to remember who you shared what with and in situations where you need to remove or modify those permissions.

Recycle bin

The **Recycle bin** shows files that were deleted by you. Files stay here for 30 days, unless you decide to delete the file or empty the recycle bin, then they are moved to the second-stage recycle bin where they stay for another 30 days unless they are manually deleted. After that, they may not be recoverable unless your organization has a backup solution in place. You can go to the second-stage bin by clicking on the **Second-stage recycle bin** link at the bottom of the main window:

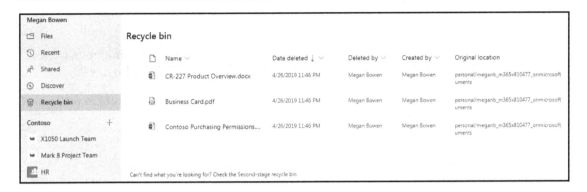

Click on the link next to the file you want and choose **Restore** or **Delete** from the action bar:

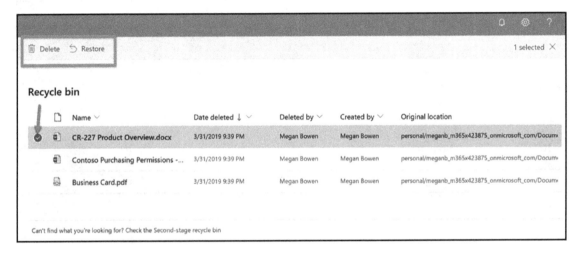

You can restore or delete individual files in this way.

#3 Sites navigation

This section gives you options for seeing files from whichever site you select. You can also see more sites if you don't see the site you want listed and/or create a new site using the links at the bottom of the section.

 You must have permissions to see the site, to see the files in that site, and you will only be able to see the files in that site that you have permission to see. You may not have permission to see every site and/or everything in the sites you can see.

To create a site, you must have the appropriate permission level to do so.

#4 Extra options

The links here take you to different places to do different things. The first link opens a new tab in your browser and takes you to the Admin Center for OneDrive for Business.

 This link will only work for you if you have OneDrive for Business or global administration permission.

The second link opens another tab where you can get apps for Windows and your devices, even Xbox One!

The last link returns you to the classic look and feel of OneDrive for Business:

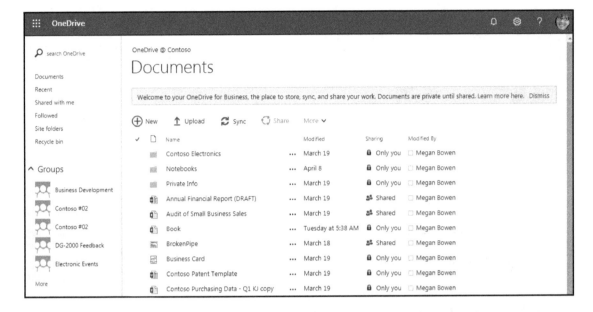

#5 Action bar

This bar is subject to change. It shows options based on where you are in your OneDrive and based on whether you have chosen an item or not. Here are some examples.

If you haven't clicked on anything, you get actions you can perform on the entire library:

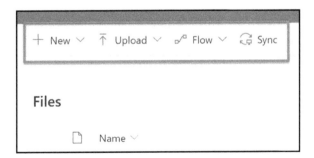

If you clicked on a file or folder, you get options based on what you selected:

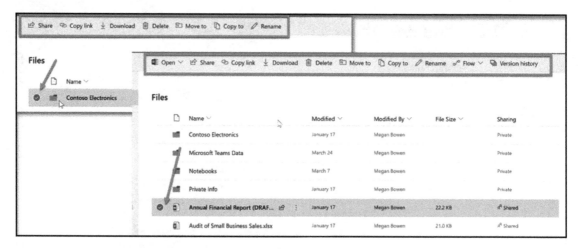

The files have three options more than the folders.

#6 View options and detail pane

View Options gives you choices for how you want files to be displayed. You can look at your files in the **List** (which is the default view), **Compact list**, or **Tiles** views:

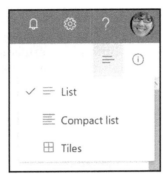

What you see in the details pane depends on whether you have not chosen anything, have chosen one file, or folder, or chosen multiple files.

If you have not chosen anything, you can see the **Activity** in this library:

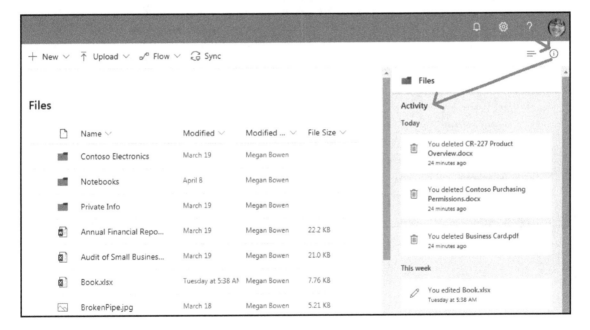

If you chose one file, you can see details for that file, including a preview of the file, the file's permissions, properties, and so forth. You may be able to change the properties in the **Properties** section if you have at least contributing permission for the file. If you have full control permission over the file, then you will be able to change the file's permission via the **Manage access** link in the **Has access** section:

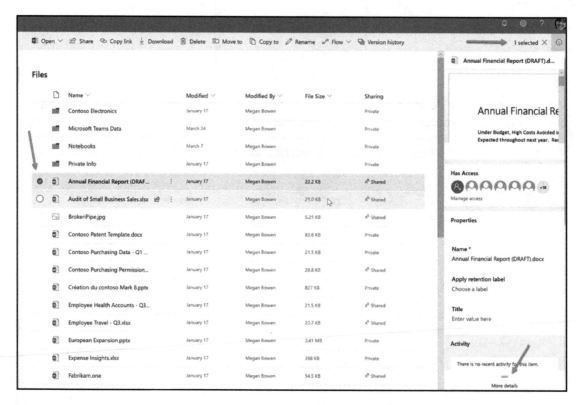

To see more details, click on the **More details** link at the bottom of the pane. To collapse this section, click on **More details** again:

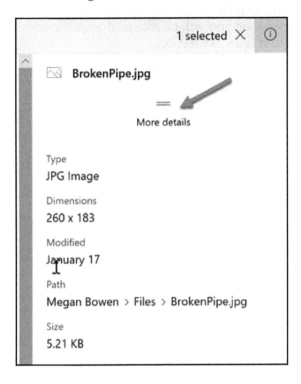

If you choose a folder, you can see details for that folder, the folder's permissions, properties, and so forth. You may be able to change the properties in the **Properties** section if you have at least contributing permission for the folder. If you have full control permission over the folder, then you will be able to change the folder's permission via the **Manage access** link in the **Has access** section:

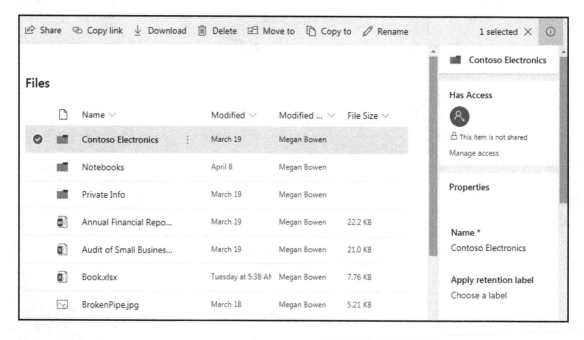

To see more details, click on the **More details** link at the bottom of the pane:

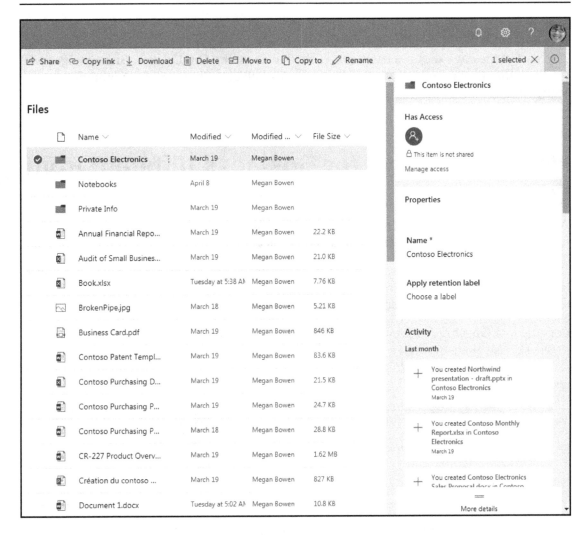

If you choose multiple files and/or folders, you only see that you selected multiple things but no details.

#7 Main window

This part of the page shows whatever is clicked on from the **OneDrive** or **Sites** navigation or shows the search results if the **See more results** link at the bottom of the preliminary search box is clicked.

How is OneDrive for Business different from OneDrive

As mentioned earlier in this chapter, OneDrive for Business and OneDrive are different in a few ways. Let's look at those differences in more detail.

The biggest difference is where you log in. OneDrive is a consumer product which is linked to your Microsoft account, formally known as Live, and OneDrive for Business is linked to Office 365, the Business version, not the Home version.

Logging into OneDrive for Business must be done through the Office 365 portal. Logging in to OneDrive is done through a Microsoft consumer page such as `https://www.msn.com/en-in/`. You can sign into your Microsoft account or choose OneDrive to sign into OneDrive faster:

The one place where you can get into either is via the OneDrive site:

The look and feel of OneDrive is also different than that of OneDrive for Business. Here is what OneDrive looks like as of April 2019:

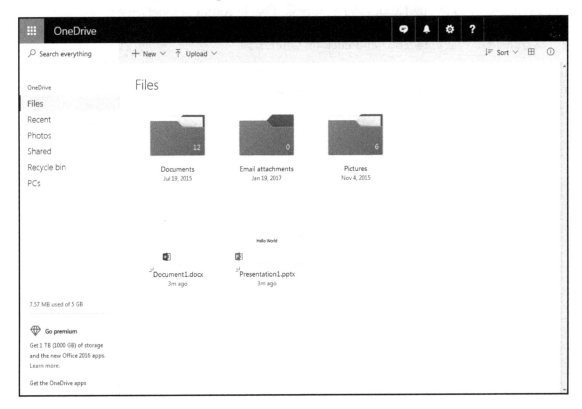

Also, the sync clients for each are two different colors. There is blue for OneDrive for Business and white for OneDrive:

The last difference you should know about as an end user is that there is no way to log into one from the other. They are separate now and more than likely, they will always be separate, which makes sense if you really stop and think about it. You really wouldn't want your personal files mixed up with your business files that your organization has the right to access at any time.

Summary

In this chapter, you learned about the history and background of OneDrive for Business. We also looked at how to get to OneDrive for Business and its parts. For more details, go to `https://support.office.com/` and click on **OneDrive**.

In `Chapter 12`, *Working with Files in Your OneDrive for Business*, you will learn about working with files in your OneDrive for Business.

12

Working with Files in Your OneDrive for Business

OneDrive for Business gives you the ability to work with your files as well as files that are shared with you. In this chapter, we will look at how you can add, edit, delete, copy, move, and share files. We will also look at the parts of an Office online file.

The topics covered in this chapter are as follows:

- Adding new files
- Editing files
- Deleting files
- Parts of the Office Online file
- Sharing files
- Move to
- Copy to

 The options in this chapter are described from the point of view of working with your files. Some of these options may not be available when working with files shared with you or files from SharePoint.

Adding new files

You can add new files in two ways: by creating them new or by uploading them.

Creating new files

To create a new file, click on the **New** dropdown on the action bar:

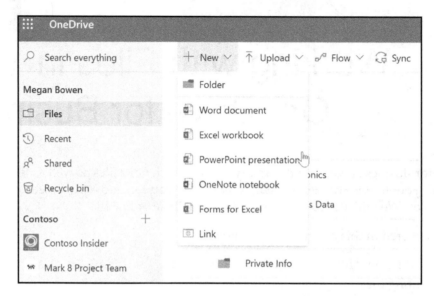

 As soon as you click on **Word document**, **PowerPoint presentation**, or **Excel workbook** and the new document opens, that document will be saved automatically to your OneDrive for Business with its default name. For example, Excel files are named `Book` (followed by a number if this one isn't the first one). If you rename it, it will be renamed during the next autosave.

You can also create a new folder or a link using any URL:

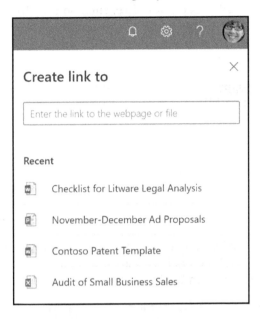

Using links is a great idea for adding access to a file that needs to be in multiple places. Using a link instead of adding that file to multiple places ensures that you have the single source of truth. Remember that adding a link to a document to multiple places does not mean that everyone with access to the library will have access to the file via the link. In order for a person to access the file via the link, they must have permission to, at least, view the file.

When you click on one of the Office file types, it opens a new file in the browser. If you need to open this file in the full version of Office, click on the **Open in Word** link before the ribbon. In this example, **Word Online** is open so you would click on **Open in Word** to open the file in the full version of Word on your desktop. In the browser, the file will autosave as you are typing, so there is no save button:

Clicking on the **Open in Word** link, will open the file in the full version of the Office app on the computer that you are working on. If you are on a computer with Office 2010, it may or may not open since Office 2010 is on the brink of reaching the end of its life as of April 2019:

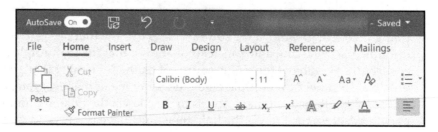

Office versions older than 2010 most likely will NOT open. Office 2013, 2016, and 2019 (depending on the build version) will open, but you may not have access to features such as **AutoSave**.

Uploading files

Click on the **Upload** dropdown on the action bar and you get the choice to upload files or folders:

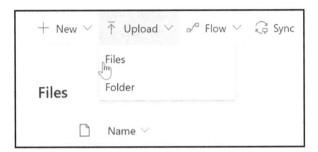

Using the **Files** action will only allow you to upload files but not folders. The **Folder** action allows you to upload a folder with its contents.

 It will copy subfolders if those folders contain files. If the subfolder is empty, it will NOT be copied.

Editing files

To open a file, click on it. If it is an Office file that you own, it will open in edit mode. If it is a file that is shared with you and you have not been given permission to edit the file, it may open in **READ ONLY** mode or in view mode. You can't edit the file in this mode but you can open it in the full Office version of Word, PowerPoint, or Excel:

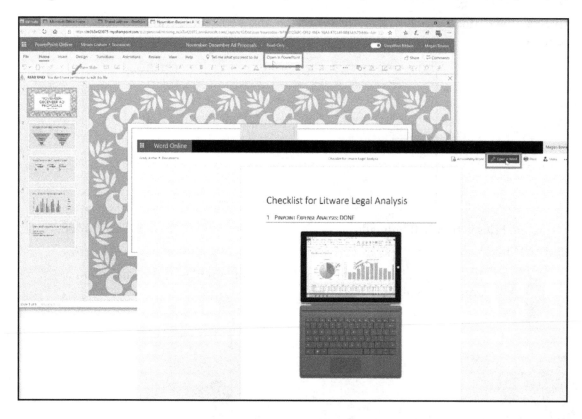

When editing a file in the browser, the file will autosave:

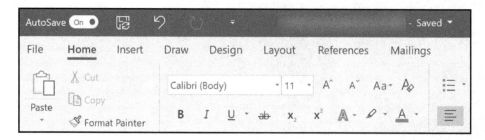

If you have the most current version of Office and you open the file in the full version of Word, PowerPoint, or Excel, it will autosave as long as the file is connected to a OneDrive or SharePoint location and **AutoSave** is turned **On**.

Deleting files

Select the file(s) and/or folder(s) you want to delete then choose **Delete** from the action bar. The deleted file(s) and/or folder(s) will go to the **Recycle Bin**:

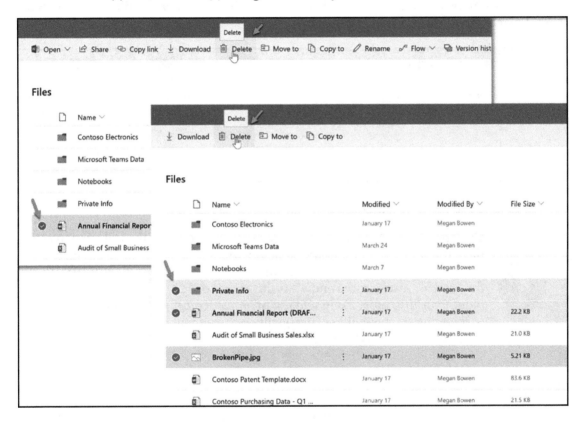

More on this in Chapter 13, *Understanding SharePoint*.

Parts of the Office Online file

When using Office Online for Word, PowerPoint, Excel, or OneNote, you can sometimes forget that you are in the online version of the file. There are some key differences you should be aware of and some things you should keep in mind.

Open in the full desktop version

There is a link at the top of each Office Online version that will open the file in the **Open in Word** link next to the tabs:

For example, if you are in **Word Online**, the link will be **Open in Word**.

 Clicking on the **Open in Word** link, will open the file in the full version of the Office app on the computer that you are working on. If you are on a computer with Office 2010, it may or may not open since Office 2010 is on the brink of reaching the end of its life as of April 2019. Office versions older than 2010 most likely will not open. Office 2013, 2016, and 2019 (depending on the build version) will open, but you may not have access to features such as **AutoSave**.

AutoSave

The file automatically saves as you are working on it! Because of this, there is no save button:

There is an indicator that lets you know if the file is saved or being saved.

Easy way to rename file

You can go the backstage of the file via the **File** tab to rename the document but there is an easier way:

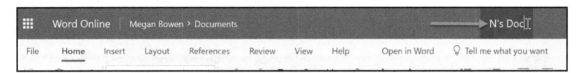

Simply click on the name in the title bar, type the name you want, and press *Enter*.

 Renaming the file is not the same as using **Save As**. If you want to use the current document as the base document for another document, use **Save As** in the backstage via the **File** tab (see *The backstage* section in this chapter).

The simplified ribbon

This ribbon style is very new and can be confusing when it first gets rolled out to your environment. You can toggle it off and on by using the toggle button in the upper right of the file:

By default, the ribbon will be simplified once it is rolled out to you.

The tabs and ribbons

In the online version of the Office file, you will have access to most or all of the tabs you would have in the full desktop version. The tabs and ribbons for Word Online and PowerPoint Online are nearly identical to the tabs in Word and PowerPoint. There is a huge hole you should be aware of for Word, though. That hole is **Track Changes**. If you need **Track Changes**, you will have to open the file in the full version of Word:

Due to the extra-special stuff that Excel does, formulas and such, Excel Online's tabs have two big holes in them. The online version is missing the tabs for **Draw** and **Formulas**. If you need those tabs, you must open Excel in its full desktop version by clicking the **Open in Excel** link:

OneNote Online's tabs look like those in the Windows 10 version of OneNote but not like OneNote on the desktop.

 As of April 2019, the desktop version of OneNote is no longer available for download in the Office download from the Office 365 portal.

Getting back to your OneDrive for Business

Sometimes, when you click on a document, it may open in the same tab instead of opening in a different tab:

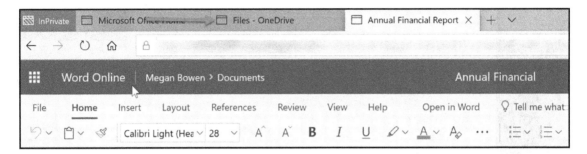

If the document opens in a different tab, look at the previous tabs. One of them will contain your files:

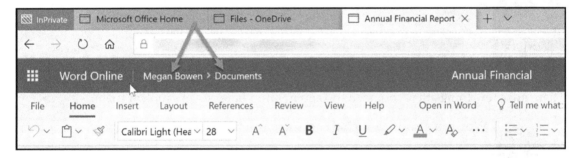

If your document opened in the same tab, click on your name, **Documents**, or, if you are in a document inside a folder, the name of the folder.

Clicking on your name or on **Documents** both take you back to **Files** in your OneDrive for Business.

The backstage

The backstage is what you see when you click on the **File** tab in any Office document, online or on the desktop:

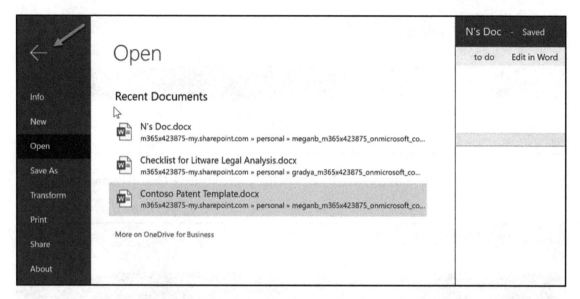

There are a few things that you need to keep in mind here, so let's look at them.

 You can always close the backstage by clicking on the back arrow.

Save As

Remember that the file autosaves, so there is no save button. Also, **Rename** is not the same thing as using **Save As**. If you want to use the current document as the base document for another document, use **Save As**:

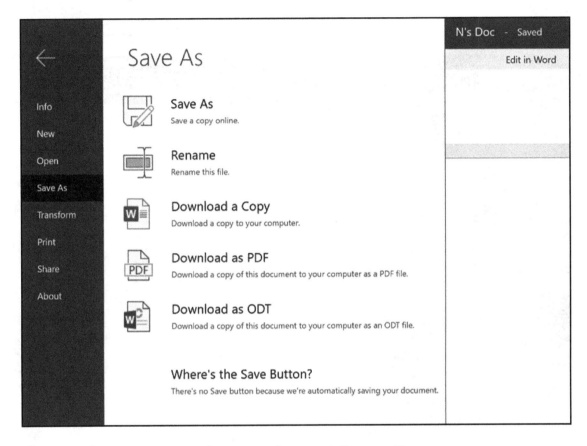

If you simply want to rename the current document, then use **Rename**.

Print

Remember that the print options you get will be dependent on the computer you are using and if that computer is hooked to a network with printers. If you are on your home computer, you may have different options for printing than those you get on your work computer:

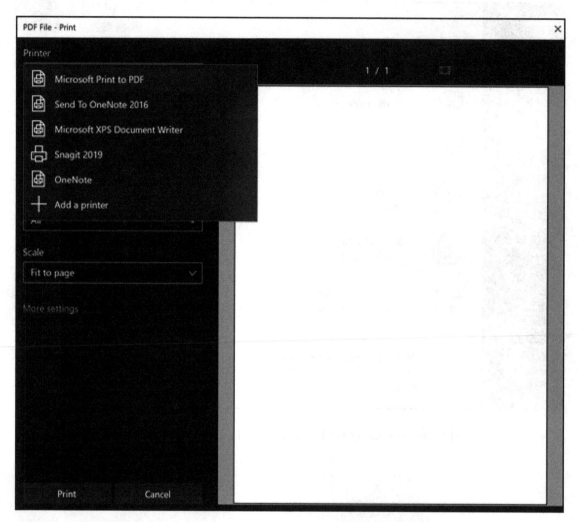

You will always have options such as **Print to PDF** or **Send to OneNote** since those options don't require a physical printer.

Sharing files

In your OneDrive for Business, you have the ability to control the access you give to others. In other words, you can give access to others at the levels of access, view, or edit, as you prefer and can remove or edit that access at any time you wish as well. Depending on the way your organization sets up your account, you may also have the ability to give access to others outside of your organization.

Giving access

You can share a file via the **Share** button inside or outside of the file itself:

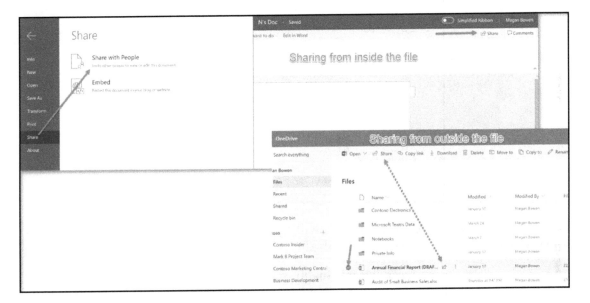

 If you are outside the file, you need to select the file first.

Any way that you go, you will get the same popup. Through this popup, you can choose the way you want to share. Let's look at the options at the bottom of the popup first:

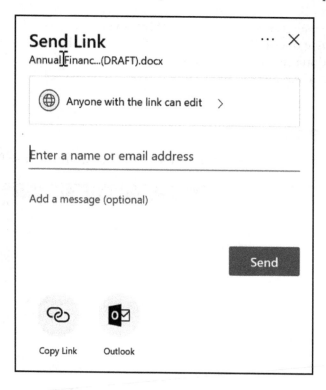

One option is to click on **Copy Link**. This will automatically copy the link to the file, which you can paste anywhere, such as in an email.

 The person receiving the link must have permission to access the file, or the link will not work for them.

The other option is to click on the **Outlook** button at the bottom which will open a new email via Outlook, or your default email app, with the file automatically attached.

Now, let's look at the main options at the top. You can see all of the options available by clicking on the bar that says **Anyone with the link** can edit. Once you choose your options, click the **Apply** button and it will take you to the first screen where you can add the name(s) (if internal to your organization) and/or email(s) (if external to your organization) and an optional message, then click the *Send* button:

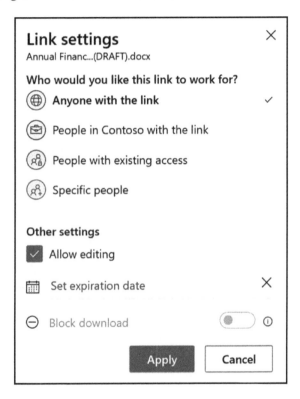

Once sent, the person(s) you listed will get an email from the system that they can use to access the file.

Editing or removing access

Once access is given, you can see which files are being shared and which aren't by looking at the **Sharing** column:

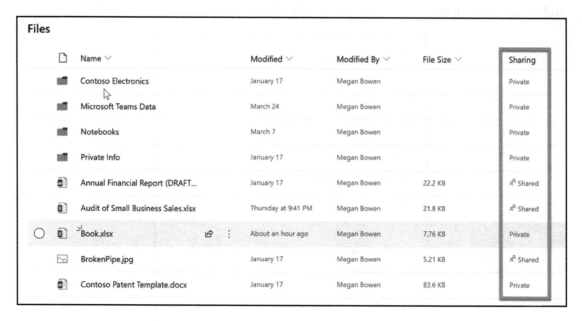

The easiest way to see who the access has been given to is to click on the **Shared** link next to the file whose access permissions you want to review. This will open the **Manage Access** side panel for that file where you can see who has direct access and any access links:

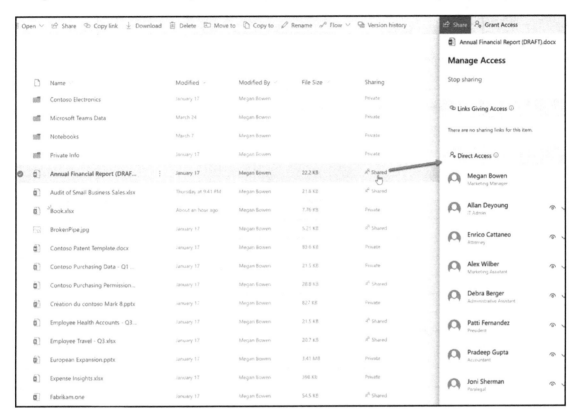

You can also share with more people via this panel using the **Share** or **Grant Access** buttons at the top.

For any links in the **Links Giving Access** section, you can see the type of link it is. Click the **Copy** button to copy the link or click the more options (**...**) button to get options for deleting the link by clicking on the **X** button or setting an expiration on the link:

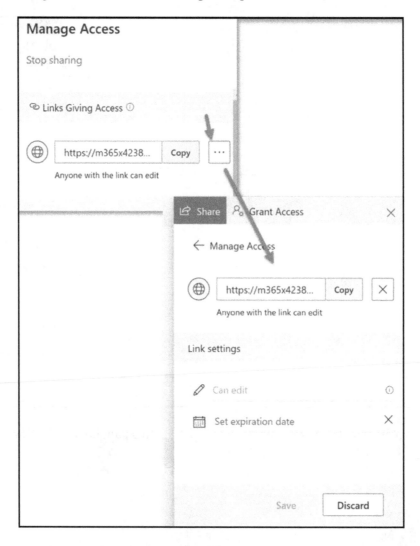

 As of April 2019, you cannot edit the link's access once created. You can only delete the link and then create another.

For those people you have given access to in the **Direct Access** section, you can see their access level via the picture indicator:

Clicking on the dropdown next to the indicator gives you options for editing or removing that person's access:

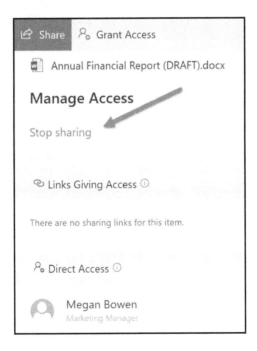

You can remove all access at one time by clicking on the **Stop sharing** link at the top of the side panel.

Things you should consider

Just like any other power, you should try your best to use it wisely. Consider using the least needed access rule. This is where you give the least amount of access needed. When determining the access you should give, ask yourself a lot of questions such as these:

- Does the person you wish to share with need to edit the file or just view the file?
- If the person(s) only needs to view, should they be able to download as well, or should that ability be blocked?
- Does that person need access for a long time or would it be better to set an expiration date on the file?
- If you created an anonymous link, would bad things happen if the link were to be shared with unintended parties or somehow get out into the wild?

Besides questioning yourself when giving access, you should also periodically review the access you have given out to determine if the access needs to change. I suggest reviewing at least monthly, but weekly would be best.

Move to

This is a fairly new capability that has been a great help to many users. This capability allows you to move files and/or folders from place to place. Once you chose the file(s) and/or folder(s) you want to move, click on the **Move to** button on the action bar. A side panel will open where you can choose to where you want to move your file(s) and/or folder(s):

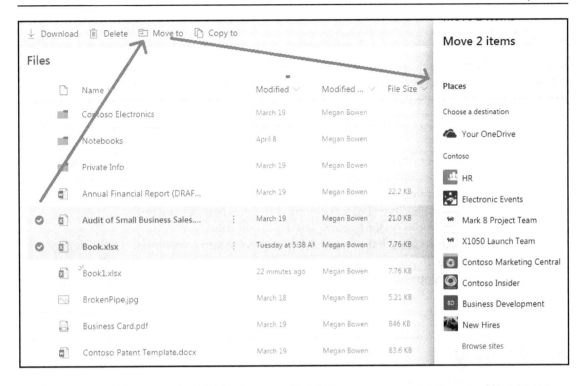

You can move files to another folder in your OneDrive or even move them to SharePoint.

Remember, this is a move, not a copy. After the operation is completed, the file(s) and/or folder(s) will no longer exist in their original place. If moving to SharePoint, you must have at least Contribute-level access permission in order to complete this operation.

In order to see a list of available SharePoint sites, you must be following that site. If you have access to the site but are unable to follow the site, contact your SharePoint administrator to see if that feature can be turned on.

Copy to

Like **Move to**, this is a fairly new capability and has been a great help to many users. This capability allows you to copy file(s) and/or folder(s) to other places. Once you have chosen the file(s) and/or folder(s) you want to copy, click on the **Copy to** button on the action bar. A side panel will open where you can choose to where you want to copy your file(s) and/or folder(s). You can copy them to another folder in your OneDrive or even to SharePoint.

Remember, this is a copy, not a move. After the operation is completed, the file(s) and/or folder(s) will exist in the original place as well as the place that you copied them to.

If copying to SharePoint, you must have at least Contribute-level access permission in order to complete this operation.

In order to see a list of available SharePoint sites, you must be following that site. If you have access to the site but are unable to follow the site, contact your SharePoint administrator to see if that feature can be turned on.

Summary

In this chapter, you learned how to add, edit, delete, copy, move, and share files. We also looked at the parts of an Office Online file. For more details, go to `https://support.office.com/` and click on **OneDrive**.

In `Chapter 13`, *Understanding SharePoint,* you will learn about SharePoint.

Section 5: Collaboration Using SharePoint

5

In this section, readers will learn about SharePoint in general and will be given specific information on making it useful.

The following chapters will be covered:

- Chapter 13, *Understanding SharePoint*
- Chapter 14, *Working with SharePoint Lists*
- Chapter 15, *Performing Different File Operations on SharePoint*
- Chapter 16, *More on Using SharePoint*

13
Understanding SharePoint

SharePoint is one of Microsoft's most widely used collaboration platforms and is both loved and hated. The reasons for the strong feelings tend to be based on how SharePoint is set up and run by any given organization.

In this chapter, we will mainly look at SharePoint Online, the version of SharePoint available via Office 365. We will also look at getting to SharePoint, navigating the SharePoint home, getting around in SharePoint, and the anatomy of SharePoint's classic and modern pages.

This chapter will cover the following topics:

- Background and history
- Editions of SharePoint
- Getting into SharePoint Online

Background and history

SharePoint is a Microsoft technology that enables content management and file sharing between users. Unlike file servers where file management is very flat, SharePoint utilizes browsers to store all the files on a centralized web location which is easily accessible by any computer by entering the site URL in an internet browser as well as the appropriate login credentials. Microsoft Office is integrated with SharePoint. This greatly assists users in viewing and editing files directly in the browser.

Out of the box, SharePoint has many templates that can be implemented. Collaborative sites can be used to share information, manage documents, publish reports, and more. One of the most used templates is the Team Site.

Let's look briefly at a timeline of SharePoint from its birth to the present day:

- **2000**: Microsoft releases the first version of SharePoint called SharePoint Portal Server 2001. It was mainly for document management and enterprise search.
- **2003:** Microsoft releases Office SharePoint Portal Server 2003 and its underlying service, **Windows SharePoint Services (WSS)**.
- **2006**: Microsoft releases SharePoint 2007 adding in new capabilities such as InfoPath Form Services and Business Data Catalog. This version was called Microsoft Office SharePoint Server 2007 or MOSS for short.
- **2010:** Microsoft releases SharePoint 2010 which included big improvements to Excel Services, InfoPath, workflows, business data services, and managed metadata. Many other features were also added.
- **2012**: Early in 2012, Microsoft released the first technical preview of SharePoint 2013 to an exclusive group of Microsoft partners. In July, the publicly available beta was released and then the final version was generally released in October. This version had a much updated look and feel, with the added-in ability to add apps from a SharePoint Store, and more.
- **2013**: The first online version of SharePoint, called SharePoint Online, was released at the end of February via Office 365. At first, it looked the same as SharePoint 2013 but, behind the scenes, there were many differences from its on-premises server sibling. Over time, SharePoint Online, or SPO, has morphed into its own product that is "evergreen" with mostly small, and sometimes large, but frequent releases. In 2015, Microsoft Office 365 Groups was released to Office 365 followed by Microsoft Teams in 2017, both of which have a SharePoint site collection behind them.
- **2016**: SharePoint 2016 was released in May 2016 with significant enhancements, such as better navigation on mobile devices, hybrid mode, expanded support for filenames special characters, support for large files, and data loss prevention capabilities identical to those in Office 365.
- **2018**: Later in the year, Microsoft released SharePoint 2019, finally bringing many of the modern interface improvements seen in SPO to the on-premises version of SharePoint.

Editions of SharePoint

SharePoint comes in a few different editions: SharePoint Foundation, SharePoint Standard, SharePoint Enterprise, and **SharePoint Online** (**SPO**). All, except SPO, are on-premises server editions and SPO is, of course, online. Each edition builds on the next, adding more capability and functionality. Since Microsoft is now thinking in a cloud-first mentality, SPO has the most capabilities and features of any of its on-premises counterparts.

Getting into SharePoint Online

Once you are logged into Office 365, you can get to SharePoint Online in two ways: via the Office 365 Home and via the app launcher. Either way you choose, you will be taken to the SharePoint home page to start.

 If you choose the app launcher, you can click on the open menu and choose **Open in new tab** to open it in a new tab.

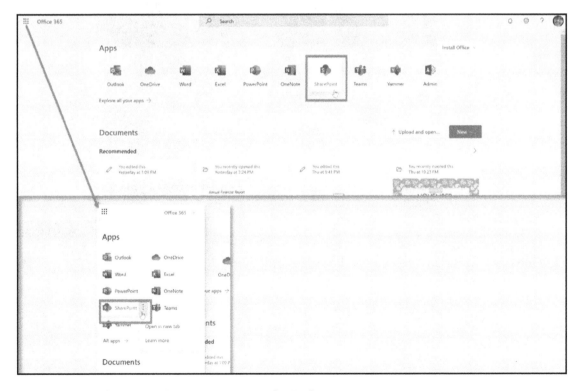

Let's look at SharePoint home in detail.

The SharePoint home

When you click on the **SharePoint** button on the Office 365 Home or on the app launcher, the SharePoint home is where you land. You can navigate from there. Let's look at the parts of this page:

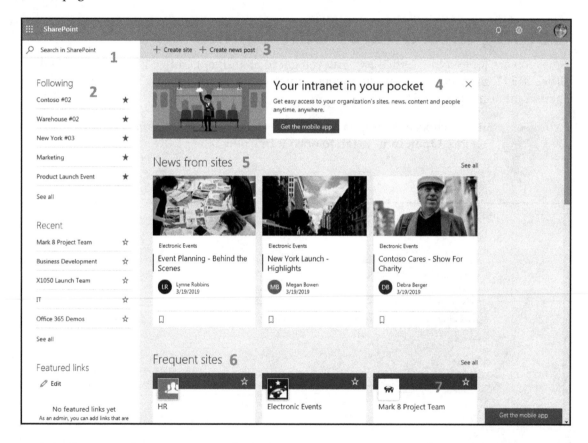

Let's look now at the components of the SharePoint home.

#1 Search

Located in the top left-hand corner, to use search, start typing in the box and the system will start offering you some preliminary results:

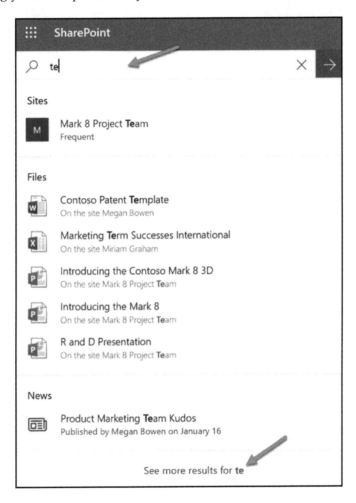

Click on the **See more results** link at the bottom of the preliminary results dropdown and you will be taken to a search page showing more results:

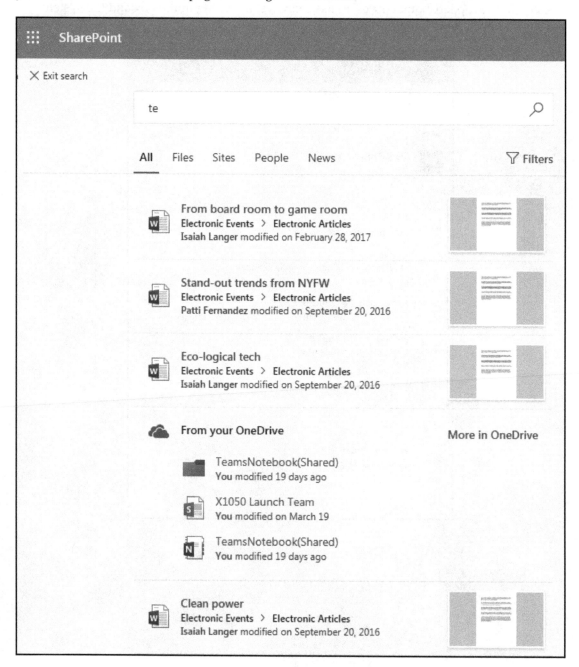

The **Filters** at the top will help to minimize your result by only showing you results of a certain type and the **Filters** button will also open a panel on the right side with options for filtering down your search results by the modified date:

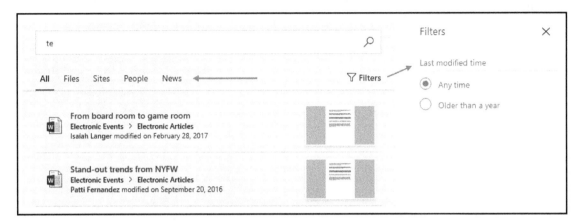

You may even encounter an option to search your OneDrive for Business:

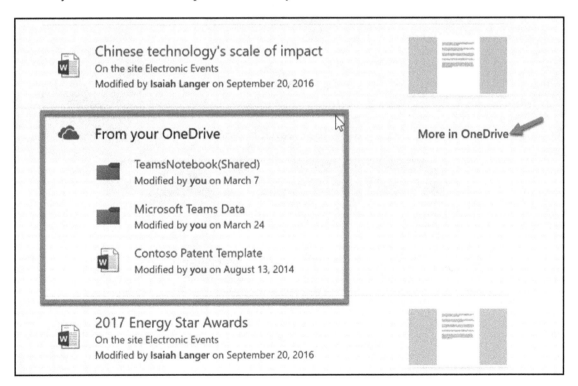

Each result has a drop-down arrow. When clicked, it will expand or collapse a section where you can see more details about that result:

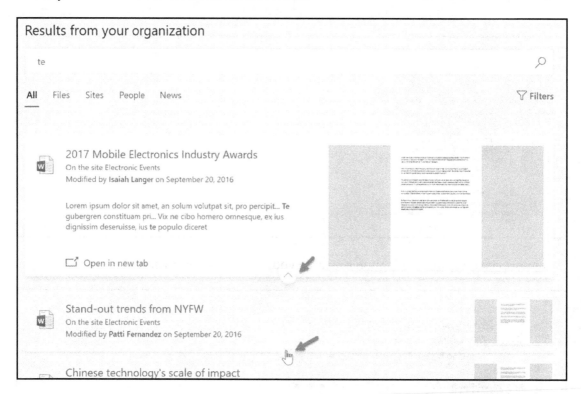

To leave the search page, click on the **X Exit search** button on the left-hand side of the page:

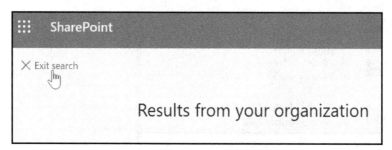

Before you click on the search box, there is text in it that says **Search in SharePoint**. This means that the search will occur in SharePoint but you will only see results that you have permission to see. So, for example, if a document meets your search criteria but you don't have permission to see it, it will not even show in your search results.

When you exit search, you will be taken back to the home page:

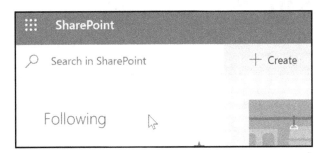

The search capability is very powerful. It is so powerful, in fact, that you may get too many results. The search will search the title of the file, web page, or site, the URL, the text contained within, and any attached metadata.

To help with getting more precise results when searching, you can use phrases and the logical operators, AND, OR, and NOT, to search just like you can with a search on the web. For example, you can search Test in Sequence NOT January which would return results containing Test in Sequence but will exclude any results with the word January. There are query syntaxes you can use that are more advanced. For more information, see https://docs.microsoft.com/en-us/sharepoint/dev/general-development/keyword-query-language-kql-syntax-reference.

#2 Left navigation

On this navigation panel, you can see any sites you are following, any recent sites you have been to, and any link that you have added.

Following

You can set sites you want to follow by clicking on the stars next to them on their site cards, or on the sites themselves:

 The ability to follow sites must be turned on. If you don't see the option to follow, ask your SharePoint administrator to turn it on.

To stop following a site, click on the star again:

Once the star is clicked, the site will disappear from this list.

Recent

Not to be confused with frequent sites on the page, the sites listed are those that you have been to recently.

Featured links

The URLs can be any that you wish to add. Simply click on the pencil to add links to anything you would like:

The links can be internal or external to your Office 365.

#3 Creation options

The first creation option, **+ Create site**, may not be available if the feature is not turned on and/or if you don't have the permission level needed to create a site:

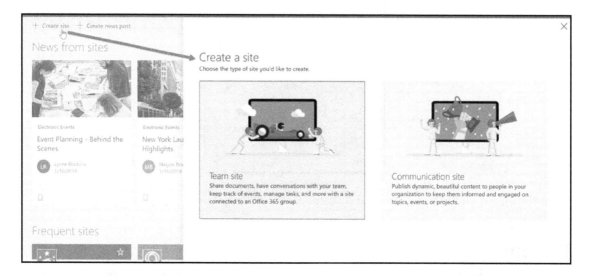

The **+ Create site** option creates modern site collections: **Communications site** and the modern **Team Site**.

Communications site collections can only be created here and in the new SharePoint Admin Center.

The modern **Team site** is not the classic site collection that is connected to an Office 365 Group. As of April 2019, modern site collections do not have all of the features and functionality of classic site collections.

The second option is + **Create news post**, which allows you to publish a news post:

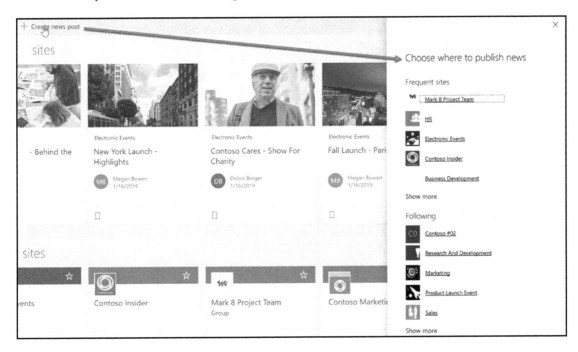

Click on the SharePoint site that you want your news post to be published to.

#4 Message

There may be a message here:

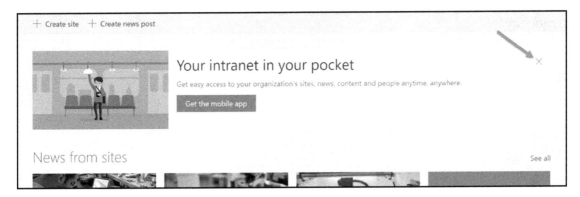

To close it, click on the **X** in the upper right.

#5 News from sites

This section shows news from **News** apps on different sites and site collections that you have access to. You can click the card to go to the article or click on the ribbon at the bottom to save the article for later:

To see more news, click on the **See all** link on the left-hand side.

#6 Frequent sites

Not to be confused with **Recent** on the left navigation, this shows the sites you go to frequently.

#7 Site card

This card shows details about your most recent activity on each site listed:

It can be helpful to see when you were last on the site or if a certain item or file on the site is getting a lot of attention.

#8 Get the mobile app

Clicking on this button will take you to a page to get the app:

You can type in your mobile number to get a text with a link to where you can download the app.

Navigating SharePoint

Once you choose a SharePoint site to go to from the SharePoint home, click on it and you will land on the site. As you move around in your site, it is important to know how to navigate. There are five options:

- **The browser's back button**: There will be times when the use of this button is a necessity:

- **Global navigation (also known as the top link bar)**: Mostly used for getting around to site collections or sub-sites, usually only links to other sites and site collections are here, but there may be links to other things as well:

- **The tiles and links**: These help you to get to other parts of the site, to other site collections, and to any other places:

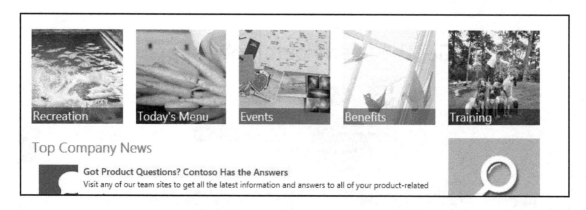

- **Left navigation (also known as the quick launch)**: This helps you move around the areas of the current site you are in. Normally, this navigation only contains links to parts of the site you are in at that moment, but sometimes links to other things and places are placed there as well:

- **The breadcrumb**: This helps you to navigate up the hierarchy from where you are. Usually, you see the breadcrumb when you are in a library and have gone down a level or more into folder(s):

Remember, for navigation, all options are on the table but its best to avoid using Option *#1* unless it's necessary. It's best to use any of the other options first. Use option *#1* when none of the others will work for you.

The anatomy of the SharePoint page

The home page of a SharePoint site has different parts. In the following screenshots, we will look at the parts of a classic page and also of a modern SharePoint page.

Your organization may have only classic or only modern site pages or it may be using a mix of both. Each site can have the home page that comes with the site as well as one or more other site pages set up for different reasons.

The classic page anatomy

The classic SharePoint page has been around longer than the modern page. You may have seen some of them in your organization's SharePoint so let's look at the parts of the classic SharePoint page:

Now, we will look at the parts of the page as they are numbered.

#1 Office 365 suite bar

This is the suite bar for Office 365 which is ever-present with the same parts but sometimes the functions of those parts change depending on where you are in Office 365. The changes on the bar in SharePoint are:

- The link to SharePoint following the app launcher
- The options under settings (gear)
- The option under help

#2 Settings

Settings change based on where you are in Office 365. When you click on the gear in SharePoint, you will see settings based on the permission where you are at that moment and what permission level you have at that place. For example, if you are in a list or a library, you will have different options than if you were on a site page. Also, you may have a lot or a smaller number of options depending on your permission level:

You may also have settings for Office 365 in general here or you may not depending on if you have received the latest roll-out of the **Settings** menu shown in the preceding screenshot.

#3 Help

Help changes based on where you are in Office 365:

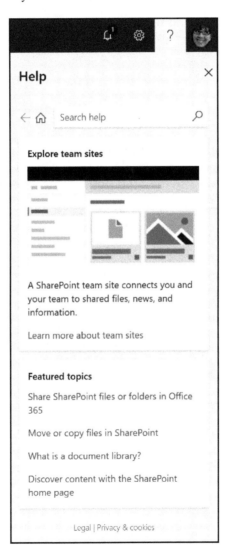

The **Help** here will be based on SharePoint since you are in SharePoint.

#4 Promoted actions bar

The bar is similar to the quick actions bar in Office which is in the upper left corner of Office applications. Instead of options like **Save**, **Undo**, **Redo**, and **Print**, you get options for sharing the site, following the site, editing the page, and full-screen mode.

 Seeing the sharing and following options depends on whether the feature is enabled in the site. Seeing the edit option depends on your permission level.

#5 Search

This search box will search based on your term(s)/phrase(s) and the scope that it is set to. Its default scope is stated in the box (for example, in the box it says **Search everything**) and the scope can be changed by clicking on the drop-down arrow and choosing a different scope:

Everything searches everything in the site collection you are in, **People** searches profiles of people in your organization, **Conversations** searches all discussion boards and news feeds, and **This Site** only searches the site you are currently in.

Once you have the scope that you want, type in your term(s) and/or phrase(s) and click the magnifying glass or press *Enter*. You will be taken to a page showing your results:

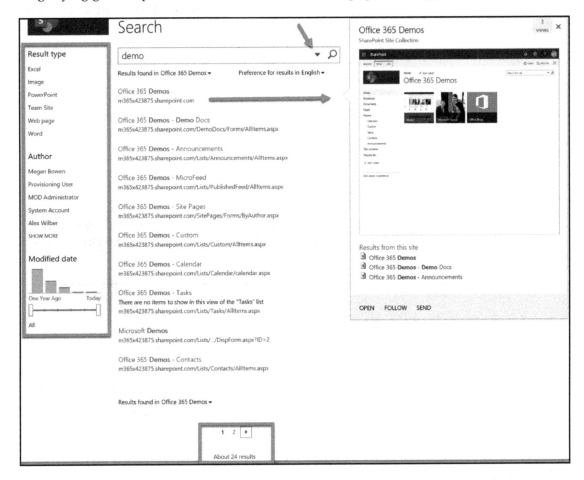

On the **Search** results page, you can see your results, refine your search by typing in a new or additional term(s) and a phrase(s), refine your search using the refiners on the left, and/or change your search scope by clicking on the drop-down arrow. At the bottom of the page, you can also see the number of results, the number of pages of results, and the arrow(s) for navigating back and forth among the pages. If you hover over a result, you get a preview popup with some actions you can do based on the type of result it is.

The search capability is very powerful. It is so powerful, in fact, that you may get back too many results. The search will search the title of the file, web page, or site, the URL, the text contained within, and any attached metadata. To help with getting more precise results when searching you can use phrases and the logical operators, AND, OR, and NOT, to search just like you can with a search on the web. For example, you can search Test in Sequence NOT January, which would return results containing Test in Sequence but will exclude any results with the word January. There are query syntaxes you can use that are more advanced. For more information, see https://docs.microsoft.com/en-us/sharepoint/dev/general-development/keyword-query-language-kql-syntax-reference.

#6 Tabs

The tabs for a page are different than those in a list or library but they all have associated ribbons with options for the place you are in except **Browse**. For example, the **Page** tab has options for working on the page:

Clicking the **Browse** tab closes any ribbons you have open so you can see the top of the page.

#7 Logo

When clicked on, the **Logo** usually takes you to the top of the site collection you are in. Sometimes, people reprogram it to take users to the home of the site they are in. The **Logo** starts as a generic logo but can be changed to use a different logo based on a picture of choice.

#8 Global navigation

The global navigation, also known as the top link bar, helps you with getting to other sites or site collections. Usually, only links to other sites and site collections are here, but there may be links to other things as well.

 The **Edit** button is only visible if you have the permission level needed to be able to edit the navigation.

#9 Left navigation

The left navigation, also known as the quick launch, helps you move around the areas of the current site you are in. Normally, this navigation only contains links to parts of the site you are in at the moment but sometimes links to other things and places are placed there as well.

 The **Edit** button is only visible if you have the permission level needed to be able to edit the navigation.

#10 Breadcrumb

When you are on a page, the breadcrumb may or may not be clickable. It may just be a title. If it is clickable, it will just take you back to the same page.

#11 Web parts and app parts

Web parts and app parts are parts that you see on the main part of the SharePoint page. They are both modular and reusable components that can be placed into any SharePoint web page. A web part can be added from the web part gallery, from a code module, or from the SharePoint Store. An app part is a display part showing a list or library.

The modern page anatomy

The classic SharePoint page has been around longer than the modern page but your organization may already be embracing the modern look for SharePoint:

Let's explore the parts of the modern SharePoint page.

#1 Office 365 Suite Bar

This is the suite bar for Office 365 which is ever-present with the same parts but sometimes the functions of those parts change depending on where you are in Office 365. The changes on the bar in SharePoint are:

- The link to SharePoint following the app launcher
- The options under settings (gear)
- The option under help

#2 Settings

Settings change based on where you are in Office 365. When you click on the gear in SharePoint, you will see settings based on the permission where you are at the moment and what permission level you have at that place. For example, if you are in a list or library, you will have different options than if you were on a site page. Also, you may have a lot or a small number of options depending on your permission level:

You may also have settings for Office 365 in general here or you may not depending on whether you have received the latest roll-out of the **Settings** menu shown in the preceding screenshot.

#3 Help

Help changes based on where you are in Office 365:

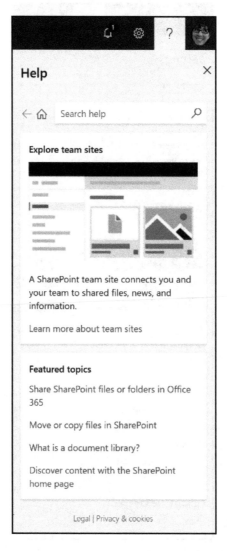

The help here will be based on SharePoint since you are in SharePoint.

#4 Promoted actions bar

The bar is similar to the quick actions bar in Office, which is in the upper left corner of Office applications. Instead of options like **Save**, **Undo**, **Redo**, and **Print**, you get options for following the site and sharing the site.

Seeing the sharing and following options depends on whether the feature is enabled in the site.

#5 Page actions bar

These are actions you can take on the page if you have the permission level to allow it. If you don't, you won't even see this bar.

#6 Global navigation

The global navigation, also known as the top link bar, helps you with getting to the other sites or site collections. Usually, only links to other sites and site collections are here but there may be links to other things as well.

The **Edit** button is only visible if you have the permission level needed to be able to edit the navigation.

#7 Logo

When clicked on, the **Logo** usually takes you to the top of the site collection you are in. Sometimes, people reprogram it to take users to the home of the site they are in. The **Logo** starts as a generic logo but can be changed to use a different logo based on a picture of choice.

#8 Breadcrumb

When you are on a page, the breadcrumb may or may not be clickable. It may just be a title. If it is clickable, it will just take you back to the same page.

#9 Search

Before you even start typing in the box, the system will start offering you some preliminary options based on who you are and what you have been working on:

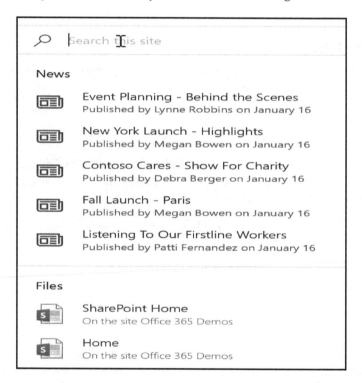

Choose one of the choices from the list or enter a term(s) and/or phrase(s) that you want to search on.

The search capability is very powerful. It is so powerful, in fact, that you may get back too many results. The search will search the title of the file, web page, or site, the URL, the text contained within, and any attached metadata. To help with getting more precise results when searching, you can use phrases and the logical operators, AND, OR, and NOT, to search just like you can with a search on the web. For example, you can search Test in Sequence NOT January, which would return results containing Test in Sequence but will exclude any results with the word January. There are query syntaxes you can use that are more advanced. For more information, see https://docs.microsoft.com/en-us/sharepoint/dev/general-development/keyword-query-language-kql-syntax-reference.

#10 Left navigation

The left navigation, also known as the quick launch, helps you move around the areas of the current site you are in. Normally, this navigation only contains links to parts of the site you are in at the moment but sometimes links to other things and places are placed there as well.

The **Edit** button is only visible if you have the permission level needed to be able to edit the navigation.

#11 Page header

The page header contains the banner and the title of the page or site. The banner may contain a picture but it can be blank.

#12 Web parts and app parts

Web parts and app parts are parts that you see on the main part of the SharePoint page. They are both modular and reusable components that can be placed into any SharePoint page. A web part can be added from the web part gallery, from a code module, or from the SharePoint Store. An app part is a display part showing a list or library.

#13 Feedback

Click this button and a side panel will open where you will have the option of giving Microsoft feedback or suggestions concerning SharePoint:

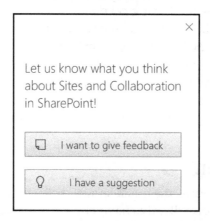

When you are giving feedback or a suggestion, remember to give as many details as you can. Try to answer the following what, when, where, how, and why questions:

- What is my feedback/suggestion? How will implementing it make a difference?
- Why am I giving this feedback/suggestion?
- Where was I and what was I doing when I encountered the issue, or where is the place that I am making a suggestion about?
- When did I experience the issue?

Giving as much detail as possible will keep Microsoft from throwing out your suggestion or feedback. It also helps others to vote your feedback or idea up. They are posted on Microsoft UserVoice for SharePoint and once 50 people vote it up, Microsoft will look at implementing it. If you can locate your feedback or idea on Microsoft SharePoint UserVoice directly, or simply post it directly on UserVoice, you can give the link to others and encourage them to vote your idea or feedback up!

Summary

In this chapter, we got a glimpse of what SharePoint is and discovered some of its history. We also looked at getting to SharePoint, navigating the SharePoint home, how to get around in SharePoint, and the anatomy of the SharePoint classic and modern pages. For more on SharePoint, go to `https://support.office.com` and click on **SharePoint**.

In `Chapter 14`, *Working with SharePoint Lists*, we are going to look at lists in SharePoint. We will look at what they are and how you can work with them.

14

Working with SharePoint Lists

SharePoint has some pretty cool ways of helping you to manage different types of data, not just files. In this chapter, we will look at the lists for managing data, the lists end uses are most likely to use that come out of the box with SharePoint, and the most-used functions you need to know about as an end user.

In this chapter, the following topics will be covered:

- What are Lists?
- The different List types
- What is a List View?
- How to add, edit, and delete list views

What are Lists?

When you think of a list, think of a spreadsheet. You can think of the **Lists** in SharePoint as spreadsheets that you and your co-workers can simultaneously use on the internet. Like a spreadsheet, the focus of the list is the data. It has columns and rows and you fill in data line by line. Each row of data in a SharePoint list is called an *item*. Unlike a spreadsheet, you can attach a file to each line of data.

 Attaching a file to a line of data in a SharePoint list is not a best practice. It can lead to a multitude of problems down the road. It is very difficult to get those files back out of the list when that data needs to be moved or the files removed from the items in the list and placed somewhere else. The best practice is to use a library (discussed in Chapter 15, *Performing Different File Operations on SharePoint*).

Like a spreadsheet, a list can be filled cell by cell using a mode called *Quick Edit*. Quick Edit will be discussed later in this section. Unlike a spreadsheet, the list also comes with a form to fill the data columns via fields. Each form of data entered is one line of data in the list:

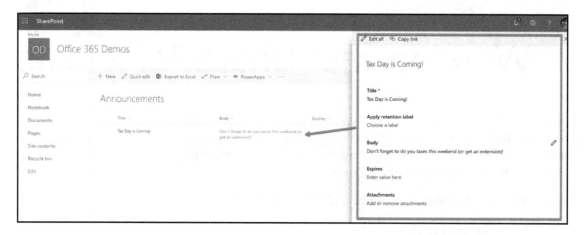

Fields with an asterisk (*) are required fields and the form cannot be saved until all required fields are filled in.

The different List types

Out of the box, SharePoint comes with lists in a few different categories. The following lists are some of the lists that you should be familiar with as an end user.

 All list types are not outlined here, only the ones you are most likely to use.

Communications

There are a few types of communications lists in SharePoint. The ones you are most likely to use are as follows:

- **Announcements**: This list type is used in classic SharePoint experiences to post announcements on the home page of a site. In the Modern Experience, the SharePoint News webpart is used instead.

- **Contacts**: This list is for keeping contact information, whether business or personal. It comes with fields for entering a person's name, addresses, company name, phone numbers, and so on.
- **Discussion board**: In this type of list, users can have an online forum, such as experience, where questions can be asked and answered in discussion threads.

Tracking

There are a few types of tracking lists in SharePoint. The ones you are most likely to use are as follows:

- **Links**: This type of list is used to track links. There are columns for putting in a title of the link (called *Description*) and for putting in the URL.
- **Calendars**: This type of list is for tracking events. There are views that look like the rest of the lists, and spreadsheet-like views, but there's also a view that looks like a calendar on this type of list. Views are explained in the *Custom lists* section. There are columns for the title of the event, start and end times, and so on.
- **Tasks**: This type of list is for tracking tasks. There are columns for the title of the task, task description, assignee, start date, task progress, and so on.
- **Survey**: This type of list, in the classic SharePoint experience, is used to track survey results. In this list, each survey question is created before the survey is opened for users. In the Modern Experience, Microsoft Forms is now the replacement for the Survey.

Custom lists

There are a few types of custom lists in SharePoint. The ones you are most likely to use are as follows:

- **Custom list**: The custom list is a list that comes with only one column, called **Title**, and the rest of the columns are added to make any type of list you want.
- **Import spreadsheet**: Historically, using this type of list was to be avoided. This list gives you the ability to import a spreadsheet and let the system create the list for you, but it was problematic. There have been improvements made to this list type and the problems may have all been resolved. If you were ever able to use this list type to create your own list, be warned that you may experience a number of issues.

What is a List View?

A view is the way you see details in the list or library. You can create multiple views on a list or library based on the different ways you would like the data to be presented.

In a view you can do the following:

- Choose the columns you want to appear
- Increase or decrease the number of columns displayed
- Choose the columns by which the information will be sorted, filtered, and/or grouped
- Add a button that enables team members to edit
- Display check boxes next to individual items so that members can select multiple items
- Add totals for items in the columns
- Apply a style
- Choose whether items are displayed in folders
- Set a limit for the number of items that can be displayed
- Set the way you want the list or library to appear when viewed on a mobile device

The most commonly-used views look like a spreadsheet with or without the lines. There are also views that make your list look like a calendar or a Gantt chart.

Adding items to any list using a list view

In a list, you can add items in two ways: through the form and through **Quick Edit** mode. Let's look at both of those ways in the Classic and Modern Experiences.

In the Classic Experience, either click on the **Items** tab and then click directly on the **New Item** button or on its dropdown, then choose **New Item** or click **+New Item** link:

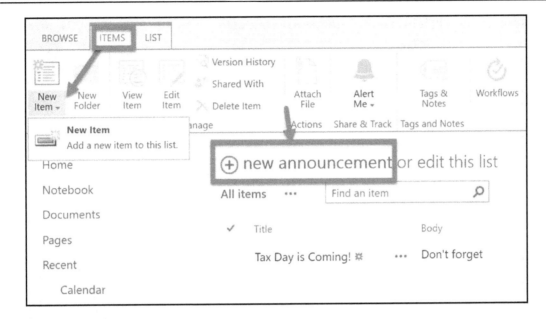

 The tab or new link may be named something else, depending on the list you are in. For example, the following diagram is of the **Announcements** list and its new link is labeled +**new announcement** instead of +**new item**.

The form opens. Fill it in and click on the **Save** button:

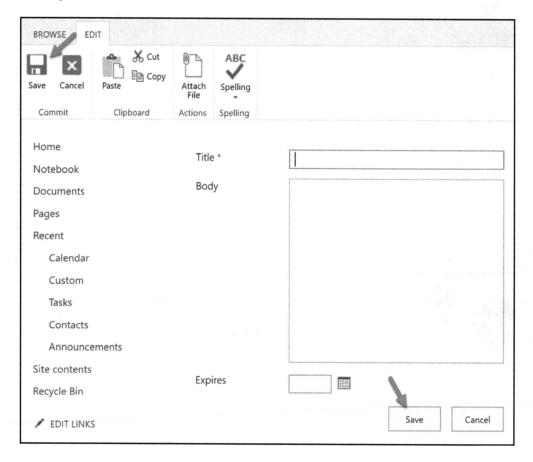

 Fields marked with an asterisk (*) are required fields; the form cannot be saved until all required fields are filled in.

In the Modern Experience, there are no tabs. Actions are performed through the actions bar. Click on the **New** button and the form will open in a side panel. Fill in the form and click the **Save** button:

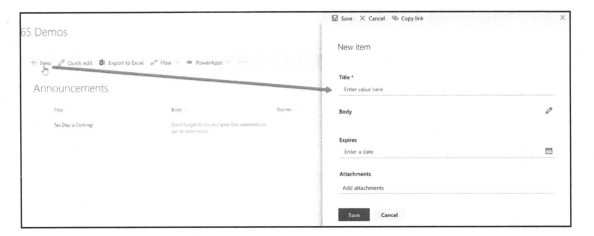

You can add new items via **Quick Edit** mode. In the Classic Experience, click on the **List** tab and then on the **Quick Edit** button, which will put the list in spreadsheet mode and you can add line by line. To stop editing, click the **Stop** link:

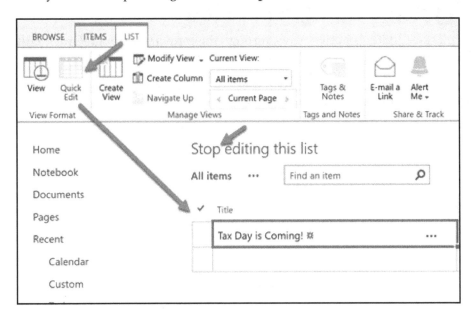

In the Modern Experience, click on the **Quick Edit** link in the action bar, which will put the list in spreadsheet mode and you can add line by line:

To stop editing, click the **Exit quick edit** link.

 Sometimes the list's view you are editing may not have all rows showing. If all required rows are not filled in, the row will not save.

Editing items using a list view

In a list, you can edit items in two ways: through the form and through **Quick Edit** mode. Let's look at both of those ways in the Classic and Modern Experiences.

In the Classic Experience, you can reopen the item for editing in three ways. One way is to click on the **Title** of the item and when it opens, click the **Edit Item** button to go from **View** mode to **Edit** mode:

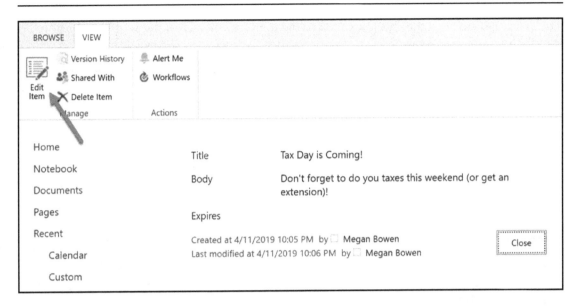

Another way is to click on the open menu next to the item and then click on **Edit Item**:

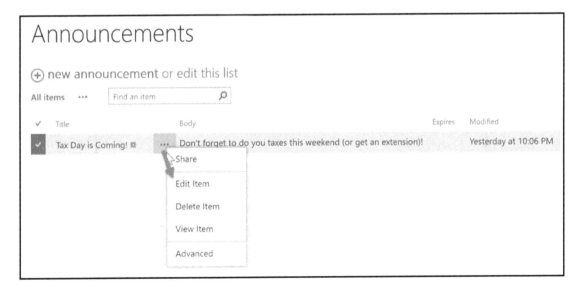

The last way is to click the checkbox next to the item and then click the **Edit Item** button on the ribbon in the **Items** tab:

In the Modern Experience, you can reopen the item for editing in four ways. One way is to click on the *Title* of the item and, when the form opens, click the **Edit all** button to go from **View** mode to **Edit** mode:

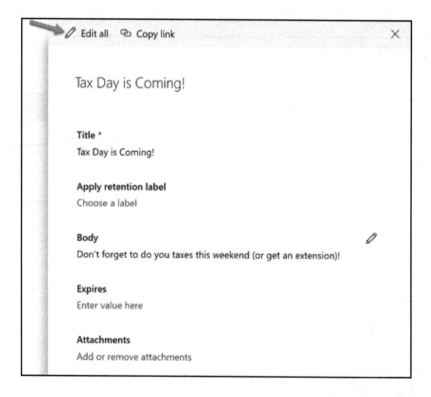

Another way is to click on the checkbox next to the item and then on the **Edit** button in the action bar to go directly into **Edit** mode:

The third way is to click on the checkbox next to the item and then on the **Show actions** menu; then click on **Edit** from the dropdown to go directly into **Edit** mode:

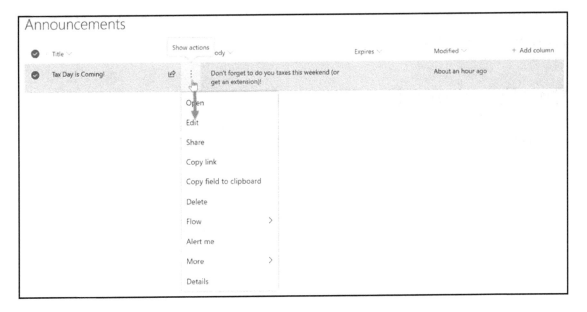

The last way is to click on the checkbox next to the item and then on the **Details Pane** icon; then click on the *Edit all* link in the **Properties** section:

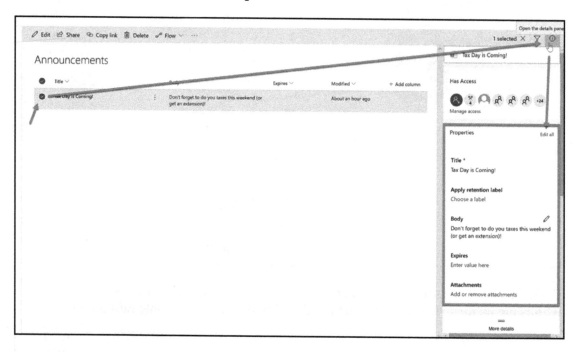

The section will then become editable.

Deleting items in a list view

In the Classic Experience, you can delete an item by clicking the checkbox next to the item, click on the **Items** tab, and then click the **Delete Item** button on the ribbon or click the open menu next to the item; then click on **Delete Item** from the dropdown:

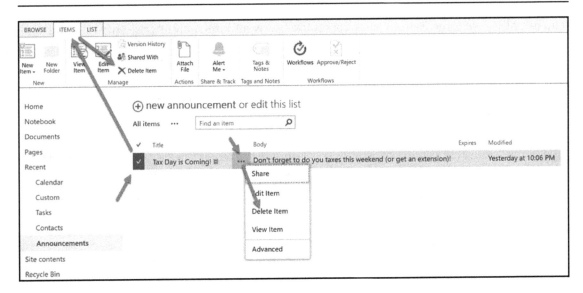

In the Modern Experience, you can delete an item by clicking the checkbox next to the item and then clicking the **Delete** button on the action bar:

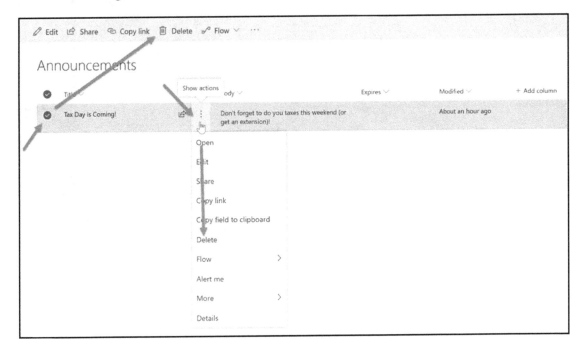

You can also delete the item by clicking on the **Show actions** menu next to the item and then clicking on **Delete** from the dropdown.

Adding/editing/deleting items in the calendar view

One of the views that can be implemented on any list or library is the **Calendar view**. The **Calendar list** automatically comes with a **Calendar view** when it is created:

This calendar view works just like the calendar in Outlook except the form is different.

Summary

In this chapter, we learned about lists, list views, and how we can add to lists in the Classic and Modern Experiences in the lists themselves. There are more ways to enter data through the webparts on a Modern SharePoint page and these methods are in flux at the time of writing. To see the latest and greatest in the Modern Experience, go to `https://support.office.com` and click on *SharePoint*.

In `Chapter 15`, *Performing Different File Operations on SharePoint*, we are going to explore libraries in SharePoint. We will look at what they are and how you can work with them.

15
Performing Different File Operations on SharePoint

SharePoint started life as a file server and now has much improved its functionality to work with files. In this chapter, we will look at the libraries that you get out of the box with SharePoint and the functions you need to know about as an end user. We will discuss how to add, edit, delete, and check files.

In this chapter, the following topics will be covered:

- What are libraries?
- The different library types
- What are library views?
- Using the document library
- Sharing files
- Moving and copying files

What are libraries?

One of the most compelling and popular features that SharePoint provides is libraries. Libraries are a great place to efficiently store and organize documents or forms. Office is tightly integrated into the SharePoint document library, adding even more functionality. Using SharePoint libraries, you can filter and group documents as well as view metadata (added as columns) for documents stored in the library.

The different library types

Out of the box, SharePoint comes with a few different types of libraries. The following are some of the libraries that you should be familiar with as an end user.

 All library types are not outlined here, only the ones you are most likely to use.

Document

Use a document library to store, organize, sync, and share documents with people. With the integration of Office, you can edit Office and PDF documents in the browser. You can co-author documents with your colleagues or check out a document to work on it one person at a time. Since all of your documents are in the same place, the latest versions of each document will be available to everyone when needed and versions will be automatically checked. Your documents can be synced to your computer so that you can access them offline.

Form

This library is home to online InfoPath forms, which are only available when the library is using the Classic Experience. If in modern, the online forms of choice are power apps, which will not work with this library.

Wiki page

This library is actually a set of easy-to-edit web pages that can be built using images, web parts, and text (these are explained in *The Classic Page Anatomy* section of Chapter 14, *Working with SharePoint Lists*).

Picture

This library gives you a place to upload and share pictures.

What is a library view?

A view is the way you see details in the list or library. You can create multiple different views on a list or library based on the different ways you would like the data to be presented.

In a view, you can do the following:

- Choose the columns you want to appear
- Increase or decrease the number of columns displayed
- Choose the columns by which the information will be sorted, filtered, and/or grouped
- Add a button that enables team members to edit
- Display check boxes next to individual items so that members can select multiple items
- Add totals for items in the columns
- Apply a style
- Choose whether items are displayed in folders
- Set a limit for the number of items that can be displayed
- Set the way you want the list or library to appear when viewed on a mobile device

The most-commonly-used views look like a spreadsheet with or without the lines. There are also views that make your list look like a calendar or a Gantt chart, and can be applied to a library as long as you have a date for the start date and a date for the end date.

Using the document library

The following will show you how to carry out common tasks using the document library, because this is the library you will spend the most time with. All functions described here can be done in any library unless otherwise noted.

Adding files

In the Classic Experience, you can add new files by creating them using the Office Web Apps (see more details in the Modern Experience explanation next) or by uploading them. When uploading, you cannot upload an entire folder or multiple files at one time:

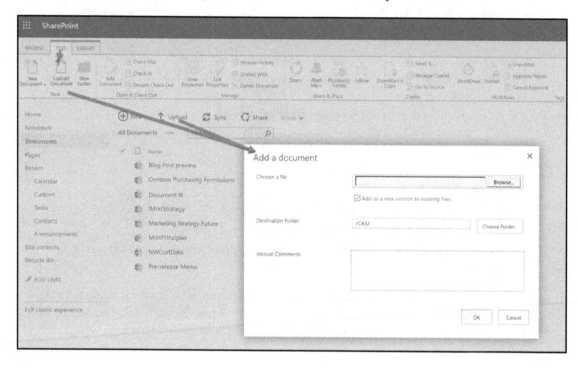

In the Modern Experience, you can add new files by creating them using the Office Web Apps or by uploading them. When adding new, you can even use a link to the file instead of having the file in multiple places:

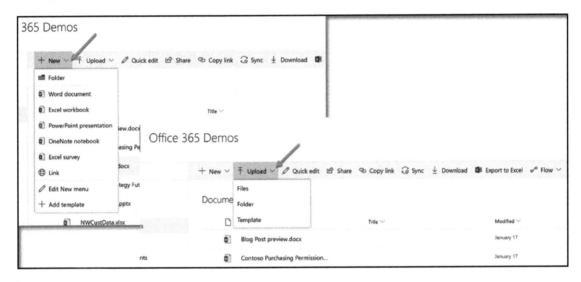

When uploading, you can choose to upload an entire folder.

Creating new files in the Modern Experience

To create a new file, click on the **New** dropdown in the action bar:

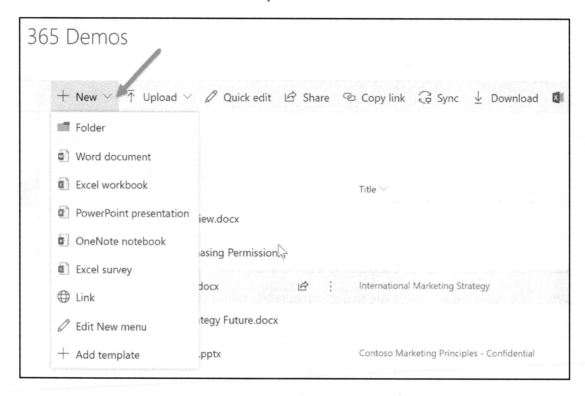

 As soon as you click on **Word document**, **PowerPoint presentation**, or **Excel workbook** and the new document opens, that document will be automatically saved to SharePoint with its default name. For example, Excel files are named `Book` (followed by a number if this one isn't the first). If you rename it, it will be renamed during the next autosave.

 Using links is a great way to add access to a file that needs to be in multiple places. Using a link instead of adding that file to multiple places ensures that you have the single source of truth. Remember, adding a link to a document to multiple places does not mean that everyone with access to the library will have access to the file via the link. In order for a person to access the file via the link, they must have permission to, at least, view the file.

You can also create a new folder or a link using any URL:

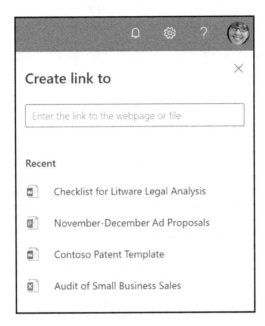

When you click on one of the Office file types, it opens a new file in the browser. If you need to open this file in the full version of Office, click on the **Open in word** link above the ribbon. In this example, **Word Online** is open so you would click on **Open in Word** to open the file in the full version of Word on your desktop. In the browser, the file will autosave as you are typing so there is no save button:

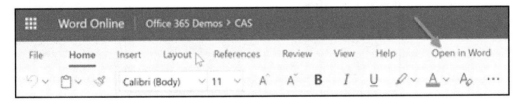

Clicking on the **Open in word** link, will open the file in the full version of the Office app on the computer that you are on. If you are on a computer with Office 2010, it may not open since Office 2010 is on the brink of reaching the end of its life (as of April 2019):

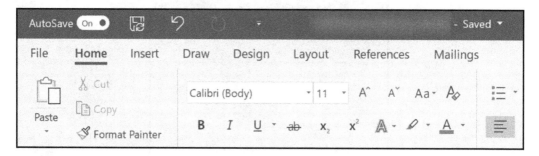

An Office version older than 2010 most likely will not open. Office 2013, 2016, and 2019 (depending on the build version) will open but you may not have access to features such as **AutoSave**.

Uploading files in the Modern Experience

Click on the **Upload** dropdown in the action bar and you get the choice to upload files or folders:

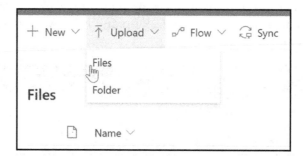

Using the **Files** action will only allow you to upload files but not folders. The **Folder** action allows you to upload a folder with its contents.

 It will copy subfolders if those folders contain files. If the subfolder is empty, it will not be copied.

Editing files

In a library, you can edit items in two ways: through the form and through **Quick Edit** mode. Let's look at both of those ways in the Classic and Modern Experiences.

In the Classic Experience, you can edit the file or its properties in two ways. One way is to click on the checkbox next to the file and then, on the **Files** tab, choose **Edit Document** to edit the document or **Edit Properties** to edit the metadata of the file. The other way is to click on the more options menu next to the file and then on the next one on the preview window and choose either **Open in Word**, **Open in Word Online**, or **Properties**:

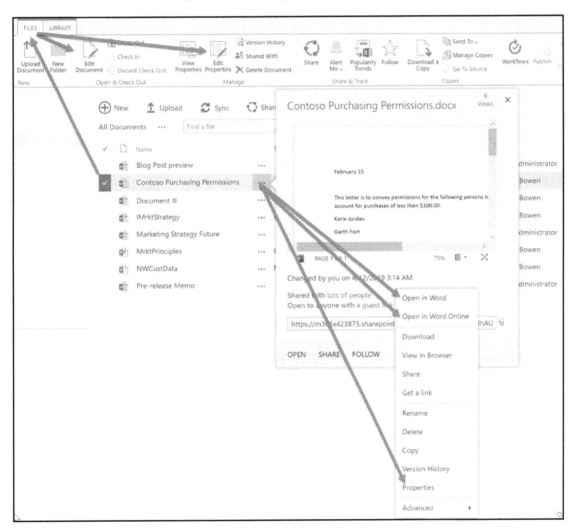

Properties are another word for metadata or columns. Some of the metadata/columns, such as **Modified**, may be system-created and cannot be modified; only user-created metadata/columns can.

In the Modern Experience, you can edit the file in three ways. One way is to click on the checkbox next to the file and then either click on the **Open** dropdown for options to **Open in Word** or **Open in Word Online** on the action bar. Alternatively, click on the **Details Pane** icon and then on **Edit all** in the **Properties** section. Click the **Edit all** button to go from **View** mode to **Edit** mode:

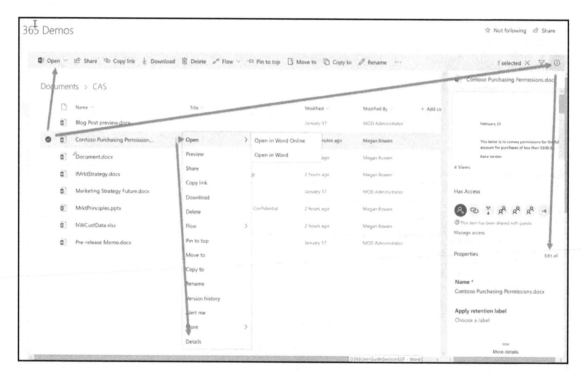

The other way is to click on the open menu next to the file and then on the next one on the preview window; then, either hover over **Open** for options to **Open in Word** or **Open in Word Online.** Alternatively, click on **Details** further down the drop down which will open the **Details** pane where you cannot **Edit all** in the **Properties** section.

Deleting files

In the Classic Experience, you can delete an item by clicking the checkbox next to the item, clicking on the **Items** tab, and then clicking the **Delete Item** button on the ribbon or clicking the open menu next to the item, and then on **Delete Item** from the dropdown:

In the Modern Experience, you can delete an item by clicking the checkbox next to the item and then clicking the **Delete** button in the action bar:

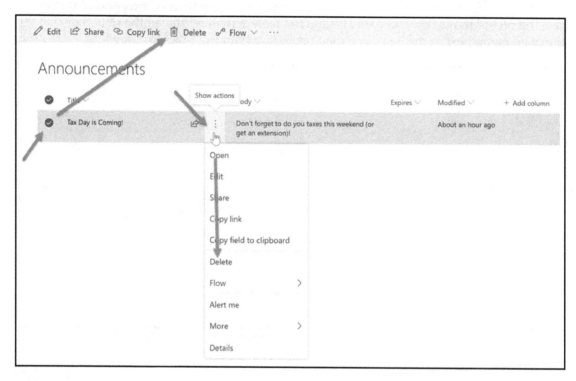

You can also delete an item by clicking on the **Show actions** menu next to the item and then clicking on **Delete** from the dropdown.

Naming conventions

Best practice is to keep the file's **Name** as short as possible and then have the **Title** as the long, descriptive name. When you upload a document, it may already have a long name. The easiest way to implement best practice is to put the library in **Quick Edit** mode after uploading the file, drag the dot in the lower-right corner over to the **Title** field, and then restructure the **Name** field:

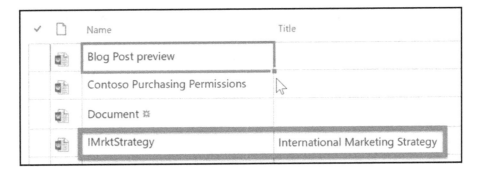

The reason for the best practice is because the **Name** field is tied to the URL of the file and, traditionally, the URL path could not go beyond 255 characters or all types of problems would occur. Older SharePoint had no way to mitigate the issue, so it was up to the users to do so. Present-day SharePoint has some safeguards and improvements to help mitigate the issue, but the best practice is still best practice.

 Although the **Title** field comes with every library, by default, the **Title** field is not in the view. If it is missing, ask your SharePoint admin to add the field to the view right after the **Name** field, as shown in the preceding screenshot.

Version history

Nowadays, by default, SharePoint libraries track version history automatically, which means the following is true:

- No more saving the same file that you modified with a different name; simply save a modified file with the same name
- Past versions can be viewed and restored, if needed
- Up to a certain number of versions of each document will be tracked

 If you are concerned that version history has not been turned on or are double-checking because your SharePoint is a bit older, talk to your SharePoint administrator.

To see the version history of a file, click on the open menu next to the file and choose **Version History** from the dropdown:

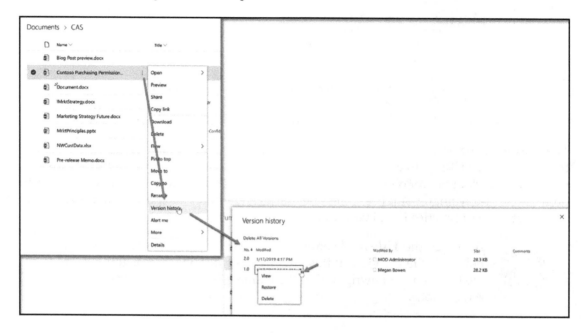

From there, you may, depending on your permission level, be able to **View**, **Restore**, and **Delete** previous versions of a file.

Checking files in or out

This feature allows users to check in/check out files so that only the person who has it checked out can edit the file. When this feature is turned on, it is on for the entire library and every file can only be edited by one person at a time.

It is important for you to remember to check the files back in once you are finished working, so others can work on them when necessary. The SharePoint admin can check in files for you but you should not rely on them.

 When you upload files, they may be checked out.

Checking out

In the Classic Experience, click on the more options menu next to the item, and then on the next more options menu on the preview window; then, hover over **Advanced** at the very bottom of the dropdown, and click on **Check Out**, or click on the checkbox next to the file, and then on the **Files** tab; then, click on **Check Out**:

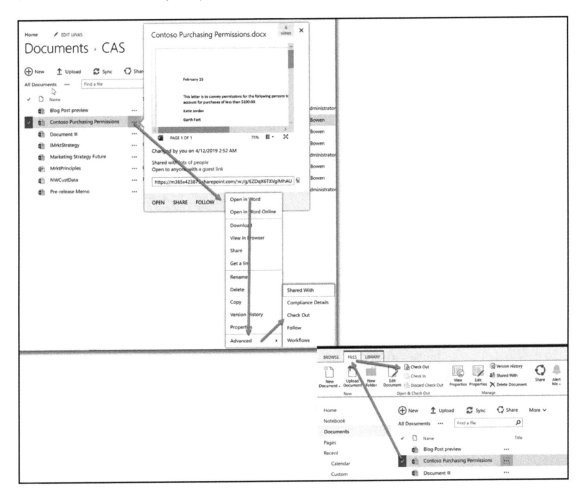

In the Modern Experience, click on the checkbox next to the file; then click on the more options menu in the action bar, and then click **Check Out** from the dropdown:

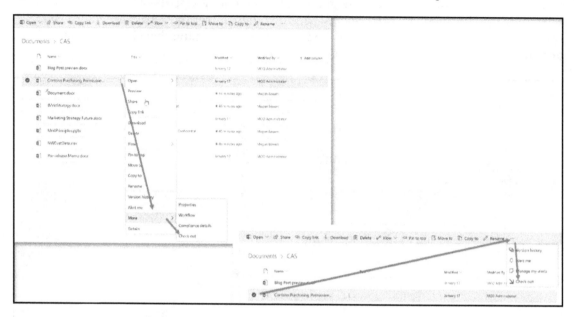

You can also click on the **Show actions** menu next to the file, hover over more at the very bottom of the dropdown, and then click on **Check Out**:

Checked-out files in the Classic and Modern Experiences are denoted with a green box with a white arrow.

Checking in

In the Classic Experience, check the box next to the file; then, on the **Files** tab, click on **Check In** or click on the more options menu; then, on the next one on the preview window; then hover over **Advanced** at the bottom of the dropdown and click on **Check In**:

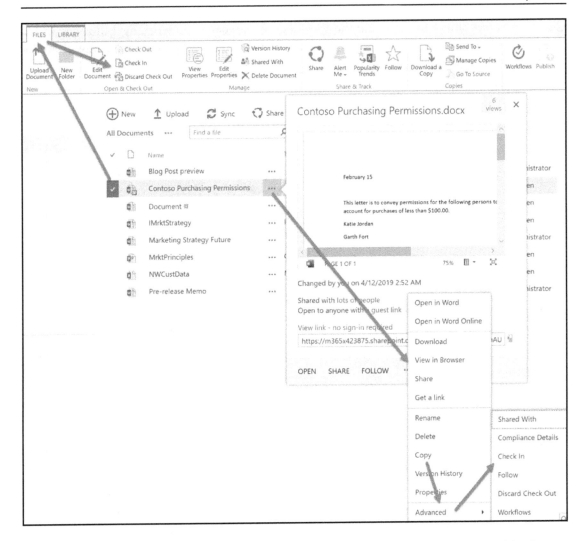

 You can also **Discard check out** but be aware that it will delete the file if it is a newly-uploaded file.

Choose whether you want to retain the check out so you can keep working, but check in your changes; then type in your comments about your change(s) and SharePoint will do the rest!

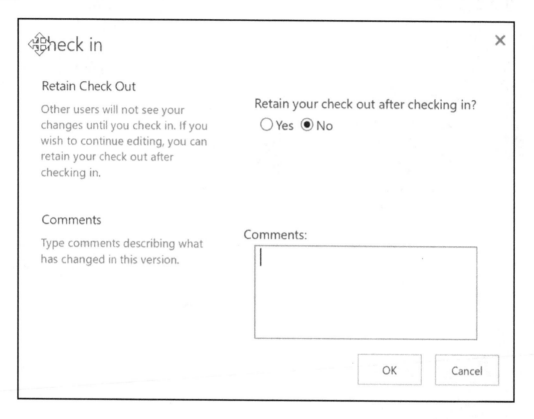

 It is best practice to be descriptive in your comments. Those comments can be seen in **Version History** and can help a person determine what is different in that version, instead of having to view the version itself.

In the Modern Experience, click on the checkbox next to the file; then click on the more options menu on the action bar, and then click **Check In** from the dropdown or click on the **Show actions** menu next to the file; hover over more at the very bottom of the dropdown, and then click on **Check In**:

Type in your comments about your change(s) and SharePoint will do the rest:

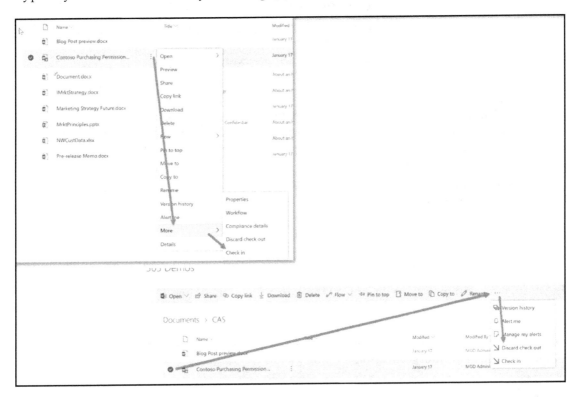

Whether you are in the Classic or Modern Experience, you may be asked to choose whether you want your version to be a major or a minor version. This will only occur if the library is configured for major and minor versions or just major versions.

Coauthoring

Coauthoring is how you and your colleagues can work on the same document at the same time. Coauthoring is awesome when you are in a work environment where everyone can collaborate in such a manner due to the collaborative culture of your organization. Also, requirements play a part in whether coauthoring is a good solution. There are times when a document is so sensitive that only one person should edit it at a time. If you find that coauthoring may be a great way to work, you and your organization should be aware of the following:

- It is recommended that no more than 10 concurrent users edit at a time. The absolute max is 99.
- If 99 coauthors have opened a single document to edit at the same time, each user after that will see a **File in use** error and the file will only open as read-only.
- More than 10 co-editors will lead to a gradually-degraded user experience with more conflicts, and users might have to go through more iterations to successfully upload their changes to the server.
- Excel is a special application and has more restrictions than other applications, so you will not be able to do some things when coauthoring.
- Coauthoring is on when **Check in/Check out** is off. **Check in/Check out** is an all-or-nothing capability. If it is on, then it is on for the entire library, but that is not so for Coauthoring. If Check in/Check Out is off, then Coauthoring is on but users can still **Check in/Check out** single files as necessary.
- You can coauthor in Word, PowerPoint, Excel, and OneNote, as well as in their online versions.

Sharing files

In SharePoint, you may have the ability to share a file with others. In others words, you would be giving access to others at the level of access, view, or edit, that you choose, but you might not have the ability to remove or edit that access once set. Depending on the way your organization set up your account, you may also have the ability to give access to others outside of your organization.

> File sharing is not a best practice and should be used with care. See the warning about *The Danger of the Share Button* in Chapter 17, *More on Using SharePoint*.

Giving access

You can share a file via the **Share** button inside or outside of the file itself:

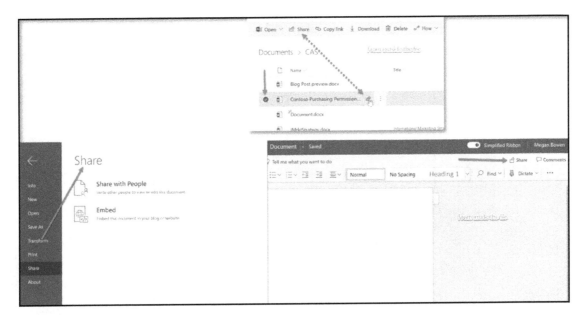

 If you are outside the file, you need to select the file first.

Any way that you go, you will get the same popup. Through this popup, you can choose the way you want to share. Let's look at the options at the bottom of the popup first:

One option is to click on **Copy Link**. This will automatically copy the link to the file, which you can paste anywhere, such as in an email.

 The person receiving the link must have permission to access the file or the link will not work for them.

The other option is to click on the **Outlook** button at the bottom, which will open a new email via Outlook, or your default Mail app, with the file automatically attached.

Now let's look at the main options at the top. You can see all of the options available by clicking on the bar that says **Anyone with the link** can edit. Once you choose your options, click the **Apply** button and it will take you to the first screen where you can add the name(s) (if internal to your organization) and/or email(s) (if external to your organization) and an optional message, and then click the **Send** button:

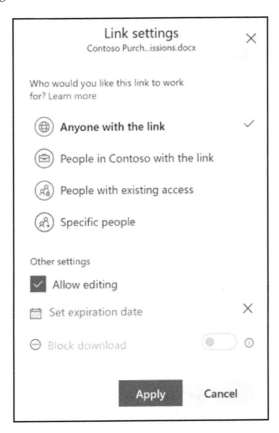

Once sent, the person(s) you listed will get an email from the system that they can use to access the file.

Editing or removing access

Once access is given, you may not have the ability to pull it back unless you have the necessary permission level. You may be able to see the permission by clicking the check box next to the file, then on the **Details** pane icon, and looking in the **Has Access** section. You may even be able to click on the **Manage Access** link to see more details:

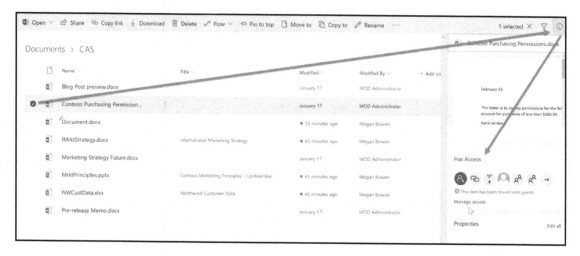

Editing and removing permissions in SharePoint is the responsibility of a person at the level of power user and up, which is outside of the scope of this book.

Move to

This is a fairly new capability that has been a great help to many users and is only available in the Modern Experience. This capability allows you to move files and/or folders from place to place. Once you have chosen the file(s) and/or folder(s) you want to move, click on the **Move To** button in the action bar. A side panel will open; here, you can choose where you want to move your file(s) and/or folder(s) to:

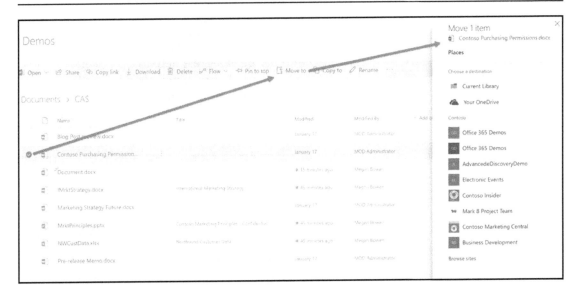

You can move to another folder in the library you are in, other places in SharePoint, or even to your OneDrive for Business.

This is a move, not a copy. After the operation is completed, the file(s) and/or folder(s) will no longer exist in the original place.

You must have access permission of at least Contribute level to complete this operation. In order to see a list of available SharePoint sites, you must be following that site. If you have access to the site but are unable to follow the site, contact your SharePoint Administrator to see whether that feature can be turned on.

Copy to

Like move to, this is a fairly new capability and has been a great help to may users, but it is also only available in the Modern Experience. This capability allows you to copy files and/or folders to other places. Once you chose the file(s) and/or folder(s) you want to copy, click on the **Copy To** button on the action bar. A side panel will open; here, you can choose where you want to copy your file(s) and/or folder(s) to:

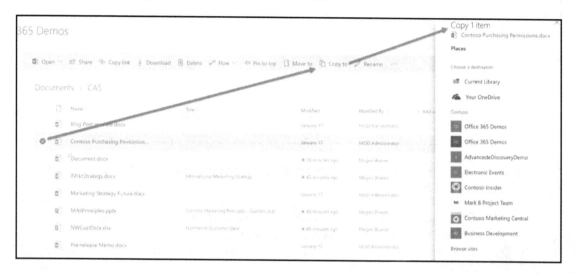

You can copy to another folder in the library, other places in SharePoint, or even to your OneDrive for Business.

 This is a copy, not a move. After the operation is completed, the file(s) and/or folder(s) will exist in the original place as well as the place you copied them to.

You must have access permission of at least Contribute level to complete this operation. In order to see a list of available SharePoint sites, you must be following that site. If you have access to the site but are unable to follow the site, contact your SharePoint Administrator to see whether that feature can be turned on.

Summary

In this chapter, you learned about the libraries that you get out of the box with SharePoint and the most-used functions you need to know about as an end user. For more on SharePoint, go to `https://support.office.com` and click on **SharePoint**.

In `Chapter 16`, *More on Using SharePoint*, we are going to explore other things you can do in SharePoint, such as creating alerts, links, and personal views.

16
More on Using SharePoint

We have already looked at a lot of the capabilities and features of SharePoint, but there is still more you should know as an end user. In this chapter, we are going to explore more capabilities, such as exporting to Excel and setting alerts. We are also going to look at the different ways you can find data in SharePoint and the dangers of using the **Share** button.

In this chapter, the following topics will be covered:

- Quick edit mode
- Exporting to Excel
- Creating a link
- Creating personal views
- Switching between views
- Different ways to find data in SharePoint
- Site contents
- Recycle bin
- The danger of the **Share** button
- SharePoint permissions and what they allow you to do
- How to request access

Quick edit mode

Quick edit mode is a way to put your list or library into a spreadsheet-like mode where you can easily make edits as in an Excel spreadsheet.

In the Classic Experience, on the **List** or **Library** tab, click on the **Quick Edit** button:

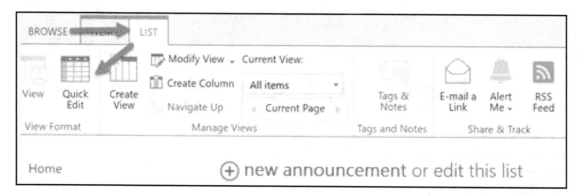

In the Modern Experience, on the action bar, click **Quick Edit**:

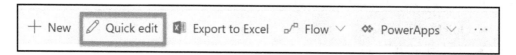

 We recommend exporting the **All Items** view so you can see all columns.

Once the **Quick Edit** is initiated, you can edit the list in a spreadsheet-like manner:

	Title	Client POC	Project Name
✓	Amnesty International, USA	none	Media Training
	Enterprise Community Partners	Vrunda Vaghela	Opportunity360
	Society of NeuroInterventional Surgery	none	Agendy of Record
	University of South Florida		Making Connections for Mental Health and Wellbeing Among Men and Boys Initiative in the U.S.
	League of Women Voters of the United States	none	Convention Video
	League of Women Voters of the United States	none	Event Concept Paper
	Equal Measure	none	New Connections
	SAMHSA/Center for Mental Health Services	none	Education for Social Inclusion Initiative: Voice Awards

There are a few things to note here:

- This operation can be done on lists and libraries.
- You can copy from a cell or cells just as you can do in Excel by clicking on the dot in the lower-right corner and dragged across the cells being copied to. See the preceding screenshot.
- You can copy and paste cells and/or columns from an Excel spreadsheet. You can even copy and paste all columns from an Excel spreadsheet as long as all of the columns match in the number of columns, the order of columns, and the type of columns.

You can exit **Quick Edit** by clicking **Exit quick edit** in the Modern Experience or the **Stop** link in the Classic Experience.

Exporting to Excel

You can export a list or a library to Excel. This can be very useful for reporting purposes.

In the Classic Experience, in the **List** or **Library** tab, click on the **Export to Excel** button:

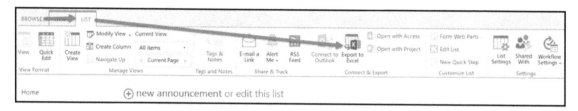

In the Modern Experience, in the action bar, click **Export to Excel**:

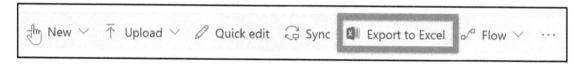

If you are prompted to confirm the operation, click **OK**.

In the **File Download** dialog box, click **Open**:

You may be prompted to enable data connections on your computer. If you think the connection is safe, click **Enable**.

There are few things to note here:

- I recommend exporting the **All items** view and then filtering the list or removing columns in Excel.
- An Excel table is created with a data connection based on a web query file (`.iqy`). Save the file as a `.csv` or `.xslx` file to prevent issues that can arise from the `.iqy` file type.
- The columns in the export are determined by the current list view.
- Filters will not apply to the export. Once data is exported, you can use the filters in Excel.

- Any page limits are ignored.
- This export is a snapshot in time. The data in the spreadsheet will not refresh as things change in SharePoint.

Now that we have learned how to export a file to Excel, let's see how to create a link.

Creating a link

Using links is a great idea for adding access to a file that needs to be in multiple places. Using a link instead of adding that file to multiple places ensures that you have the single source of truth. Using links only works in the Modern Experience.

 Adding a link to a document to multiple libraries does not mean that everyone with access to the library will have access to the file via the link. In order for a person to access the file via the link, they must have permission to, at least, view the file.

Go to the list or library of your choice and, in the action bar, click **New** and then choose **Link** from the dropdown:

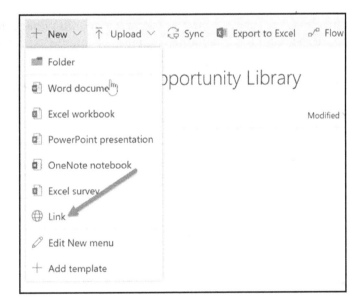

Once the **Link** choice is clicked, you can type or copy in any link you want, or choose from some of the choices you are presented with:

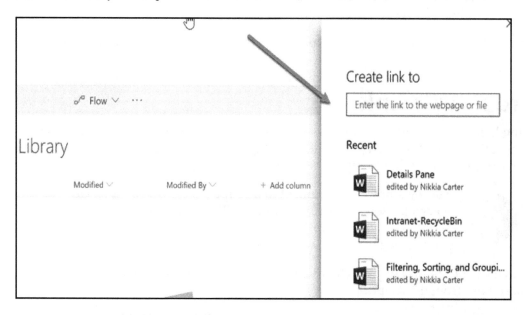

If you type or copy in a link, the system will give the link a default name before it is created. You can choose to accept the link name or change the name to something else, then click **Create**:

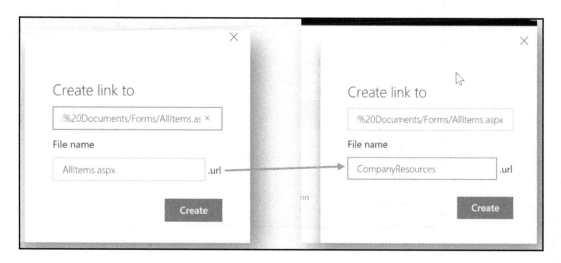

If you choose from one of the system-provided choices, the link will be created without giving you the opportunity to change the link name, but you can rename the link afterwards by clicking on the open menu (the three dots) and choosing **Rename** from the dropdown:

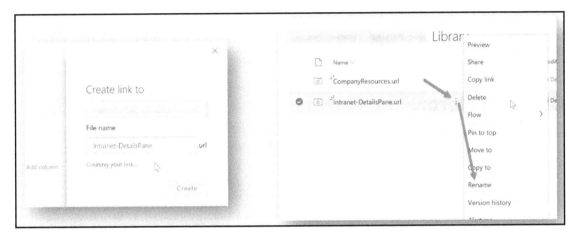

This operation can be done on lists and libraries, inside of the actual list or library. This action cannot be done via a list or library web part:

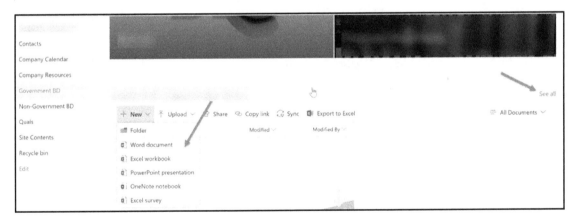

If you are on a page and want to easily get to that web part's list or library, click on the **See all** link on the right side of the web part.

Alerts

An alert is a notification that lets you know when things have changed or have been added in SharePoint lists/libraries. These notifications can be very useful. One way they can be helpful is for use with issues tracking project tasks, or tasks lists. If you are responsible for responding to trouble tickets or tasks when they are submitted, you will likely want a notification as soon as an item is created or edited. An alert can be set on the entire list or library, or on specific files or items.

Creating alerts

In the Classic Experience, click on the **List** or **Library** tab, and then on **Set alert on this list** or **Set alert on this library** under the **Alert Me** drop down to set on the entire list/library; alternatively, click the checkbox next to item(s) or file(s), and then on the **Items** or **Files** tab; click on **Set alert on this item** or **Set alert on this file** under the **Alert Me** dropdown to set on item(s) or file(s):

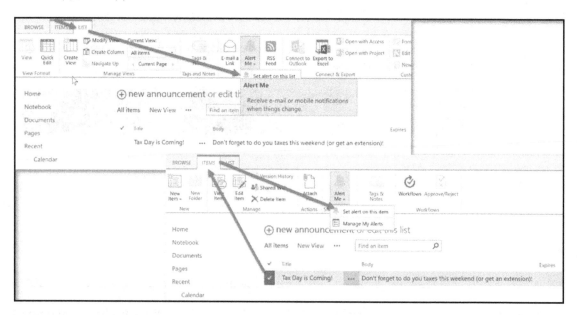

For an entire list or library, fill out this form and click **OK**:

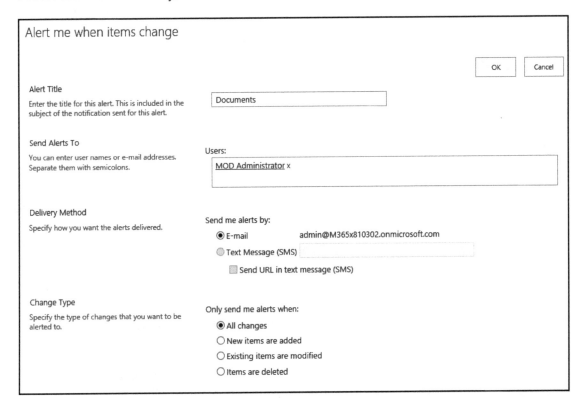

You'll probably want to leave the **Title** as is so or may add the site name so you can manage them easier later.

You can set alerts for yourself and/or others. If you set them for others, you will not be able to manage the alerts unless you are a site owner or above.

For items or files, fill out this form and click **OK:**

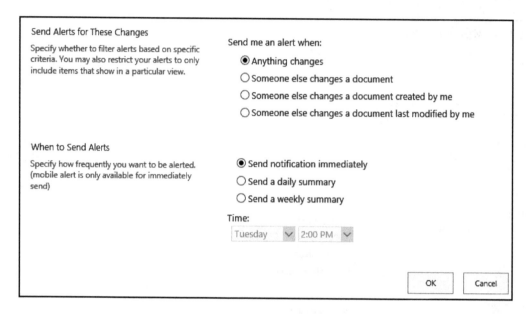

You may have noticed that the form for the item or file, and the list or library are slightly different but are basically the same.

Managing alerts

To manage your alerts, first go to the **List**, **Library**, **Files**, or **Items** tab of any list or library in the site where you set your alert; then click on **Manage My Alerts** on the **Alert Me** dropdown:

You can delete and modify alerts here as well as create new ones:

To modify an alert, simply click on the alert and make changes to the form. To delete an alert, click the checkbox next to it and then click **Delete Selected Alerts**.

I highly recommended that you create them using the method detailed in the *Creating alerts* section.

More on views

When working in a list or library, you may wish that you could change the way the list or library looks by doing things such as ordering the columns differently, hiding or showing columns, grouping items or files, or hiding the folders. As an end user, you can create your own views on any list or library you have access to. A personal view is a view only you have access to and can see. You can create up to 10 personal views per list or library. Let's look at how you can create your own personal view.

Creating a personal view

Once in the list or library of your choosing, there are three ways get to the page where you can create a new view: via the Classic Experience, via the Modern Experience, or via the list or library **Settings**.

To get to the page for creating a new view in the Classic Experience, click on the **List** or **Library** tab (or the **Calendar** tab), and then click on the **Create View** button on the ribbon:

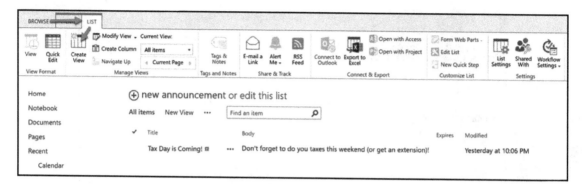

 You can use the **Modify View** button to modify any personal views or, if you have the required permission level, public views. Clicking on that button will take you to the same page you will go to in order to create a new view. You just need to make sure you have switched to the view you want to edit first.

To get to the page for creating a new view in the Modern Experience, click on the **View Options** menu on the right side and then click on **Save view as**:

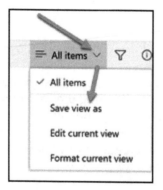

Give the view a name and click the **Save** button. You will be switched to that new view. Next, you will want to edit it, so click on the **View Options** menu again and then on **Edit current view**:

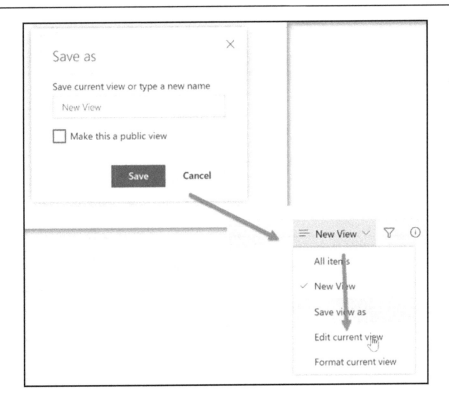

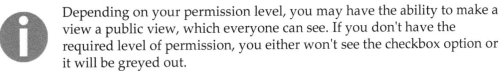

Depending on your permission level, you may have the ability to make a view a public view, which everyone can see. If you don't have the required level of permission, you either won't see the checkbox option or it will be greyed out.

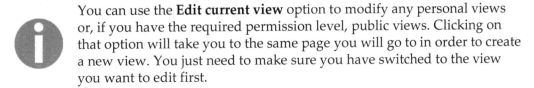

You can use the **Edit current view** option to modify any personal views or, if you have the required permission level, public views. Clicking on that option will take you to the same page you will go to in order to create a new view. You just need to make sure you have switched to the view you want to edit first.

The last way to get to the page for creating a new view is through the list or library's **Settings**.

In the Classic Experience, click on the **List** or **Library** (or **Calendar**) tab and then on the **Settings** button:

Next, choose the type of view you want to create or use an existing view as your starter:

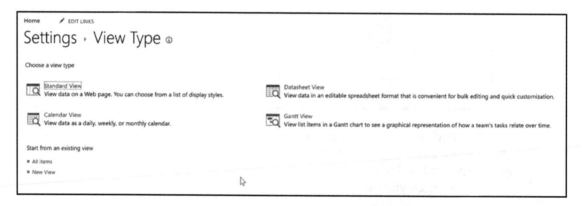

In the Modern Experience, click on the gear icon and then on **List Settings** or **Library Settings**:

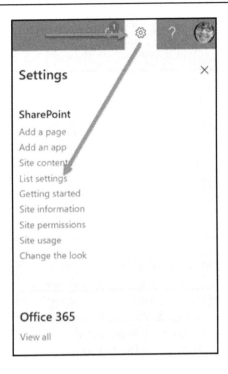

Once on the **Settings** page, scroll down to the **Views** section and click on **Create View**:

 If you want to modify any personal views or, if you have the required permission level, public views, click on the view and it will take you to the same page you will go to in order to create a new view.

Once on the **Edit View** page, you will have a lot of options for creating the new view. First things first, give it a name:

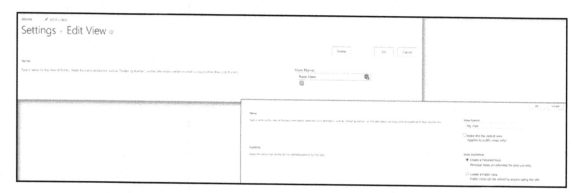

 Depending on your permission level, you may have the ability to make a view a public view, which everyone can see. If you don't have the required level of permission, you either won't see the radio button option or it will be greyed out. If you do have the option to make the view public, you can choose to make the view the default view so it will be the first one a user sees when they go to the list or library.

Next, you can choose which columns would like to show in the view and in what order:

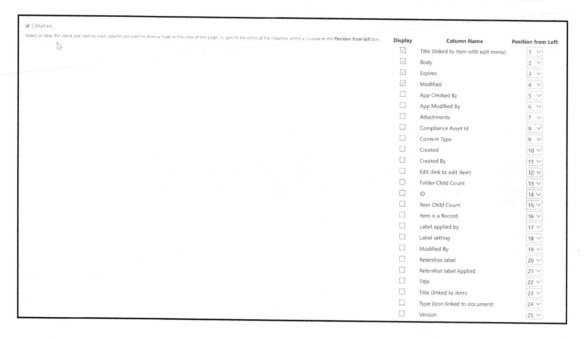

Make sure you check the box next to all columns you want to show in the view or they will not even if you change that column's order.

In the next two sections, you can choose to **Sort** by a primary and/or secondary column in ascending or descending order and/or to **Filter** by one or many columns in ascending or descending order. Click on **Show More Columns...**to add more columns to filter by:

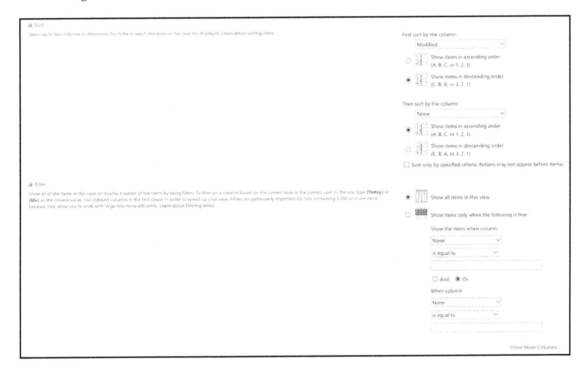

In the next three sections, you can choose to enable **Tabular View**, to **Group By** a primary and/or secondary column in ascending or descending order in a specified number of collapsed or expanded groups by default per page and/or to **Totals** certain columns in order to calculate the **Count**, **Average**, **Maximum**, **Minimum**, **Sum**, **Std Deviation**, or **Variance**:

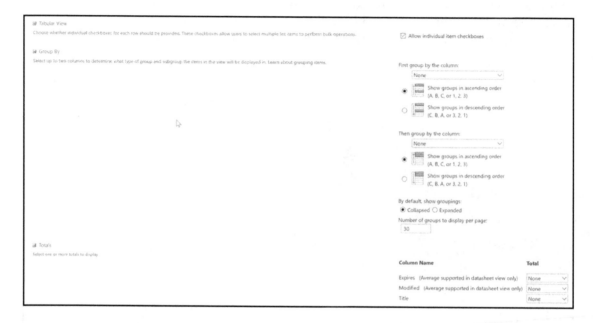

In the last three sections, you can choose to change the **Style**, to show the items in **Folders**, if any, and/or to change the number of items to display. Click the **OK** button to save your view:

Here is the result:

In this view, I added **Grouping** on the **Modified** column.

Switching between views (to view, edit, or delete)

There are three ways to switch the view: two ways via the Classic Experience and one way via the Modern Experience.

In the Modern Experience, click on the **View Options** menu in the upper-right corner and choose the view you want:

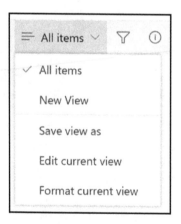

In the Classic Experience, click on the **List** or **Library** tab, then on the **Current Views** dropdown to choose the view you want, or, under the **+New** button, click on the view you want:

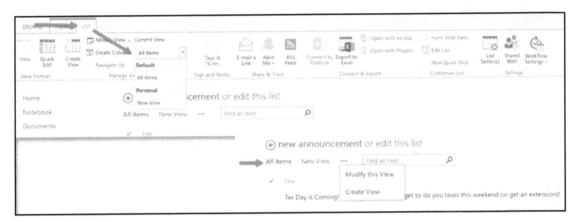

More views may be available in the more options dropdown.

 To edit or delete a view, switch to it before opening it in edit mode. If you want to delete it, a **Delete** button is located at the top or bottom of the **Edit View** page.

The different ways you can find data

When searching in SharePoint, you have two main ways to find data:

- Via the site
- Via the list or library

Besides searching, you also have the ability to find things by using **Filtering**.

Let's look at all three of these ways.

How to use list/library filtering

Instead of searching, you may want to filter the list or library by the metadata columns in the list or library. To do so, click on the drop-down arrow of the column you want to filter by, hover over **Filter By**, and choose from the options:

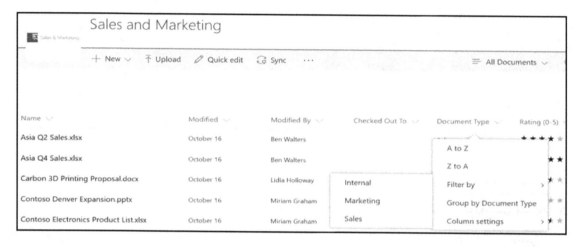

To release the filter, hover over the column, click on the dropdown, and choose **Clear filters**. Repeat to clear any and all filters you want to clear.

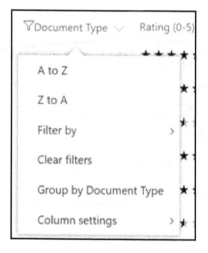

You can filter multiple columns at once.

How to use searching in a list/library

The search box for the list or library only searches the list or library you are in:

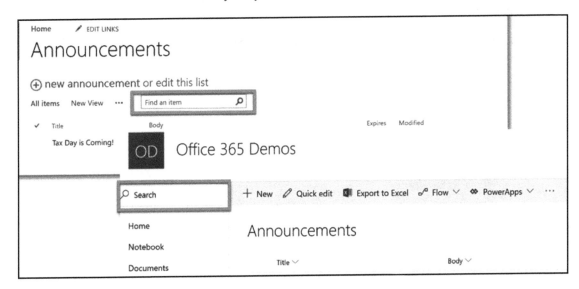

In the Classic Experience, if items were very recently added to the list or library, they may not show up in a search immediately. They may need to be indexed by the system or manually. The system usually crawls every 156 minutes.

How to search sites in SharePoint

This search will search the contents of the current site you are in and any sub-sites' contents and their sub-sites, down the hierarchy. If you are at the top of the site collection, it will search the entire site collection. For more details, see *The Anatomy of the SharePoint Page, The Classic Page Anatomy, Search,* and *The Anatomy of the SharePoint Page, The Modern Page Anatomy, Search* portions of `Chapter 13`, *Understanding SharePoint*.

Searching via the SharePoint home

This search will search across all site collections you have access to. For more details, see *The SharePoint Home* and *Search* section of `Chapter 13`, *Understanding SharePoint*.

Site contents

The **Site contents** shows you the contents of the site you are currently in. It will show you the site's lists, libraries, apps, and sub-sites.

In the Classic or Modern Experience, go to **Site Contents** by clicking the link on the left navigation:

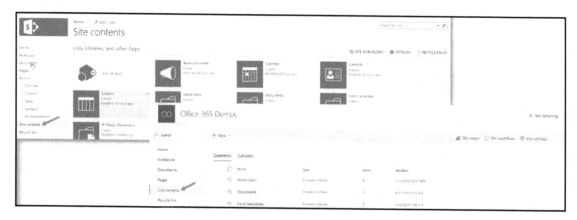

You can also click on the gear and choose **Site contents** from the dropdown.

The recycle bin

In SharePoint, the recycle bin functions similarly to how it works in Windows. When you delete a file or item from a library or a list, it goes to the recycle bin.

In the Classic or Modern Experience, click on **Recycle Bin** on the left navigation or, if the link isn't there, go to **Site content** (also on the left navigation or under the gear) and click on **Recycle Bin** in the upper-right corner:

In the **Recycle Bin**, you can choose an item:

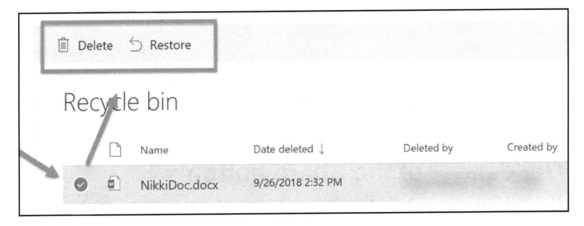

To restore a deleted item in the recycle bin, simply click it and click **Restore**.

To delete an item permanently from the recycle bin, select it in the recycle bin and click on **Delete**.

 Items stay in this recycle bin for 30 days, unless manually deleted, then go the site-collection administrator's recycle bin and stays there for 30 days, unless manually deleted. After that, consider it gone. The site-collection administrator's recycle bin is only accessible to site-collection admins and above.

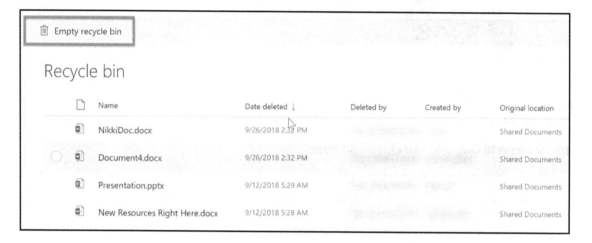

You can delete all of the contents of the recycle bin by unselecting any checked items and clicking the **Empty Recycle Bin** link.

The danger of the Share button

When you share a file using the **Share** button, you may inadvertently break the permission structure, leaving a mess for the person trying to make sure everyone has proper permissions, and/or give permission to someone you shouldn't. This is one of those powers that you need to consider very carefully before using. Do not assume that it is OK to use just because it is enabled. If you find you have the ability to share with anyone, you may want to check with your organization's leadership before proceeding.

Just like any other power, you should try your best to use it wisely. Consider using the least-needed access rule. This is where you give the least amount of access needed. When determining the access you should give, ask yourself these questions:

- Does the person you wish to share with need to edit the file or just view the file?
- If the person only needs to view the file, should they be able to download it as well or should that ability be blocked?
- Does that person need access for a long time or would it be better to set an expiration?
- If you created an anonymous link, would bad things happen if the link is shared with unintended parties or somehow gets "out into the wild"?

SharePoint permissions and what they allow you to do

SharePoint's access control is made up of permission levels and security groups.

Permission levels are groupings of permissions that give a user the ability to have a certain level of access to be able to do certain things. Here is a list of permission levels, straight from SharePoint. Most levels are out of the box but some are custom-made:

Permissions · Permission Levels ⓘ

Permission Level	Description
Full Control	Has full control.
Design	Can view, add, update, delete, approve, and customize.
Manage Hierarchy	Can create sites and edit pages, list items, and documents.
Approve	Can edit and approve pages, list items, and documents.
Contribute	Can view, add, update, and delete.
Read	Can view only.
Restricted Read	Can view pages and documents, but cannot view historical versions or review user rights information.
Limited Access	Can view specific lists, document libraries, list items, folders, or documents when given permissions.
View Only	Members of this group can view pages, list items, and documents. If the document has a server-side file handler available, they can only view the document using the server-side file handler.
Edit	Can view, add, edit, but cannot delete.
Site Content Control	Has control over content and permissions within a site.
Contribute & Approve	Can view, add, update, delete and approve pages, list items and documents.
Approve and Manage List	Approve list item or document; Can create and delete lists, add or remove columns in a list, and add or remove public views of a list.
Records Center Web Service Submitters	Submit content to this site using Web Services.
Restricted Interfaces for Translation	Can open lists and folders, and use remote interfaces.

Groups are collections of users who have the same permission level. The use of groups greatly enhances and simplifies the permissions-management process for administrators. It is easier to manage groups than to manage the permission of every user individually.

As a member of a site, you usually have unrestricted access to all the content of the site; however, certain lists or libraries on the site may be restricted for security purposes.

How to request access

When you are denied access to a resource, you might not have to find the correct administrator's email address, identify the resource you want access to, and compose an explanation on why you need access. If the **Let us know why you need access...** window opens when you try to access something in SharePoint, you can enter information pertaining to the access you would like to request, and your request will be routed automatically:

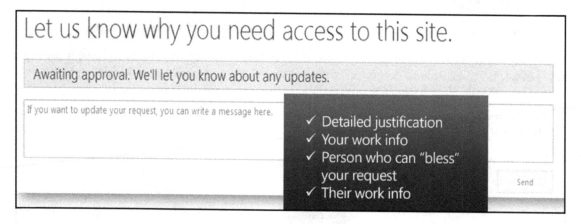

Make sure you include all of the details in the preceding screenshot. Including all of these details will help with speeding up the request.

 Sometimes this box is not wired correctly to send notifications to the right person or they may miss the notification. I would not wait longer than a couple of days before reaching out and, if I had to reach out, I would notify the SharePoint admin that I had sent the request using the **Let us know why you need access...** form so that the problem can be corrected for the next time a request is sent this way.

Summary

In this chapter, we looked at more capabilities, such as exporting to Excel and setting alerts. We also looked at the different ways you can find data in SharePoint and the dangers of using the **Share** button. Then we discussed the permissions levels that give access, and how you can request access when needed.

For more on SharePoint, go to `https://support.office.com` and click on **SharePoint**.

Other Books You May Enjoy

If you enjoyed this book, you may be interested in these other books by Packt:

Mastering Office 365 Administration
Thomas Carpe, Nikkia Carter, Alara Rogers

ISBN: 978-1-78728-863-8

- Get an understanding of the vast Office 365 feature set
- Learn how workloads and applications interact and integrate with each other
- Connect PowerShell to various Office 365 services and perform tasks.
- Learn to manage Skype for Business Online
- Get support and monitor Office 365 service health
- Manage and administer identities and groups efficiently

Office 365 Essentials
Nuno Árias Silva

ISBN: 978-1-78862-207-3

- Learn how to implement Office 365 from scratch and how to use best practices to be a successful Office 365 professional
- Understand Microsoft productivity services to take your organization or business to the next level by increasing productivity.
- Learn how workloads and applications interact and integrate with each other
- Learn to manage Skype for Business Online
- Get support and monitor service health with Office 365
- Manage and administer identities and groups efficiently

Leave a review - let other readers know what you think

Please share your thoughts on this book with others by leaving a review on the site that you bought it from. If you purchased the book from Amazon, please leave us an honest review on this book's Amazon page. This is vital so that other potential readers can see and use your unbiased opinion to make purchasing decisions, we can understand what our customers think about our products, and our authors can see your feedback on the title that they have worked with Packt to create. It will only take a few minutes of your time, but is valuable to other potential customers, our authors, and Packt. Thank you!

Index

A

access
  requesting 430
action bar, OneDrive for Business 289
action bar, OWA mail parts
  categories menu 95
  Junk menu 94
  Move to menu 95
  New menu 93
  open menu 97
alerts
  about 410
  creating 410, 412
  managing 412
anatomy, of SharePoint page
  classic page anatomy 343
  modern page anatomy 350

B

browsers, Office 365
  Chrome 15
  edge 15
  Firefox 15
  Internet Explorer 11 (IE11) 14
  Safari 15
Business Productivity Online Suite (BPOS) 7

C

calendar view
  items, adding 372
  items, deleting 372
  items, editing 372
calendar, OWA calendar parts 141
calendars and groups, OWA calendar parts 143
calls, Microsoft Teams
  initiating 256
calls, Skype for Business
  initiating 240
classic SharePoint page
  anatomy 343
  breadcrumb 349
  global navigation 349
  help 345
  left navigation 349
  Logo 348
  Office 365 suite bar 343
  promoted actions bar 346
  search 346, 347
  settings 344
  tabs 348
  web parts and app parts 349
coauthoring 394
communications lists
  about 360
  contacts 361
  discussion board 361
contacts, Microsoft Teams
  call contacts, adding 252, 254, 255
  chat contacts, adding to groups 250, 251
  working with 248
contacts, Skype for Business
  calls 226
  copying 227
  email 226
  groups, working with 228
  instant messaging 226
  meeting invites 226
  moving 227
  options by dropdown 225
  options by hovering 224
  privacy relationship 228
  removing 226
  tag for status change alerts 227

working with 224
copy to capability 400
creation options, SharePoint home 336, 337
custom lists
about 361
spreadsheet, importing 361

D

data
finding, ways 423
details pane, OneDrive for Business 291, 294
document library
files, adding 378
files, creating in Modern Experience 380
using 377

E

email rules, creating
about 180
via Outlook 182
via Outlook, for web 181
email signature, creating via Outlook
about 176
forward used 177
new used 177
reply email used 177
via file backstage 178
email signature, creating
about 175
via Outlook on web 176
Excel
exporting to 406, 407
Exchange Online, parts
about 83
calendar 84
contacts 85
email 84
tasks 86
Exchange Online
about 80
Outlook, via app launcher 81, 82
Outlook, via Office 365 Home 80, 81
Exchange
about 10, 71, 72
history 72, 73, 74, 76, 77, 80

extra options, OneDrive for Business 288

F

file sharing, OneDrive for Business
about 313
access, editing 316, 318
access, providing 313
access, removing 317, 319
considerations 320
copy link option 314
editing 319
Outlook button option 314
via share button 313
files, OneDrive for Business
copying 322
deleting 305
editing 304, 305
moving 320
new files, adding 299
new files, creating 300, 301, 302
Office Online file 306
sharing 313
uploading 303
files, sharing
about 394
access, editing 398
access, granting 395, 397
access, removing 398
files
checking in 390, 392
checking out 388, 389, 390
deleting 385
editing 383, 384
naming conventions 386
forwarding email, setting
setting 182
via Outlook 184, 185, 186
via Outlook on web 183
frequent sites, SharePoint home 338

H

home page
about 18
app launcher/switcher 19
help 22, 24, 26

notifications 20, 22
Office 365 link 20
profile picture 28
settings 22
suite bar 18

I

instant messaging, Microsoft Teams 255
instant messaging, Skype for Business
  about 229
  add more participants button 239
  call buttons 231
  IM button 231
  message area 231
  message options 231
  more options button 237
  participants list 238
  presentation button 232, 234, 235, 237
  text box 231

L

left navigation, SharePoint home
  about 333
  featured links 335
  following 334
  recent 335
libraries 375
library types
  about 376
  document 376
  form 376
  pictures 376
  wiki page 376
library view 377
licensing
  about 64
  Office 365 commercial 65
  Office 365 consumer 64
link
  creating 407, 409
List View
  about 362
  items, adding to any list 362
  used, for deleting items 370
  used, for editing items 366, 370

list/library filtering
  using 424
list/library
  searching, using 425
lists
  about 359
  communications 360
  custom lists 361
  tracking 361
  types 360

M

main window, OneDrive for Business 296
meeting invite, Microsoft Teams
  sending 270
  sending, via Outlook on your desktop 274, 275
  sending, via Teams 270, 272, 273
meeting invite, Skype for Business
  sending 241
  sending, via Outlook on your desktop 242
  sending, via Outlook online 241
meetings, Microsoft Teams
  working in 265, 266, 270
meetings, Skype for Business
  initiating 240
message, SharePoint home 337
Microsoft Teams
  about 10, 245
  background 192
  calls, initiating 256
  contacts, working with 248
  history 192
  instant messaging 255
  meeting invite, sending 270
  meeting, working in 265
  presence settings, exploring 246
  Teams, working with 256
mobile app, SharePoint home 339
Modern Experience
  files, creating 380, 382
  files, uploading 382
modern SharePoint page
  about 350
  breadcrumb 354
  global navigation 353

help 352
left navigation 355
Logo 353
Office 365 Suite Bar 350
page actions bar 353
page header 355
promoted actions bar 353
search 354
settings 351
web parts and app parts 355
month calendar navigation, OWA calendar parts
142
month/year navigation, OWA calendar parts 141
move to capability 398
my account, profile picture
account security phone numbers, updating 47,
48
app passwords, managing 48, 49
app permissions 50, 51
contact preferences 45
install status 38, 39
organization privacy statement 46
password 43, 44
personal info 35, 36, 37
security and privacy 42, 43
security verification, additional 47
settings 52, 53
subscriptions 40, 42

N

navigation, SharePoint
options 340

O

Office 365 commercial
business plans 65, 66
enterprise plans 66
Office 365, services
about 9
compliance 12
Exchange 10
Microsoft Teams 10, 11
Office Professional or Professional Plus
applications for desktop 12
office web and mobile apps 12

OneDrive for Business 11
privacy 12
security 12
SharePoint 11
Skype for Business 10
transparency 12
Office 365
about 7
browsers 14, 15
logging in 13, 14
requisites 7
versions 8
Office Online file
autosave 306
backstage 310
going, back to OneDrive for Business 309
opening, in full desktop version 306
parts 306
print options 312
renaming 307
save as, using 311
simplified ribbon 307
tabs and ribbons 308
OneDrive for Business
about 11, 279
action bar 289, 290
details pane 291, 293, 294
exploring 280, 281
extra options 288, 289
files, working with 299
history 279
main window 296
parts 282
search box 282, 284
sites navigation 287
versus, OneDrive 296
view options 290
your OneDrive navigation 285
out of office reply
setting 178
setting, via Outlook 180
setting, via Outlook on web 179
Outlook apps, OWA calendar parts 144
Outlook backstage
about 107

exit 116
feedback 115
info 108
Office Account 112, 114
open & export 109
options 116
print 112
save as 110
save attachments 111
Outlook calendar, parts
about 144
calendar 153
calendar navigation 152, 153
calendars, list 154
Outlook apps 154
search 153
tabs 147
tell me what you want to do box 151
weather 152
Outlook mail, parts
about 102, 104
email accounts, list 124
Email options 126
email, display 105
emails, list 104
favorites 122
filters 106
focused and other filters 105
folder 119
help 120
Home 117, 118
Outlook apps 124
ribbons 117
search 107
Send/receive 119
tabs 107
view 120
Outlook
apps 174
contact details pane 173
left navigation 170
list of contacts 171
parts of contacts 164
search and filtering 171
tabs 166

Tell me what you want to do box 170
via app launcher 82
via Office 365 Home 80
OWA calendar, parts
about 128
action bar 130
add calendar 132
calendar 141
calendar views 141
calendars and groups 143
interested calendars 135
interesting calendars 132
month calendar navigation 142
month/year navigation 141
new 130
Outlook apps 144
print 139
search 142
selected days events 142
share 136, 139
OWA mail, parts
about 88
action bar 92
email message, displaying 90
email options 101
emails, list 89
filter 92
focused and other filters 91
folders 100
Mark all as read 98
Outlook apps 101
permissions 100
search 99
OWA
parts of people (contacts) 158

P

parts of people (contacts), OWA
action bar 160
left navigation 163
main window 162
outlook apps 164
search 162
Parts of Teams
about 208

Back and forward buttons 211
close button 210
left navigation 211
location and menu 212
main app screen 214
maximize button 210
minimise button 210
New chat button 210
profile picture 210
public/private indicator 213
search box 209
tab, adding 212
tabs 212
personal settings
  configuring 55, 56
  search box 57
presence settings, Microsoft Teams
  appear away 248
  available 247
  aways 247
  be right back 248
  busy 247
  do not disturb 247
  exploring 246
  offline 248
  unknown 248
presence settings, Skype for Business
  appear away 224
  available 222
  aways 223
  be right back 223
  busy 223
  do not disturb 223
  off work 224
  offline 224
  setting 222
  unknown 224
presence, Skype for business
  exit 196
  green/available 194
  real/busy 195
  red with dash/do not disturb 195
  reset status 196
  sign out 196
  white with question mark/unknown 196

white/offline 196
yellow/appear away 195
yellow/be right back 195
yellow/off work 195
profile picture, home page
  about 29, 30
  for Microsoft Teams 54
  my account 34
  my profile 30, 31, 32

Q

quick edit mode 403, 405

R

recycle bin functions 426

S

search box, OneDrive for Business 282, 284
search box, personal settings
  app settings 64
  language and time zone 63
  software 61, 62
  start page 60, 61
  themes 58, 60
search, OWA calendar parts 142
search, SharePoint home 330, 332, 333
selected days events, OWA calendar parts 142
Share button
  limitations 428
SharePoint home
  creation options 336
  frequent sites 338
  get mobile app 339
  left navigation 333
  message 337
  news from sites 338
  search 329, 331, 333
  searching via 425
  site card 338
SharePoint Online (SPO) 327
SharePoint page
  anatomy 342
SharePoint
  about 11, 325
  editions 327

history 325
home 328
navigating 340
permission levels 429
permissions 429
sites, searching 425
timeline 326
site card, SharePoint home 338
site contents
about 426
sites navigation, OneDrive for Business 287
Skype for Business, getting into
about 214
via app 215
via Office 365 214
Skype for Business, parts
about 192
add people button 203, 204
contacts 198
conversations 199
finding someone 202, 203
location 196, 197
main section 206
meetings 200
personal note 194
photo 197
presence 194
primary device, selecting 206
settings 200
sub-tabs 204
Skype for Business
about 10, 191, 192
calls, initiating 239
contacts, working with 224
instant messaging 229
meeting invite, sending 241
meetings, initiating 240
presence settings 222
using 221
sub-tabs, Skype for Business
contacts 204
conversations 205

T

tabs, Outlook 167
tabs, Outlook calendar
folder 149
help 151
home 148
Outlook backstage 148
send/receive 149
view 150
Teams, getting into
about 215
via app 216, 218
via Office 365 216
Teams, Microsoft Teams
creating 262
joining 262
main window 262
more options, for selected Team's channel 260
more options, for Teams and channels 258
privacy indicator 257
tabs 260
Teams and channels panel 257
Teams settings, managing 264
way forward with 219
working in 256

V

version history
tracking 387
view options, OneDrive for Business 290
views
about 413
personal view, creating 413, 417, 421
switching, between 422

Y

your OneDrive navigation, OneDrive for Business
recent 285
Recycle bin 286, 287
shared 286

CPSIA information can be obtained
at www.ICGtesting.com
Printed in the USA
LVHW101555050820
662459LV00014B/2117

9 781789 809312